Teaching Towards Musical Understanding

A Handbook for the Elementary Grades

Amanda P. Montgomery

University of Alberta

Prentice Hall

Toronto

National Library of Canada Cataloguing in Publication Data

Montgomery, Amanda Palmer
    Teaching towards musical understanding : a handbook for the elementary grades

ISBN 0-13-017394-0

1. School music—Instruction and study. I. Title.

MT930.M787 2002   372.87   C2001-903633-7

The musical hand signals in Table 9.2, page 187, are reproduced from Robert W. Winslow and Leon Dallin (1992). *Music Skills for Classroom Teachers*, 8th ed. Dubuque, IA: Wm. C. Brown Publishers. Reproduced with the permission of McGraw-Hill Education, A Division of The McGraw-Hill Companies.

ISBN 0-13-017394-0

Vice President, Editorial Director: Michael Young
Acquisitions Editor: Andrew Wellner
Marketing Manager: Christine Cozens
Signing Representative: Andrew Wellner
Developmental Editor: Martina van de Velde
Production Editor: Avivah Wargon
Copy Editor: Ruth Pincoe
Production Manager: Wendy Moran
Page Layout: Debbie Kumpf
Creative Director: Mary Opper
Interior Design: Sarah Battersby
Cover Design: Sarah Battersby
Cover Image: Comstock

29 30 31 DPC 11 10 09

Printed and bound in Canada

To the memory of Jean Sinor, my mentor, teacher, colleague, and friend.

Special thanks also to my loving husband Jim, whose patience, support, and quiet wisdom made this book possible; and to my daughter Emaline, whose love of music was a constant inspiration.

Contents

Preface

This textbook has been written to provide a valuable resource for two populations of music teachers: pre-service university students majoring in education or music who are enrolled in undergraduate elementary music education methods classes; and elementary music teachers currently working in the field who are looking for additional theoretical and pedagogical information with which to build a stronger music curriculum.

Teaching Towards Musical Understanding was inspired by the growing need within our profession for a Canadian textbook on elementary music education that features Canadian song materials and resources. In addition, my own university teaching over the last two decades has indicated to me the increasing importance of providing undergraduate students with significant connections between theory and practice. As a result, one of the unique strengths of this book is the highlighting of recent research in elementary music education side by side with the pedagogical implications of such research.

This book is written to provide pre-service and experienced teachers with the knowledge needed to help children develop musical understanding: *the ability to think and act musically with personal meaning*. Each of the five main parts of the book provides the reader with significant information regarding a quality general music curriculum for students in Kindergarten to Grade 6 to help accomplish this goal. Margin textboxes throughout the book highlight important concepts discussed in each of the 18 chapters.

Part I—Setting the Stage—provides foundational information about the nature of music, the nature of music education and musical understanding, and the principles of elementary school music instruction (Chapters 1–2). This conceptual material provides a meaningful framework through which readers may view Chapters 4 to 17 on classroom pedagogy and curricular planning. Part I also includes an overview of the equipment, resources, and physical environment desirable for a balanced music curriculum in the elementary grades (Chapter 3).

Part II—Authentic Musical Experiences—surveys the musical experiences through which children should encounter music in the elementary school classroom, including singing (Chapter 4), playing classroom instruments (Chapter 5), improvising and composing (Chapter 6), listening to music (Chapter 7), moving with music (Chapter 8), and reading and writing music (Chapter 9). Each chapter provides essential information on the various developmental issues to be considered when utilizing particular musical experiences with children of elementary school age.

Part III—Classroom Activities—presents specific pedagogical information on daily classroom activities that can be designed by the elementary music teacher to help children learn about the structure of music, through the eight classroom experiences discussed in Part II. These six chapters present classroom activities for learning about beat, tempo and metre (Chapter 10), rhythm (Chapter 11), pitch (Chapter 12), dynamics, timbre, and expressive elements (Chapter 13), form (Chapter 14), and harmony and texture (Chapter 15) in a sound-before-symbol progression within a developmentally appropriate simple-to-complex teaching order.

Part IV—Curricular Planning—presents critical information on the process of long-range planning, including the role of student assessment and evaluation and the daily task of lesson planning (Chapters 16–17). The two sample lesson plans provided in Chapter 16 utilize music activities and strategies discussed in Chapters 4–15.

Part V—Finale—provides the pre-service elementary music teacher with closing thoughts about the role of the elementary educator in providing quality music instruction for children (Chapter 18).

The Appendix (pp. 337–350) provides an overview of musical symbols for use by pre-service education students who need a reference tool on musical notation, and the Glossary (pp. 351–363) enables readers to find definitions for bolded terms used throughout the book at a glance. The Music Index at the end of the text lists all the music in the book as well as all the recommended selections of recorded music, and the Subject Index will be helpful for research and reference purposes.

Depending on their level of experience, readers may choose to focus on different chapters of the book in a variety of sequences. For example, pre-service education students who need a grounding in music fundamentals might wish to concentrate their early reading on Part III (Classroom Activities), using the children's activities recommended in these chapters to become more comfortable with musical terms and musical notation. The Appendix can also serve as an important reference in this regard. Chapters in Parts II and IV might then be added as determined appropriate by individual university method course instructors.

Pre-service university music students, on the other hand, might want to focus their early reading on Part II (Authentic Musical Experiences) to learn about the general developmental needs of elementary school children in relation to activities such as singing or playing instruments, followed by the more specific pedagogical chapters in Part III and the curricular planning chapters in Part IV.

I recommend that *both* populations of pre-service students begin their initial reading of this textbook with Part I, in order to obtain a thorough grounding in the foundational issues of elementary school music teaching (for example, organizing instruction through sound-before-symbol, planning for multiple perspectives, presentation of concepts in a spiral progression). The final thoughts presented in Part V provide an excellent closing to the reading process.

Experienced elementary music teachers can use this book as appropriate to their specific needs. Although a cover-to-cover reading will provide a refreshing new look at the principles of elementary music teaching, individual chapters (such as Chapter 6, on improvising and composing experiences with children) may be read as unique units to provide an experienced teacher with helpful hints on enhancing current practices in elementary school music education.

It is important to note that this textbook is not intended as a "recipe book" for elementary music instruction. Although beginning teachers will find specific guidance with regard to issues such as the selection of age-appropriate music and materials, the creation of a learner-centred environment, the use of authentic experiences which place the child in the centre of the music making–composing–listening, or the need to value individual response, it is hoped that individual teachers will bring these ideas to life through creative lesson planning that takes into full account the specific needs of the children in their personal classrooms. Providing the significant tools for children to reach towards musical understanding is a gift we can give to students only after careful planning as teachers. I hope this book will provide the necessary resource with which to carry out this process successfully. After all, the aesthetic lives of our Canadian children deserve nothing less!

Acknowledgments

I wish to thank James Montgomery for his expertise as official photographer for this book, and Robert de Frece for his creative energy in writing the two new Orff arrangements included in Chapter 5. I would also like to thank my colleagues across the country who provided important feedback as reviewers during the writing process of the book: Ki Adams, Memorial University of Newfoundland; Rodger J. Beatty, Brock University; Carol Beynon, University of Western Ontario; Eugenia Costa-Giomi, McGill University; Deryl Edwards, University of Toronto; Dianne Edwards, Ontario Institute for Studies in Education, University of Toronto; Lori-Anne Dolloff, University of Toronto; Betty Hanley, University of Victoria; Sheila MacKenzie-Brown, Okanagan University College; Victoria Meredith, University of Western Ontario; Robert Petersen, University College of the Cariboo; Brian Roberts, Memorial University of Newfoundland; and Michael Wilson, University of Ottawa.

About the Author

Dr. Amanda Montgomery is a professor in the Faculty of Education at the University of Alberta, where she teaches both undergraduate and graduate courses in music education. She also teaches music to the kindergarten-to-grade-3 children enrolled in the Department of Elementary Education's Child Study Centre. Formerly a professor at the University of Western Ontario and the University of Prince Edward Island, Dr. Montgomery received her graduate degrees with distinction from Indiana University School of Music.

As Past-President of the Canadian Music Educators Association and the Kodály Society of Canada and as an active workshop clinician, Dr. Montgomery provides leadership to many music educators across Canada. Her research includes studies in early childhood music, musical preference, and teacher education. She has published articles in several national and international journals.

PART ONE

Setting the Stage

Part I provides the important foundational information needed for building a quality elementary music curriculum. Chapter 1 discusses the nature of music and music education, presenting implications for the development of children's musical understanding. Chapter 2 considers the context of an elementary music education curriculum organized to maximize the development of individual children's musical understanding through engagement with the structure of music. The principles of instruction for elementary school music are broadly presented, providing a framework through which to view the subsequent chapters on classroom experiences (Part II) and activities (Part III). Chapter 3 provides a brief overview of the equipment, resources, and physical environment that should ideally be available to the teacher in the elementary school music classroom.

CHAPTER 1

Introduction

SYNOPSIS

Chapter 1 discusses the nature of music, drawing parallels to language development. Evidence is presented that musical semantics is culturally and stylistically bound with implications for elementary music education. Musical understanding is defined in conjunction with a brief description of curricula designed to teach for this purpose.

The Nature of Music

All humans have the capacity for musical thinking.

According to John Blacking (1973), "music is humanly organized sound." Indeed, music is a fundamental human resource which presumably is borne out of the need for humans to express themselves beyond the simple use of words. As J.W. Goethe suggested, music begins where words end (attributed).

In the last two decades of the twentieth century, psychologists such as Howard Gardner (1983) popularized the theory that all humans are born with a combination of several ways of viewing the world. He termed this **multiple intelligence**—*the bio-psychological potential to think in certain ways.* According to Gardner, there are eight ways of thinking: linguistic, logical-mathematical, spatial, bodily-kinesthetic, naturalist, interpersonal, intrapersonal, and musical.

Such theories have reinforced the view of ethnomusicologists that *all humans have the capacity to think musically.* Indeed, although different cultures around the world have created unique forms for musical thinking, ethnomusicological research indicates that individuals within all cultures utilize this form of intelligence to some degree in order to communicate within their culture through the medium of music (Hodges and Haack, 1998).

Music education plays an important role in this communication process, as such instruction can intensify and enhance each individual's capacity to think musically. For Canadians, elementary school music plays a critical role, since it is often the only formal music instruction children receive before adulthood. Across the country, quality music education in the pre-school years is often limited, and in many provinces, school music becomes an elective after grade six or eight. Although private music instruction attempts to fill the gap, access to it is often restricted by the financial resources of individual families. Indeed, by default, Canadian elementary music teachers often find themselves with the opportunity to play a heightened role in the process of nurturing children's abilities as musical thinkers (Montgomery, 2000).

For the purposes of planning elementary school music education, it is interesting to note that the development of **musical intelligence** shows similarities to the development of **linguistic intelligence**. As Sloboda (1985) suggests,

1. Language and music are universal to all humans and specific to humans.
2. Language and music are capable of generating an unlimited number of novel sequences.
3. The natural medium for both language and music is auditory-vocal.
4. Children seem to have a natural ability to learn the rules of language and music through exposure to examples.
5. Receptive skills precede productive skills in the development process. (pp. 17–21)

Structurally, language and music also share some similarities. Language breaks down into three logical components:

1. **phoneme**: the smallest sound unit in language
2. **syntax**: the rules governing the combination of phonemes into sound sequences
3. **semantics**: the way in which meaning is assigned to or carried by these sound sequences

Music also appears to follow this structure, at least in the first category, in that the smallest sound unit of music is characterized as a **musical phoneme—** *a note distinguished by frequency (pitch) and duration (length)* (Sloboda, 1985). Whether such phonology shows direct correlation to language syntax is more debatable, since musical syntax is more than a simple set of rules governing the combining of musical phonemes into sound sequences.

In language, syntax is used to combine sounds in such a way as to communicate a particular meaningful idea. Music, on the other hand, generally has a much broader conception with a "plasticity and a richness that [verbal] language does not" (Aiello, 1994, p. 55). For example, composers often utilize great freedom within the syntax of a particular musical style in order to create novelty or to tamper with the listener's expectations. Such expectations would undoubtedly be different for various individuals based on each person's experience and comfort level with the particulars of that musical style. Indeed, such multi-dimensionality led Sloboda (1985) to suggest that **musical syntax** may be "best understood as relating to propensities of listeners to infer particular underlying structures from note sequences rather then the generative processes of composers" (p. 57).

Musical semantics, then, can probably best be thought of as *socially and culturally bound within the confines of a musical syntax shared to some degree by*

People make sense of the music they encounter through cognition of the structural components in music as those components relate to their lives within a culture.

the individuals within that culture. If listeners are unfamiliar with the rules regarding the organization of sound sequences within a particular style (for example, jazz, Baroque art music, or First Nations chants), then the ability of those listeners to derive deep personal meaning from that music may be limited. In other words, personal relevance for an individual can only be heightened when he or she is able to make sense of the musical patterning (the syntax) that is critical to a particular musical style within a culture (Heller and Campbell, 1981).

This implies that a working knowledge of a variety of structural properties (pitch, rhythm, timbre, etc.) combined with the syntax (rules) for the organization of these properties appropriate within a culture's music is important in order to achieve a deep, personal experience with music. As Fiske (1990) suggests,

> **Musical meaning is a reflection of the extent of the listener's ability to determine relationships between tones, to construct patterns based upon those relationships, and to perceive the function of identified patterns within the development of the composition as a whole. (p. 81)**

As a result, we can say that people make sense of the music they encounter not through pre-determined semantic meaning as in speech, but rather *through musical cognition of the structural components of that music as it relates to their personal lives within a culture.* This says personal meaning comes from a *combination* of the child's cognitive response to the sonic properties in the music *and* the social, emotional, and spiritual background that the child brings to that music. Realistically, **music** should be thought of, not as a fixed product, but rather as *an ever-changing experience that is dependent on the dynamics of human interaction with that music.*

Music should be thought of as an ever-changing experience dependent on the dynamics of human interaction with that music.

Music education can play an important role in strengthening children's interaction with music by providing them with a pedagogy designed to lead them towards gaining a working knowledge of the structural components and syntax of music. As Koopman (1997) states, "Teaching pupils to concentrate on the sensuous and structural properties of musical works is the best way of assuring that music gets an even deeper meaning for them" (p. 43). In addition, a sensitive and caring teacher—one who is cognizant of the importance of the social, emotional, and spiritual background that each child brings to the musical experience—is critical since both a knowledge of musical structure and syntax and an awareness of what is brought to the music by an individual play a part in making musical meaning. Such a teacher will expect, and value, multiple meaning-making by students.

Teaching Towards Musical Understanding

Musical understanding is defined as the ability to think and act musically with personal meaning.

Musical understanding—*the ability to think and act musically with personal meaning*—involves students using their knowledge of musical structure and syntax acquired during classroom experiences in order to think, to act flexibly, and to ultimately bring personal intervention to any of their musical encounters.

An elementary music curriculum designed to teach towards musical understanding stimulates, enhances, and intensifies a child's natural cognitive response

Elementary music
education should
help children
learn how to
perceive,
compare, relate,
and make sense
of the structural
patterns of music
they encounter in
their everyday
lives.

Elementary
classroom music
should engage
children in the
authentic music
experiences of
performing,
composing, and
listening.

to music—that is, her or his musical intelligence. Such music education is designed to help children learn how to perceive, compare, relate, and talk about musical structure in order to heighten their ability to make sense of the music they encounter in their everyday lives.

This dynamic approach to teaching provides children with a diversity of hands-on experiences (singing, composing, etc.) with musical style(s) that allow each child to become aurally, kinesthetically, and cognitively familiar with the possibilities for patterning of **musical structure** (syntax) in that music. This musical structure is traditionally divided into parts called the **elements of music**:

1. **beat**: the steady pulse underlying music
2. **tempo**: the speed (fast or slow) of the beat
3. **metre**: the periodic accenting of specific beats.
4. **rhythm**: varied durations of notes or silences over an underlying beat
5. **dynamics**: the loudness or softness of notes
6. **timbre**: the tone colour of an instrument or voice
7. **pitch**: the highness or lowness of a note
8. **form**: the way music is structured into an organized journey
9. **harmony and texture**: the simultaneous sounding of two or more notes; the nature of those multiple sounds
10. **expressive elements**: the particular emphasis given to a note during performance

Since children learn best while engaged in active, concrete, authentic experiences, such musical structure and syntactical implications within a musical style are experienced while engaged in the three ways in which they encounter music in their world:

1. as **performers**—*makers of music*
2. as **composers**—*creators of music*
3. as **listeners**—*consumers of music*

Classroom experiences through which children experience these three musical modes include:

1. singing
2. playing classroom instruments
3. improvising
4. composing
5. listening
6. reading music
7. writing music
8. moving to music

Musical skills are certainly critical for development in the elementary grades, as they provide children with strong psychomotor tools for experiencing the "stuff" of music—the unique ways in which the musical elements are arranged. However, a curriculum designed to teach towards musical understanding

To achieve
musical
understanding,
children need to
reflect, analyze,
and interpret the
music they
encounter and
the actions they
take regarding
that music.

requires children to do more than simply learn the musical skills necessary for success as musicians. To achieve musical understanding, children need to be asked to reflect, analyze, and interpret both the music (i.e., the structure) they encounter and the actions (i.e., the skills) they take regarding that music. In other words, children need opportunities to internalize and interpret their growing knowledge of musical structure in order to work towards making informed, artistic, and meaningful musical decisions, whether as performers, composers, or listeners.

According to Perkins (1998), children with understanding in a subject area have "the ability to think and act flexibly with what [one knows]" (p. 40). Musical understanding requires students to make musical connections and relationships when they encounter or create music in their environment. As Howard Gardner (1999) states:

> If a person understands music ... if a person can think musically, that means he or she has certain categories, certain institutions, certain schemas that came out of his or her exposure to previous music ... It means when a person approaches a new work of music, or even creates one, that person can draw on that knowledge. (p. 15)

Thus children approaching musical understanding should be able to use their knowledge of musical structure and syntax acquired during classroom experiences with music to develop personal meaning out of sound.

Elementary music
education should
give students
experience with
musical style or
syntax so that
they can move
towards novel
ways of
interpreting and
creating.

Educators such as Newton (2000) believe that "understanding moves from the authorized or public understanding to a personal one" (p. 23). Presumably, elementary music education should help students to gain experience with the standards of normalcy within whatever musical style and syntax is being studied in order to build the confidence to bridge towards novel ways of interpreting and creating. Whether they are active as performers, listeners, or composers, children must become familiar with the commonly occurring structural patterning in a given musical style in order to increase their abilities to make meaningful and artistic decisions within that style.

Selection of music for these experiences merits careful consideration since children need practice with the syntax and patterning of a musical style in order to make meaningful decisions within that style. Given the global economy and technological leaps of the late twentieth century, it is likely that the diversity of musical styles available to children in their everyday lives will only increase over the next two decades. As a result, the need to help children come to an understanding of numerous musical styles is increasing.

Music
multiculturalism
is part of a
growing reality
for children.

Such **musical multiculturalism** suggests the educational appropriateness of providing children with classroom experiences with musical syntax and patterning from a variety of musical styles. Educators such as Elliot (1996) caution, however, that "musical diversity should not be sought at the expense of musical depth" (p. 9). Since it often takes considerable time to become comfortable with the musical patterns of any one style, there may be limits to the amount of time in the elementary grades that can actually be spent on developing sensitivity to several different styles. In reality, building depth in musical understanding may ultimately require teachers to make thoughtful decisions regarding which musical styles to include or exclude in the elementary curriculum. As Koopman (1997) points out,

There are many aspects of musical form that are not idiosyncratic to one particular tradition but can be found in most, if not all traditions, for instance, the development of rhythmic and melodic ideas, the use of contrasting sections, patterns of tension and release, or the exploration of sound resources ... Thus, responsiveness to musical form provides a basis for meaningfully relating to music of whatever tradition. By furthering children's responsiveness to the properties of musical works [in some styles] as such, we assure that they gain a passport to music of all cultures. (p. 45)

In summary, Figure 1.1 provides a graphic description of a curriculum designed to promote musical understanding. Children lucky enough to participate in such a curriculum should gain the skills necessary for building the understanding to think, to act flexibly, and to ultimately bring personal intervention to all their future musical encounters. Chapter 2 will discuss the context required to bring such curricula to life.

Figure 1.1. • A CURRICULUM DESIGNED TO TEACH TOWARDS MUSICAL UNDERSTANDING

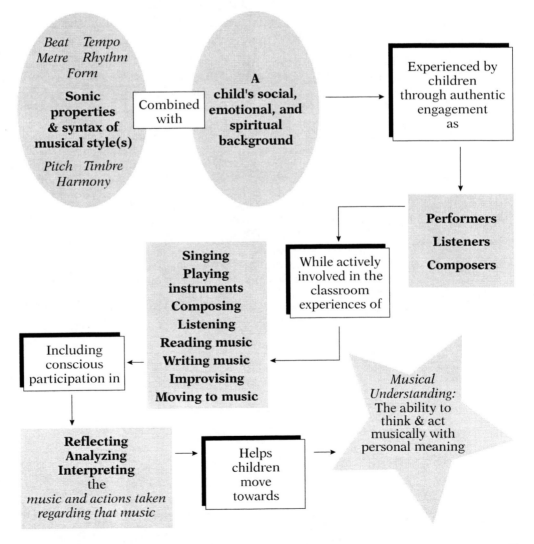

Questions for Discussion and Practice

1. Briefly discuss how language and music are related. Highlight the similarities and differences.

2. Why is music more of a dynamic experience rather than a fixed product?

3. Why is a working knowledge of musical structure important in order to derive personal meaning through musical listening?

4. List and define the ten elements of music that make up musical structure. Describe the structural aspects of one song from this book in relation to these ten elements.

5. Define musical understanding. Outline the components of a curriculum designed to teach for musical understanding.

References

Aiello, R. (1994). Music and language. In R. Aiello and J. Sloboda (Eds.), *Musical Perceptions*. Oxford: Oxford University Press.

Blacking, J. (1973). *How Musical Is Man?* Seattle: University of Washington Press.

Elliot, D. (1996). Consciousness, culture, and curriculum. *International Journal of Research in Music Education, 28,* 1–15.

Fiske, H. (1990). *Music and Mind*. Queenston: The Edwin Mellen Press.

Gardner, H. (1983). *Frames of Mind*. New York: Basic Books.

Gardner, H. (1999). Keynote address from the cognitive processes of children engaging in musical activities conference: honouring M.P. Zimmerman. *Bulletin of the Council for Research in Music Education, 142,* 9–21.

Heller, J., and Campbell, W. (1981). A theoretical model of music perception and talent. *Bulletin of the Council for Research in Music Education, 66–7,* 20–24.

Hodges, D., and Haack, P. (1998). The influence of music on human behavior. In D. Hodges (Ed.) *Handbook of Music Psychology*. IMR Press: University of Texas at San Antonio.

Koopman, C. (1997). Music as language: An analogy to be pursued with caution. *International Journal of Music Education, 29,* 40–46.

Montgomery, A. (2000). Elementary school music: Reflections for the future. In B. Hanley and B. Roberts (Eds.), *Looking Forward: Challenges to Canadian Music Education*. Victoria: Canadian Music Educators Association.

Newton, D.(2000). *Teaching for Understanding*. New York: Routledge.

Perkins, D. (1998). What is understanding? In M. Stone (Ed.) *Teaching for Understanding: Linking Research to Practice*. San Francisco: Jossey-Bass.

Sloboda, J. (1985). *The Musical Mind: The Cognitive Psychology of Music*. Oxford: Clarendon Press.

CHAPTER 2

Context for Teaching

SYNOPSIS

Chapter 2 considers the context of a curriculum organized to maximize the development of musical understanding. Topics discussed include: choice of musical style(s); sequencing of musical concepts; presentation of concepts in a spiral progression; planning for multiple learning perspectives; using developmentally-appropriate classroom activities; organizing instruction through sound-before-symbol; music literacy; group and individual instruction; and supporting student reflection.

Introduction

Elementary music education should deepen children's ability to make meaningful music decisions.

Elementary music education has the potential to contribute significantly to the development of children's musical understanding. As stated in Chapter 1, curricula designed for such a purpose should be rooted in the authentic musical experience of *performers, composers,* and *listeners.* Students need classroom instruction that deepens their abilities to make meaningful musical decisions when engaged in any of these three modes of musical encounter.

Experiencing the structural components and syntax of music through active engagement with various styles of music forms the critical core for this curriculum. Children require a working knowledge of how such structure (i.e., the musical elements: beat, tempo, and metre; rhythm; pitch; dynamics; form; timbre; harmony and texture) is utilized in musical patterning in order to make sense of the music they encounter, whatever the musical mode of experience.

Children require a
working
knowledge of the
ten elements of
musical structure.

For example, as listeners, children need to perceive and determine relationships in musical patterning in order to derive meaning through the music listening experience. As performers, children need to perceive and determine these structural relationships in order to make artistic or expressive decisions regarding musical performance. And as composers, children need a working knowledge of musical components in order to abstract some of these for re-construction into unique, personalized musical compositions.

Selecting Musical Styles

Selection of music for these experiences merits careful consideration. As discussed in Chapter 1, personal relevance regarding musical structure and syntax is stylistically and culturally based. This implies that children need practice with syntax and patterning from any given musical style in order to make meaningful musical decisions within that style. However, building depth in musical understanding takes time and requires thoughtful decisions on the part of teachers regarding which musical styles to include in the elementary curriculum.

Musical styles selected by teachers for use in Kindergarten through Grades 6–8 might include one or more from the following list:

1. *European-influenced Canadian folk songs* (lullabies, chants, singing games, Orff arrangements, etc.)

2. *traditional songs of the Inuit and First Nations peoples* (for example, lullabies, chants, children's songs, ceremonial music, dances)

3. *Western art music* (for example, instrumental and choral music from the **Baroque**, **Classical**, and **Romantic** periods)

4. *Western twentieth-century musical theatre and film music* (Broadway tunes, Hollywood movie themes, etc.)

5. *Western twentieth-century jazz* (**Dixieland**, **bebop**, **swing**, etc.)

6. *Western twentieth-century popular music* (rock, pop, hip hop, country and western, etc.)

7. *instrumental and vocal music from other parts of the world* (including Africa, Asia, the Middle East, and Australia)

The demographic make-up of individual classrooms may dictate the style most appropriate for beginning instruction, since knowledge of musical syntax should be broadened from the known to the unknown. Most Canadian elementary music textbooks, however, concentrate on music from group 1 (European-influenced Canadian folksongs) for early performing experiences, augmented by music from group 3 (Western art music) for listening examples. Teachers interested in beginning with music from other cultural styles (for example, vocal music from Africa or Asia) because of unique school populations will need to do considerable research in order to find a suitable repertoire for children. Parents or ethnic community groups near the school may be helpful in this regard. The Internet may also prove to be a valuable resource for teachers in search of such repertoire.

The fact that singing or chanting exists in many cultures makes this type of music an excellent entry point. Research indicates that singing is a common strategy utilized by teachers in Canada, and plays a central role in many elementary music classrooms across the country (Shand, 1982; Montgomery, 1990). Teachers generally plan for children in Kindergarten or Grade 1 to begin their exposure to music with simple children's songs and games while progressing to experiences with more complex kinds of music, regardless of the musical style selected for initial instruction.

Sequencing Musical Concepts

A curriculum designed to promote musical understanding includes a subdivision of the various elements of musical structure (pitch, rhythm, etc.) into smaller units called **musical concepts** or constructs; for example, concepts of pitch include, among others, high and low notes, melodic contour, and the major scale. These musical concepts are generally sequenced into an *easy-to-complex teaching order* based on the profession's growing knowledge of how children learn music. As Zimmerman (1993) states, "Sequential teaching in music organizes material in a way that simplifies the musical environment and enables the child to build on it for future use" (p. 16). Sequencing, then, is used by teachers to help organize content into a logical order for effective classroom practice.

Such sequencing does not imply that students should study all the musical concepts from one element (for example, all the concepts from rhythm followed by all the concepts from pitch, and so on) before proceeding to the concepts from another element. Rather, it implies that children gain experience with musical structure in a **spiral progression**: that is, *children study progressively more sophisticated musical concepts from all ten elements of music during each consecutive grade level.* Thus, the purpose of the easy-to-complex sequence of musical concepts is to select the simplest concepts from each of the ten musical elements for Kindergarten, leaving the most complex for teaching in Grade 6.

In Canada, such sequencing has traditionally been available through provincial or school board curriculum guides. The recent publication *Achieving Musical Understanding: Skills and Concepts for Pre-Kindergarten to Grade Eight* (CMEA and CMEC, 2001) adds an excellent resource. The chart on pp. 12–13 provides the author's recommendations for the general progression of teaching these musical concepts in the elementary grades.

Please note that although sequencing guidelines are helpful for beginning teachers, more experienced instructors should view such recommendations as merely starting points for curriculum construction. Indeed, teachers need to modify, stretch, and redirect sequencing suggestions so as to make them congruent with the unique population of children they teach. In addition, each individual musical style studied may emphasize the patterning of one particular musical concept over another. Thus, successful learning in the elementary music class is dependent on the active role played by teachers in making sequencing decisions for their individual classrooms.

Recommended Sequence for Introducing Musical Concepts in the Elementary Grades

Beat, Tempo, and Metre

1. beat (Kindergarten—Grade 1)
2. beat vs. rhythm (Kindergarten—Grade 1)
3. tempo: fast vs. slow (Kindergarten—Grade 1)
4. metre: accented beat, bar lines, 2/4 metre (Grades 1—2)
5. 3/4 metre (Grade 3)
6. 4/4 metre (Grade 4)
7. 6/8 metre (Grade 5)
8. compound metres: 5/4, 6/4, 9/8, etc. (Grade 6)

Dynamics

1. loud vs. soft (forte vs. piano) (Kindergarten/Grade 1)
2. *crescendo* and *decrescendo* (Grade 2)
3. dynamic levels: pp, mp, ff, etc. (Grades 3—6)
4. *sforzando* (*sfz*) (Grade 4)
5. as appropriate (Grades 5—6)

Rhythm

1. rhythm (Kindergarten—Grade 1)
2. beat vs. rhythm (Kindergarten—Grade 1)
3. individual rhythmic values and patterns:
   - *tah, ti-ti*, quarter rest (Grade 1)
   - *ta-ah, ta-a-ah*, half note and dotted half rest (Grade 2)
   - *ti-ka-ti-ka; ti ti-ka; ti-ka ti*, sixteenth rest (Grade 3)
   - *ta-a-a-ah*; whole rest; *syn-co-pa* (Grade 4)
   - *tim-ka; tam-ti* (Grade 5)
   - *ti-ti-ti; tah-ti*, 6/8 metre (Grade 5)
   - *trip-o-let* (Grade 6)

Pitch

1. high vs. low (Kindergarten—Grade 1)
2. melodic contour (Grade 1)
3. individual pitches: tonic sol-fa names (Grades 1—6)
   - *soh—mi, lah* (Grade 1)
   - *doh, re* (Grade 2)
   - low *soh, lah* (Grade 3)
   - high *doh* (Grade 4)
   - *fa, ti* (Grade 5)
   - *fi, si* (Grade 6)
4. staff, treble clef, and absolute pitch names (Grades 3—4)
5. accidentals (Grade 4)
6. key signatures (Grades 4—5)
7. scales: major and minor (Grade 5)
8. scales: blues, chromatic, whole tone (Grade 6)

Harmony and Texture
1. monophonic singing (Kindergarten)
2. easy rhythmic *ostinati* (Grade 1)
3. pedal tones (Grade 1)
4. easy *bordun* patterns (Grade 2)
5. easy rounds (Grades 2–3)
6. easy melodic *ostinati* (Grades 2–3)
7. easy partner songs (Grades 2–3)
8. easy descants (Grades 2-3)
9. more complex rhythmic and melodic *ostinati* (Grades 4–6)
10. more complex *borduns* (Grades 4–6)
11. more difficult rounds and canons (Grades 4–6)
12. polyphonic two-part singing (Grades 4–6)
13. polyphonic three-part singing (Grades 5–6)
14. chords: I, IV, and V (Grades 5–6)

Form
1. phrase (Grade 1)
2. phrase form (Grades 1–2)
3. introduction and *coda* (Grade 2)
4. sectional form:
   - binary and ternary (Grade 3)
   - rondo (Grade 4)
   - theme and variations (Grade 5)
   - fugue (Grade 6)

Timbre
1. four voices (Kindergarten–Grade 1)
2. body percussion (Grades 1–2)
3. non-pitched percussion (Grades 1–6)
4. pitched percussion (Grades 1–6)
5. orchestral families (Grades 2–3)
6. orchestral instruments (Grades 4–6)
7. recorder (Grades 4–6)
8. other instruments (Grades 4–6)

Expressive Elements
1. *staccato* (Grades 2–3)
2. *legato* (Grades 2–3)
3. *fermata* (Grades 4–6)
4. other elements (as appropriate)

Planning for Multiple Learning Perspectives

Curricula designed to guide children towards musical understanding need to be **learner-centred**. This means teachers should incorporate classroom strategies that *promote learning in ways that allow individual students to reach their potential* *through the most positive routes possible*. Because children are unique in their learning styles (for example, some are better kinesthetic learners, while others are better visual learners), classroom experiences with music should be as broad as possible. When learning about any of the ten musical elements, children should be provided with classroom lessons that involve a variety and balance of experiences. Musical experiences of this type include:

A learner-centred curriculum takes individual learning styles into account.

1. singing music
2. playing music with classroom instruments
3. moving to music
4. listening to music
5. improvising music
6. reading music
7. writing music
8. composing music

Such multiple exploration of the individual components of musical structure (i.e., musical concepts) is integral to the development of musical understanding. As Davidson and Scripp (1992) suggest,

> Through activity, discrimination, and thoughtful observation, multiple perspectives of the same event or object are generated, differentiated from one another, and during reconsideration, integrated into a new and more comprehensive understanding. (p. 400)

Thus, in any given school year, children should be given the opportunity to become familiar with the musical concepts appropriate for study at their grade level through *each* of these eight important experiences.

It is also important for teachers to be sensitive to the fact that individual children may respond differently to the manipulation of musical structure. For example, children bring varying social, emotional, and spiritual backgrounds to the musical experience: a piece of music with loud dynamics may make one child feel exuberant but frighten another. Teachers are cautioned not to offer suggestions as to how the implementation of particular structural concepts in music should make a child feel (for example, that music in a **major key** should make one feel happy or that music in a **minor key** suggests sadness). A child's individual emotional response to the manipulation of various aspects of musical structure should be honoured and respected.

A quality elementary music curriculum utilizes a multitude of music experiences.

Developmental Appropriateness

Classroom activities should be developmentally appropriate.

Daily classroom activities (for example, keeping the beat while singing a song) involving any of the eight musical experiences need to be **developmentally appropriate**: that is, they should *match the children's cognitive, psychomotor, and socio-emotional development levels*. This means, for example, determining which songs are appropriate for Grade 1 students based on the development of their vocal range. Or, determining whether to ask children to first move to the beat using their arms or their feet should be based on their development of moving body parts. Children will have greater chances of understanding a given musical concept if the classroom activities incorporating that structural component are good matches for their psychomotor, cognitive, or socio-emotional levels. Recommendations regarding such planning are included in Chapters 4–15.

Sound before Symbol

The sound-before-symbol teaching process begins with aural, kinesthetic, and oral experiences in music.

Developmental appropriateness in elementary music also involves organizing instruction around the **sound-before-symbol teaching process**. Similar to the way many cultures around the world learn music (Sloboda, 1985; Campbell, 1991), research indicates that sound-before-symbol is a powerful tool for nurturing children's musical understanding (Zimmerman, 1993).

Sound-before-symbol provides a teaching process by which children *experience music aurally, kinesthetically, and orally first, before labelling and reading its symbolic representation*. Through this four-step process, children develop a working knowledge of musical structure in the most natural way possible. The description of these four steps below includes a specific classroom example involving rhythm.

Step 1 – Aural, kinesthetic, and oral: Students participate in aural, kinesthetic, and oral activities with music – musical concepts from the ten musical elements are experienced unconsciously without reference to label or symbol.

Example: While singing, students clap the rhythm of a rote song that contains rhythmic patterns made up of quarter notes and eighth notes.

Step 2 – Label: Students learn the verbal and visual labelling (names and notational symbols) of musical concepts from the ten elements of music.

Example: Students learn the names and notational symbols for quarter notes and eighth notes using music they have previously experienced aurally, kinesthetically, and orally.

Step 3 – Reinforce: Students gain practice in recognizing labels and/or notational symbols of musical concepts combined with the practice of translating those symbols into meaningful musical response.

Example: Students read, from notation, the rhythm of a new song that contains rhythmic patterns made up of quarter notes and eighth notes while singing or playing classroom instruments.

Step 4 – Create: Students create new music using the notational symbols of musical concepts in a unique and personal way

Example: Students compose a short song that contains rhythmic patterns made up of quarter notes and eighth notes.

The length of instruction planned for each of these four teaching steps logically depends on the age and experience of the children. Younger children (Kindergarten–Grade 3) need considerably more aural, kinesthetic, and oral experiences since most are at the beginning of their encounters with musical structure and patterning. Older elementary school students (Grades 4–6), who are building upon a larger repertoire of musical sounds, might require less time for aural, kinesthetic, and oral activities, leaving more time for in-depth development during symbolic response.

Regardless of the grade level, instruction that focuses on a particular musical concept during any given year should provide children with classroom activities involving *each* of the four steps. Such teaching practice will help students reach a point in their learning where, as performers, listeners, or composers, they can make meaningful and artistic decisions regarding musical patterning with that concept. Recommendations for successfully organizing daily classroom activities around the sound-before-symbol process are discussed in Chapters 10–15.

Music Literacy

Musical literacy provides students with independent access to musical style.

Historically, it is interesting to note that many of the significant elementary music education leaders of the twentieth century, including Émile Jaques-Dalcroze (1865–1950), Zoltán Kodály (1882–1967), and Carl Orff (1895–1982), organized their teaching approaches around the sound-before-symbol process. Although each emphasized different pedagogical tools for achieving musical understanding (movement with Jaques-Dalcroze, singing with Kodály, and playing instuments with Orff) all three centred their curriculum planning around the sound-before-symbol process (Montgomery, 1997).

According to Campbell (1991), "Reading and writing music should follow a rich and prolonged period of aural experiences. It is in this combination that children can develop a more thorough musical understanding" (p. 212). One of the main reasons that Kodály- and Orff-inspired curricula had such an impact on Canadian elementary school music during the last three decades of the twentieth century may well have been due to their success at organizing beginning instruction around aural, kinesthetic, and oral experiences. Such curricular organization paved the way for teachers of these curricula to subsequently lead students towards the acquisition of **musical literacy**—*the reading and writing of musical notation.*

Clearly, it is critical for children to develop musical literacy in order to move towards a comprehensive musical understanding. Indeed, children need skills in reading and writing music in order to fully experience two of the authentic modes of musical encounter discussed earlier in this chapter: performing and composing. For example, children without skills in musical literacy are wholly dependent on experts being available to teach them a piece of music by **rote** (*orally without the use of notation*) so that they might perform it. Similarly, students who lack musical literacy must rely on the presence of an expert whenever they want to compose a piece of music and write it down (or notate it on a computer). Without musical literacy, students have little independent access to multiple musical styles thereby limiting their chances of deriving personal meaning from any music other than what is "given" to them by someone else.

Musical literacy also opens the door for students to have the opportunity to perform music that is too long or too complex to learn by rote. In addition, musical literacy provides students with the opportunity to experience the history of music through performance by playing music that was written hundreds of years ago. Thus, the development of reading and writing skills in music is an important component of a curriculum designed to promote the development of a comprehensive musical understanding.

The Classroom Environment

Daily planning should include activities for both group and individual instruction.

Planning for this comprehensive curriculum also requires careful consideration as to the kind of instruction utilized on a daily basis. Such planning should include classroom opportunities for both group and individual instruction. Children need to extend the knowledge acquired through whole-class instruction through to activities that require them to problem-solve as individuals. For example, after practising writing rhythmic patterns of music with the whole class, children could be given individual baggies of popsicle sticks and asked to "write" rhythms from additional songs by themselves on the floor. This kind of activity is important as individual practice with musical decision making is necessary in order to move towards informed practice.

It is also important to give children the opportunity to reflect on the actions they take regarding music, whether as performers, as listeners, or as composers. This means classroom instruction, whether group or individual, should include time for children to talk about, explain, and interpret the decisions they make regarding the music they experience during an activity. Such discussions play a significant role in developing musical understanding as children need practice at carefully thinking through the various options available to them in a variety of musical experiences.

Children need a supportive classroom environment for reflection.

For successful discussions, CMEA and CMEC (2001) recommends that teachers provide a classroom environment that supports children

- asking questions,
- taking risks,
- solving problems,
- analyzing their work, and
- valuing the work of others.

This encouraging classroom environment should help children to gain the confidence and flexibility necessary to begin to bring personal intervention to all of their musical encounters. Physical parameters regarding this environment are discussed in Chapter 3.

Questions for Discussion and Practice

1. Discuss some of the challenges teachers face when selecting musical styles for inclusion in the elementary grades. Search the Internet and make a list of helpful Web sites where you might find a variety of music to use with children in the elementary classroom.

2. How are musical concepts organized for use in the elementary music curriculum? What is meant by a learner-centred classroom in elementary music?

3. Discuss the sound-before-symbol teaching process. What role does it play in organizing instruction for the elementary music class? Give another teaching example for each of the four steps of the process.

4. Why is the development of musical literacy important in an elementary music curriculum designed to teach for musical understanding?

5. What role does reflection play in elementary school music? Why is it important for children's development?

References

Campbell, P. (1991). *Lessons for the World: A Cross-Cultural Guide to Music Teaching and Learning*. New York: Schirmer Books.

CMEA and CMEC. (2001). *Achieving Musical Understanding: Concepts and Skills for Pre-Kindergarten to Grade 8*. Toronto: Coalition for Music Education in Canada.

Davidson, L., and Scripp, L. (1992). Surveying the coordinates of cognitive skills in music. In R. Colwell (Ed.), *Handbook of Research on Music Teaching and Learning*. New York: Schirmer Books.

Montgomery, A. (1990). The effect of selected factors on the use of instructional time by elementary music specialists in Atlantic Canada. *Canadian Journal of Research in Music Education, 32(3)*, 48–61.

Montgomery, A. (1997). Orff or Kodály: What's all the fuss? *The Canadian Music Educator, 39(1)*, 11–13.

Shand, P. (1982). Part I: The status of music education in Canada. *The Canadian Music Educator, 23(3)*, 18–30.

Sloboda, J. (1985). *The Musical Mind*. Oxford: Clarendon Press.

Zimmerman, M. (1993). Psychological theory and music learning. In R. Colwell (Ed.) *Basic Concepts in Music Education II*. Niwot, Colorado: University Press.

CHAPTER 3

The Musical Classroom

SYNOPSIS

Chapter 3 describes the equipment, resources, and physical environment required for successful instruction in the elementary music classroom. Discussion on various aspects of the music teacher follows, with particular reference to challenges in the Canadian classroom.

Equipment, Resources, and Physical Environment

The music classroom needs to be set up in such a way as to facilitate children's growth in musical understanding. Discussion in Chapter 2 regarding the context of such a curriculum gives important clues as to the physical parameters necessary for providing a positive learning environment for this growth.

Special consideration needs to be given to the physical organization of a classroom that will provide for children's authentic experiences in performing, listening, and creating. As discussed in Chapter 2, this means utilizing a balanced curriculum involving children in the broad musical activities of *singing, playing classroom instruments, moving to music, listening to music, improvising, composing,* and *reading and writing music.* How, then, may the classroom be set up in order to promote such successful instruction?

The elementary music classroom should have adequate open floor space to support a variety of movement activities.

For *movement*, there must be enough space in the room for children to participate in a variety of activities—both **structured movement** (for example, action songs, singing games, and dances) and **creative or exploratory movement** (for example, movement used to interpret music). Furniture should be minimal, and the floor carpeted for safety (to prevent slipping). A smaller room can potentially serve multiple purposes for music instruction if chairs or risers can be folded up and placed against the wall during movement activities.

Concrete accessories that children can use during creative movement to illustrate particular music patterning, such as scarves and ribbons (for melodic contour, phrases, etc.), balls (for accented beats, etc.), yarn (for melodic contour), large elastic bands (for dynamics), and hoops (for phrase form) should be readily available. In addition, teachers need access to excellent resources that contain authentic examples of children's singing games and dances appropriate to the musical style being explored.

Successful experience with *singing* requires space for the children to be able to sit or stand with excellent posture. If the children are not sitting on the floor, chairs or foldable risers work best in this regard, as sitting at a desk makes it difficult to maintain a good singing position. Teachers should have access to excellent collections of song materials that contain a variety of rhymes, chants, folk songs, **canons**, **partner songs**, and choral music (in two and three parts) appropriate to the musical style(s) selected for study. A classroom filing cabinet for music storage is also useful. The addition of puppets or similar concrete visuals will serve as handy classroom props for motivating younger children during individual singing experiences or for dramatizing the text of a song.

If song materials are in published music textbooks such as *Canada Is Music* (Harrison and Harrison, 2000) or sheet-music form (for example, Telfer 1993), there should be enough copies for complete class sets at each grade level. Teachers who use single copies of songs that are in the public domain (i.e., songs not under copyright) will need appropriate music notation software to generate multiple copies for students. When using single copies of songs that are covered by copyright (and therefore may not be duplicated), an overhead projector or a computer with LEG projector may be needed when the instructor wants to teach the song to the children using notation. A tape recorder or a CD burner with a quality microphone can also be an effective classroom tool for providing feedback to students regarding their singing performance.

Listening activities require a high-quality stereo system with the capacity to play CDs, tapes, and mp3s. Speakers should be placed so that the music may be heard clearly, even at the back of the room. An individual listening station with a table, chairs and headphones, and a computer workstation with Internet access are also useful classroom tools for children working on independent projects. Listening resources should include a large music library containing quality CDs or tapes of a variety of music from the musical styles selected for study. CD sets containing music from a particular time period (for example, the Baroque era) or style (for example, jazz) can be economical additions for building such a library.

Composing activities require the availability of a variety of classroom materials and resources in the music classroom. Younger children might use popsicle sticks (thin wooden sticks about 10 cm. long), note heads (round wooden discs, bingo chips, etc.), and staff boards for writing muical compositions, while older children may prefer to use large poster boards and markers or more traditional pencils and paper. A computer with a MIDI station attached is also a valuable classroom resource for student composing.

Children should have access to a wide variety of instruments on which to try out their compositions: a piano, recorders, and both pitched and non-pitched percussion instruments. Video equipment for documenting the performance of student compositions can also be useful for creating a permanent record of the students' work.

Classroom activities involving *performing on instruments* or *improvising on instruments* require the availability of a wide variety of quality instruments. **Non-**

Authentic experiences with composing, improvising, and performing require the availability of a wide variety of classroom instruments.

Individual learning activities work best when students have access to a diversity of resources.

The acoustics of the music room need careful consideration.

pitched percussion instruments (*percussion instruments that produce only one tone or note*, such as rhythm sticks, triangles, wood blocks, or hand drums) are especially useful at all grade levels for experiencing timbral (sound colour) and rhythmic patterning in music. **Pitched percussion instruments** (*percussion instruments that produce more than one note*, such as xylophones, glockenspiels, or metallophones), and **recorders** (*small flute-like instruments belonging to the woodwind family*) allow children to experience melodic and harmonic concepts in music. Some teachers use **ukuleles** or guitars for accompaniment purposes as well. A piano, of course, is helpful, both for accompanying choral music in the upper grades and for facilitating creative movement activities in the lower elementary grades.

All music classroom activities require the availability of a variety of tools to enhance learning for children whose strengths lie in the visual domain. These include items such as felt boards, whiteboards, and magnetic staff boards where the teacher can use an assortment of concrete visuals to illustrate musical patterning. Portable boards are desirable for the early elementary grades because they can be placed in an easily viewable space for younger children sitting on the floor. Smaller felt boards or white boards can also be used by children during individual instructional activities (such as writing the melody of a song).

The classroom itself should be well lit and ventilated with considerable attention given to the acoustical properties of the space. Children developing aural sensitivity to musical structure need to be able to hear music clearly without interference from external sounds (such as clanky heaters!). Ideally the walls of the music classroom should be covered with colourful pictures and posters that attract children's attention as they enter. Most music teachers enjoy putting together bulletin boards that illustrate children's musical work, using photographs, posters, and actual musical compositions. All in all, the music classroom should be an exciting place for children to come to!

The Music Teacher

The ideal music classroom, as described in this chapter, clearly can only be as effective as the music teacher who provides the instruction. Successful elementary music teachers in the past have often found themselves having to work in much less stimulating classroom environments than described above, and yet have made significant contributions to the development of their students' musical understanding. How can this be?

The *key* to such successful teaching lies in the teacher's knowledge and competence in the subject matter of music (Krehbiel, 1990; Barry, 1992; Bressler, 1993; Brown, 1993; Vandenberg, 1993; Montgomery, 1994, 1995a). Perhaps, unlike any other curriculum area in the elementary grades, teachers of music must serve as live models for children's development of subject-matter competence. Although performing music plays only a partial role in the elementary music classroom, teachers must feel comfortable with such daily skills as teaching a song by rote (orally), modelling proper vocal production, or demonstrating proper playing technique on classroom instruments. Music teachers should have a competent knowledge of musical structure and musical styles, and they must also feel comfortable with their own musicianship. Add to these attributes an understanding of developmentally appropriate music activities, a working knowledge of the sound-before-symbol process, data about how various children learn, and a comfort level with motivating and managing classroom behaviour, and one has identified the makings of an excellent elementary music teacher!

Canadian elementary school music education is generally taught by two classifications of teachers: **music specialists** (*individuals with university-level training in music and music education*) and **classroom teachers** (*teachers with university-level training in general elementary education*). Music specialists carry the strength of several years of university-level music classes with special training in elementary music methods. Although classroom teachers with a Bachelor of Education degree have received heightened education in the art of teaching children, they often receive only one, or maybe two, classes in music or elementary music methods. As a result, classroom teachers often feel much less comfortable with their personal musicianship than do their music-specialist colleagues (Montgomery, 1995b).

Ideally, Canadian elementary school music curricula taught by classroom teachers should be augmented by teacher partnerships with music specialists. This might mean a sharing of planning, resources, weekly classroom instruction, and/or assessment by both of these teachers. Economic cutbacks in many provinces during the close of the twentieth century, however, have made this kind of significant linkage difficult to sustain. Classroom teachers left on their own to shoulder the entire responsibility of music instruction for their particular grade level in the new millennium may need to attend additional university classes during the summer months in order to gain more confidence in their personal music skills. Singing in a community choir or learning to play a musical instrument as an adult are two activities that may help classroom teachers become more at ease with the daily musicianship tasks required of them as elementary music teachers.

This textbook should provide a useful resource for elementary music teachers—whether music specialists or classroom teachers—as they plan for excellent classroom instruction. Readers will find special attention to details regarding the development of children's musical understanding in Chapters 1 to 3. Discussion of the developmental appropriateness and sequencing of content and classroom activities for singing, moving, composing etc. is covered in Chapters 4 to 9. Pedagogical ideas for building children's knowledge of musical structure and its patterning in musical style through the sound-before-symbol process are presented in Chapters 10 to 15. Chapters 16 and 17 present advice on lesson planning, providing for authentic assessment. Chapter 18 presents a discussion of challenges facing elementary music teachers over the next twenty years. All of this information should provide teachers with significant ideas for curriculum organization.

Readers should understand that no single resource, can, of course, provide all the details necessary for developing effective music instruction in the elementary grades. This textbook, however, provides an excellent beginning for those teachers interested in helping children build the musical understanding necessary to think, to act flexibly, and to ultimately bring personal intervention to all their future musical encounters.

Questions for Discussion and Practice

1. Describe the physical parameters of an elementary music classroom designed to help children participate in the authentic musical experiences of performing, composing, and listening.

2. What equipment is helpful for providing affective music instruction in the elementary grades. How might the lack of access to these items affect curricula?

3. What resources would be useful for an elementary music teacher to have in the classroom?

4. Briefly describe the difference between a music specialist and a classroom teacher. How could a partnership between the two benefit students in the elementary grades?

5. Discuss the issue of personal musicianship. What role does this play in the life of an elementary music teacher? List some ideas for teachers to continue this development beyond their undergraduate university education.

References

Barry, N. (1992). Music and education in the elementary music method class. *Journal of Research in Music Education, 39,* 248–61.

Bressler, L. (1993). Music in a double-bind: Instruction by non-specialists in elementary schools. *Bulletin of the Council for Research in Music Education, 115,* 1–13.

Brown, E. (1993). *Elementary music education curricula in public schools in Canada.* Unpublished doctoral dissertation, Northwestern University, Chicago, Illinois.

Harrison, J., and Harrison, H. (2000). *Canada Is Music—3/4 and 5/6.* Toronto: Gordon V. Thompson Music.

Krehbiel, H. (1990). *Illinois fine-arts: Elementary classroom teachers perceptions of music instruction.* Unpublished doctoral dissertation, University of Illinois, Urbana-Champaign, Illinois.

Montgomery, A. (1994). Competencies in music teaching for the elementary grades. *Canadian Journal of Research in Music Education, 35(4),* 25–35.

Montgomery, A. (1995a). The importance of music teaching competencies as rated by elementary classroom teachers and university methods' instructors. *Canadian Journal of Research in Music Education, 36(7),* 19–26.

Montgomery, A. (1995b). Training Canadian Kodály educators for the year 2000. *Alla Breve: National Journal of the Kodály Society of Canada, 39(1),* 11–13.

Telfer, N. (1993) *Songs of the Outports.* San Diego, CA: Neil A. Kjos Music.

Vandenburg, G. (1993). *Northern California classroom teachers' perceptions of their preparation to teach music in grades 2–5.* Unpublished doctoral dissertation, University of San Francisco, San Francisco, California.

PART TWO

Authentic Musical Experiences

Part II provides overviews of the three modes children engage in when encountering music: as performers—makers of music; as composers—creators of music; and as listeners—consumers of music. Chapters 4 to 7 discuss elementary school experiences that authentically involve children in these modes: singing, playing classroom instruments, improvising and composing, and listening to music. Important information relating to the developmental needs of the elementary school child for each experience is presented, along with sample classroom materials and activities.

Chapter 8 discusses the power of accompanying music with movement in the elementary grades, and presents strategies for facilitating positive music-movement experiences with children. Chapter 9 discusses the role of musical literacy in the child's development of a comprehensive musical understanding. Recommended teaching sequences for helping children gain the important skills of reading and writing music are included.

CHAPTER 4

Singing

SYNOPSIS

Chapter 4 discusses the role of making music through singing in the elementary school classroom. Topics include background on children's singing development, a description of the teacher vocal model, criteria for selecting songs for elementary classroom singing, rote vs. note teaching of a new song, techniques for helping beginning singers, advice on moving towards two- and three-part singing, and thoughts on elementary school children's choirs.

Children's Singing

Singing is a natural expression of music for children. Babies as young as a few months enjoy babbling and vocalizing on a variety of pitches accessible to their voices. By one to two years of age, this spontaneous singing becomes more complex with children improvising brief melodic phrases several times, substituting different words or nonsense syllables during each repetition. By age three, many children begin to imitate small parts of chants and songs sung to them by their caregivers, often with their own personal variations. By the end of pre-school (ages 4 to 5) most children can begin to successfully reproduce whole songs that are presented to them orally by rote.

Elementary school music teachers have the wonderful opportunity of beginning their work with children at this critical moment in a child's singing development. Indeed, this is the time when many children are ready to discover the difference between their singing voice and their talking voice, thus leading the way to the use of a beautiful, clear head tone. Teachers with an understanding of this developmental process can do a great deal in the classroom to facilitate positive growth in this direction.

In addition, researchers have determined that Kindergarten-age children tend to learn songs in several drafts; they absorb the words of the song first, followed by the rhythm, melodic contour, discrete pitches, and finally a sense of the tonality (Davidson, 1985; Hargreaves, 1986; Dowling, 1984, 1988; Veenker, 1999). Therefore, the early elementary grades are an important time period in the child's development when carefully considered classroom instruction can make a significant difference in helping children to move towards a positive beginning with singing.

Teacher Vocal Modelling

Children will imitate directly the quality of singing they hear from adult models. As a result, educators such as Bartle (1988) suggest teachers use a voice that is clear, relaxed, resonant, and in tune. Use of an extensive **vibrato** in the voice is not recommended as research indicates that children match pitch more accurately from a non-vibrato vocal model (Yarborough et al., 1992).

The ideal singing quality for children is a *light, natural treble* called the **head voice**. This beautiful upper singing register of the child's voice, although easily mastered, may be unfamiliar to many children who during their pre-school years heard and imitated the lower register chest voices used by pop singers or characters on their favourite television programs. In the early elementary grades, the use of the head voice can be encouraged in the classroom by using children's songs that contain only notes in the upper part of the child's natural singing **range**.

Upper part of range

Songs containing notes in the lower third of the child's range

Lower part of range

should be avoided, as this may promote the children's use of a more throaty chest voice (Goetze, et al., 1990).

Female elementary music teachers may also be used to singing mainly in the lower range of their voices, and will need to practise in order to become comfortable with singing children's songs in the proper higher vocal register. Be assured that the rewards of such effort are tremendous, giving teachers the musical skill necessary to motivate children towards using their beautiful head voices when singing.

Posture and Breathing

*Singing requires
excellent posture
and breath
support.*

Teachers should learn to model a good singer's posture, as tone quality is affected by all the muscles in the body. Singers should stand tall, with one foot slightly in front of the other and the weight on the balls of the feet; the chest should be high but comfortable, and the shoulders slightly back, down, and relaxed. When seated, singers should hold the upper body in the same position as for standing, sitting at the front edge of the chair with both feet flat on the floor. Avoid stiffness in the head, neck, or jaw muscles, since such tension usually finds its way into the singing voice.

Breath support is important for singers to ensure a steady flow of air to sustain the singing tone. Many teachers may be accustomed to using **clavicular breathing** (*a shallow upper-chest type of breathing that causes the shoulders to rise during inhalation*) and will not be familiar with the art of **deep breathing** (*a lower-chest type of breathing that utilizes the diaphragm*). Teachers will need to practise initiating and sustaining vocal sound using the proper diaphragm muscles in order to model deep breathing behaviour for their students during singing.

The **diaphragm** is *a large muscular membrane that separates the abdominal and chest cavities*. During proper deep breathing, the diaphragm contracts downward, directing the internal organs down and out with the abdominal and intercostal (lower rib) muscles. This movement allows the lungs in the lower chest to expand more fully when taking in air. The upper chest and shoulders should remain still during this natural breathing action so as to avoid tension in the throat and neck.

To simulate what this is like, lie comfortably on your back on the floor with your hands resting gently on your lower abdomen, and breathe normally. Since your shoulder muscles can't help out in this position, you will be able to feel the diaphragm and abdominal muscles at work. To do this from a standing position, lean forward from the waist until your upper body is parallel with the floor. Put your hands on the lower abdomen area and breathe slowly and deeply. Here again, the shoulder muscles will have a hard time moving, and you should be able to feel the proper muscles at work.

The same diaphragm and abdominal muscles should be used to sustain the singing voice. Practise with the following exercises may help to achieve this:

1. Take a proper deep breath, then blow out the air towards the flame of an imaginary candle. Think of keeping the flame pointing steadily away from you but don't blow it out completely. This exercise should help you feel the diaphragm and abdominal muscles moving gradually inward and upward, back into place, forcing the air out of your lungs to prepare for the next breath.

2. Take a deep breath, then try to achieve the same feeling of steady, controlled exhalation while making a hissing sound. This exercise illustrates the steady pressure needed to produce a consistent sound.

3. Now, with your hands on your abdomen at waist level, sing a series of short "ha-ha-ha-ha" sounds on a comfortable pitch. You should be able to feel your lower abdominal muscles at work.

4. Finally, sing phrases of a favourite song. As you do so, attempt to simulate this same steady flow of air. Remember, singing is like an athletic activity; it requires excellent breath control for success!

Making a Beautiful Sound

In order to produce a clear, resonant vocal sound, it is important to maintain a relaxed, dropped jaw and tongue. These few simple exercises will help you to get a feel for how a good singing tone should be made.

1. Choose a comfortable pitch, open your mouth as if you were beginning a yawn, and sing "ah."

2. Repeat exercise 1, but this time close your lips—but not your jaw—and begin to hum. You should feel a buzzing sensation forward in your face. Keeping relaxed, shift your hum to other pitches above and below your starting note, moving up one step at a time and then down again.

3. Begin to hum once again, but this time add vowels after the beginning hum to create sounds such as "hummoo-moo-moo," "hummoh-moh-moh," "hummah-mah-mah," etc. Move up and down again to different notes, always maintaining a dropped jaw and and open throat. Remember to keep your jaw relaxed

4. Now, try maintaining this jaw and throat position while you sing a favourite song. Make sure you are breathing properly!

Vocal Expression

Artistic performance begins in the elementary grades.

Teachers should also keep in mind the importance of modelling expressive singing for elementary music students. Whether the piece is a simple chant or a more complex folksong, expressive singing goes beyond simple rhythmic and melodic accuracy. To express the text and the mood of the song, teachers need to consider appropriate tempo, dynamics, and articulation. Facial expression and eye contact are also critical to communicate the meaning of a song. Young children will imitate a song sung by the teacher with tenderness or with vigour, thereby providing the teacher with a golden opportunity to establish the importance of beautiful artistic performance within a style.

The Male Teacher's Voice

Research indicates that early elementary school children match pitches more accurately from a female singing model rather than from a male one, since male voices actually sound an octave lower than the child's voice (Sims et al., 1982; Green, 1987; Cooper, 1992). This does not mean, however, that men should be discouraged from becoming elementary music teachers. Rather, male teachers should be aware that they may need to use additional sound models—such as a child's voice, a **recorder** (*a small flute-like woodwind instrument*), or a **xylophone** (*a wooden barred pitched percussion instrument*)—to help them teach a song accurately to the children (Goetze et al., 1990). The piano is usually not a good alternative for modeling a singing phrase with young children, as research indicates that keyboard instrumental models are much less effective than vocal ones (Stadler, 1990). Some men try using their **falsetto voice,** (*an imitation soprano-like voice achieved by singing lightly one octave higher than a male's normal vocal range*), but this is useful only if the falsetto voice has a good, clear, tone quality. As soon as the children are consistently able to match pitches from any of the recommended alternatives, a male teacher should resume using his regular voice, as this will help the children to imitate beautiful artistic singing.

Remember that children's singing should stay light, free, and unforced at all times. Younger voices tend to be sweet, soft, and even breathy, and should not be pushed to sound louder. With care, the child's voice develops naturally over time. Thoughtful selection of repertoire, combined with joyful singing and positive instructional techniques, can result in a powerful performance experience for children moving towards growth in musical understanding.

Criteria for Selecting Songs

Songs in the elementary music classroom should match the vocal developmental level of the students.

Much of the success in children's singing during the elementary grades depends on the teacher's knowledge of how to pick an appropriate repertoire for children. As was discussed in Chapter 2, children need a learner-centered environment that matches their cognitive, psychomotor, and socio-emotional levels of development. Never is this more true than in the selection of songs for classroom singing. Vocal modelling is important, but becomes totally irrelevant if the song being taught is too difficult or too easy for the children's voices.

Here are some important musical criteria to consider when selecting songs for classroom singing:

1. *range:* the distance between the highest and lowest notes in the song
2. *note placement:* the placement of the song range in relation to the child's natural singing range (in other words, the portion of the child's voice that is used in the song)
3. *starting note:* the first note of the song that the child sings
4. *melodic contour and intervals:* the linear shape of the melody and the **interval** distance between individual notes: for example, notes can be connected by **repeat** (*same note*), by **step** (*interval of a 2nd*), by **skip** (*interval of a 3rd*), or by **leap** (*interval of a 4th or more*)
5. *rhythm:* the type of rhythm (from simple to complex, in terms of note values and combinations)
6. *length:* the length of the song; the number of measures without repeats
7. *harmonic texture:* the nature and number of independent vocal parts; for example, songs might be **monophonic** (*having one vocal part*) or **polyphonic** (*having two or more independent vocal parts*).

All seven of these criteria must be considered as to psychomotor applicability (the physical capability of the child's voice at various age levels) during the song selection process. The text of the song is also important in relation to the child's socio-emotional level, but should be considered only after examining the melodic and rhythmic elements of the song.

Table 4.1 outlines selection criteria for three age groups: the early grades (Kindergarten–Grade 2); the middle grades (Grades 3–4); and the later elementary grades (Grades 5–6).

Table 4.1
Criteria for Selecting Songs for the Elementary Grades

Criteria	Kindergarten to Grade 2	Grades 3 and 4	Grades 5 and 6
Range (distance between lowest and highest notes)	1 to 6 notes	1 to 8 notes	1 to 10 notes (with special consideration for the changing voice)
Note placement in child's singing voice	all notes in upper part of child's singing range	most notes in upper part of child's singing range	notes in any part of the child's singing range
Starting note	or higher	or higher desirable but not required	any note in the child's singing range
Melodic contour and intervals (repeated notes, steps, skips, and leaps)	melodies containing only repeated notes, steps, and skips; avoid leaps if possible.	melodies containing only repeated notes, steps, skips, and small leaps (up to a 5th)	melodies containing repeated notes, steps, skips, and leaps up to an octave (8 notes)
Rhythm	simple rhythms made up of half notes, quarter notes, eighth notes, and sixteenth notes; avoid long sustained notes such as whole notes	simple rhythms (as for the early grades) with the addition of syncopated rhythms and longer note values	rhythms as for the earlier grades, with the addition of complexities such as dotted rhythms and triplets
Length	short songs (4–16 measures) with lots of repetition	longer songs with multiple verses; some repetition is still desirable	longer songs with multiple verses; some repetition is still desirable.
Texture (monophonic or polyphonic)	monophonic repertoire only	monophonic repertoire plus simple polyphonic structures (for example, rounds, canons, partner songs, and simple two-part songs with *ostinati*, descants, or counter-melodies)	monophonic songs, polyphonic rounds and canons, plus polyphonic two- and three-part choral arrangements
Text	appropriate to age group	appropriate to age group	appropriate to age group

As is recommended in Table 4.1, songs for the early grades should be short; the range should be one to six notes, falling in the upper part of the child's singing voice, and the melody should contain only repeated notes, steps, and skips; the rhythm should be simple and the texture monophonic (one part). An excellent example of a song for Grade 1 that fits these criteria is *Savez-vous planter des choux*.

Savez-vous planter des choux?

Traditional French Canadian folk song
English text by A. Montgomery

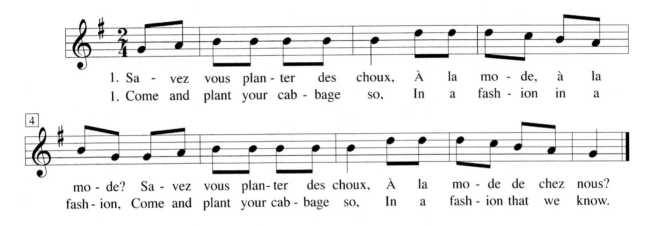

1. Sa - vez vous plan - ter des choux, À la mo - de, à la
1. Come and plant your cab - bage so, In a fash - ion in a

mo - de? Sa - vez vous plan - ter des choux, À la mo - de de chez nous?
fash - ion, Come and plant your cab - bage so, In a fash - ion that we know.

2. On les plante avec les pieds,
   À la mode, à la mode,
   On les plante avec les pieds,
   À la mode de chez nous.

3. On les plante avec les mains,
   À la mode, à la mode,
   On les plante avec les mains,
   À la mode de chez nous.

4. On les plante avec le nez,
   À la mode, à la mode,
   On les plante avec le nez,
   À la mode de chez nous.

2. We can plant them with our feet,
   In a fashion, in a fashion,
   We can plant them with our feet,
   In a fashion that we know.

3. We can plant them with our hands,
   In a fashion, in a fashion,
   We can plant them with our feet,
   In a fashion that we know.

4. We can plant them with our nose,
   In a fashion, in a fashion,
   We can plant them with our nose,
   In a fashion that we know.

Songs for Grades 3–4 should be slightly more complex in relation to all seven criteria, with the addition of some **polyphonic songs** *(songs having two or more independent vocal parts)* to the repertoire. For Grades 5–6 choose songs with larger ranges and more complex rhythms, and include many more two- and three-part polyphonic choral arrangements. Excellent examples of songs meeting these criteria are *Iroquois Lullaby* for Grade 3, and *I'll Give My Love an Apple* for Grades 5–6.

Iroquois Lullaby

Traditional First Nations song
English text and arrangement by A. Montgomery

I'll Give My Love an Apple

Traditional Maritime folk song

1. I'll — give my love an ap - ple with - out — e'er a core, I'll — give my love a dwell - ing with - out e'er — a door, I'll — give my love a pa - lace where - in she — might — be, That — she might un - lock it with - out e'er — a key.

2. How can there be an apple without e'er a core,
   How can there be a dwelling without e'er a door,
   How can there be a palace wherein she might be,
   That she might unlock it without e'er a key.

3. My head is an apple without e'er a core,
   My mind is a dwelling without e'er a door,
   My heart is a palace wherein she might be,
   That she can unlock it without e'er a key.

This version of I'll Give My Love an Apple was collected by Helen Creighton.
It is used here with permission of Nova Scotia Archives and Records Management, Halifax, Nova Scotia, Canada.

The criteria listed in Table 4.1 are, of course, guidelines that should be adjusted depending on the experience of the children in the classroom. However, these criteria provide excellent basic standards for selecting children's songs. Although research confirms that children's singing accuracy varies widely in any one grade level (Cooper, 1992), careful selection of song material can make an important contribution towards a positive singing experience for all of the children in the class.

The Changing Voice

The changing voice must be given extra consideration in the upper elementary grades.

There is one further aspect of the child's voice in the elementary grades to consider regarding repertoire. As children, especially boys, reach puberty (ages ten and a half to twelve and a half), their voices begin to change, becoming lower in pitch and heavier sounding. Physically, the male vocal cords and larynx become larger. During this transition stage (which can last anywhere from a few weeks to several months) boys may lose control of their voices; the sound sometimes becomes squeaky and there is a loss in range within the A–A octave.

This, of course, can be very embarrassing for young male singers, who need a sensitive teacher to help them through this growth period. Boys should be encouraged to continue singing during this time, but the teacher will need to make some adjustments in repertoire choices. Music in three parts—labelled I, II, and III—can be used, with the unchanged voices singing the upper part and the changing or changed voices singing either the middle or lower parts. The "number" labelling will avoid the social stigma sometimes associated with voice parts designated as "soprano" or "treble." Include open discussion of what happens when the voice changes so that children have some knowledge of what to expect when they reach this important transition period. Careful instruction combined with sensitive teaching should result in a positive singing experience for children right through puberty and beyond.

Teaching a New Song to Children

There are two different methods for teaching a new song to children:

1. by **rote:** teaching orally without notation
2. by **note:** teaching using some or all of the notation

Teaching by Rote

Rote singing is most commonly used in the early elementary grades when children's music literacy is only just developing. In the later grades, teachers might use rote teaching and/or a combination of rote singing and note reading, depending on the difficulty of the song and the children's development with reading musical notation.

Rote teaching of a song is traditionally done in one of two ways:

1. With the **whole-song** or **global approach** children echo back the whole song during each repetition.

2. With the **phrase-by-phrase approach** children echo back the song one phrase at a time.

These two approaches share certain techniques at the beginning of the process but vary in the actual steps for teaching the song.

To begin teaching a song by rote, a teacher might briefly introduce the song using a **concrete motivator** such as a puppet (for example, a rabbit puppet for a rabbit song), an item of clothing (perhaps a conductor's hat for a train song), or a picture (for example, a map of Africa for an African song) to arouse the children's interest. Once their attention is focused, the teacher sings the entire song to the students, asking the class to listen for a particular aspect, such as the words of the text. Then the teacher sings the song a second, or even a third time, posing additional questions about the text or asking the class to listen for specific musical elements, such as dynamics, repetition in the melody, or repetition in the rhythm.

At this juncture, the teacher must decide whether to continue singing the song in its entirety (the whole-song approach) or break the song into individual phrases (the phrase-by-phrase approach). Shorter songs lend themselves to the whole-song approach, whereas longer songs are most successfully taught with the phrase-by-phrase approach. In addition, younger children (Kindergarten–Grade 1) may have greater success when taught using the whole-song approach because of their desire to sing along with the teacher (Klinger et al., 1998).

To use the *whole-song approach*, the teacher gives the starting pitch and tempo to the children by singing

One, two, read-y and sing

in tempo and on the correct pitch, and gestures to the children to begin. Then the teacher sings the song softly along with the children. After each repetition, the teacher sings an example of an appropriate note, rhythm, or text correction for the children to try in their next attempt at singing the song. The children might be asked to tap the beat or clap the rhythm to help keep focus while singing. It is important for the teacher to stop singing along with the children after the first few repetitions in order to hear their vocal progress.

To use the *phrase-by-phrase approach*, the teacher asks the children to keep the beat while she or he sings the first phrase of the song. The children should be directed to echo back the phrase immediately after, without missing a beat between phrases. Corrections can be made after hearing the children echo each phrase or after the first time the whole song has been sung. If the children have difficulty with a particular phrase, the teacher can show the rise and fall of the melody (the melodic contour) with his or her hand while singing. Again, it is important to remember to not always sing with the children during each of their repetitions, in order to hear them clearly and make corrections. When ready, the children should attempt to sing the whole song without the teacher's help.

A variation of the rote method that combines both rote and note teaching is called the **rote-note observation method.** Here, *the children are given the music to look at while the teacher sings the song.* The children are asked to use their eyes and fingers to follow along with the music as the teacher sings. After each repetition, the teacher might ask questions about the song such as "Which phrase ends on a half note?", "Where are the phrases that repeat?", or "Which phrase ends on *re*?" Although the teacher eventually teaches the song by either whole-song or the phrase-by-phrase method, the rote-note observation method gives the child an opportunity to begin to associate sounds with symbols and provides excellent practice for moving closer towards musical independence.

The measure of success for any rote method is how accurately and pleasurably the children sing the song without help from the teacher. Remember that not all of this comes in one lesson; further repetitions will be necessary on subsequent days. When the song is repeated during later lessons, add something unique to the singing, such as movement or instrumental accompaniment, or ask the children to find musical concepts so that interest is continually sustained. Teachers should remember to always give a starting pitch and tempo along with a "starting" gesture as they start singing, so that the children have a solid beginning every time they sing.

Teaching by Note

Teaching a new song using the note method helps children to work on their musical literacy.

The second method for teaching a new song—*note teaching*—helps to build children's independence with singing by improving their ability to read music. Here, the teacher gives the children copies of the music with which to learn the song. Depending on the grade level of the class, a teacher might begin by asking the children to identify elements such as the key, time signature, and starting note. Most teachers then ask the children to sight-read the rhythmic notation first, since rhythm is usually easier to master than pitch (Moore et al., 1997). Children can read the rhythm by clapping, by chanting **rhythmic syllables** (*tah, ti-ti*, etc., see Chapter 9), or by a combination of the two.

Next, the children should be guided to look for melodic passages they might recognize from previous songs. Invite them to sight-read these passages using either a neutral syllable (such as "loo") or **tonic sol-fa** syllables (*doh, re, mi*, etc., see Chapter 9). Give the starting pitch each time a new section is begun. Next, the children can be challenged to read new melodic passages in the song using any of these techniques. This should be done slowly, possibly with several stops and starts. The teacher may eventually need to sing the song all the way through in order to help the children get a clearer picture of the complete song. Finally, the children should attempt the song in its entirety, with text, and without the teacher's help.

Whatever method is used for teaching a new song, it is important to give the children time during later lessons to *look at the music more closely to discover the rhythmic and melodic structural patterns* used in the music. Because singing is an activity that may help children to work towards developing musical understanding, recognition of these patterns and their manipulations in music is an important step toward gaining the ability to make meaningful and artistic decisions with future music. Classroom activities for this kind of *reflection* with singing are described in Chapters 10–15.

Strategies for Helping Beginners to Sing in Tune

Research suggests that there are four prerequisites for singing in tune (Goetze et al., 1990):

1. **pitch discrimination**: the ability to determine one pitch from another and to hear a succession of pitches
2. **pitch production**: the ability to manipulate one's singing voice throughout a range of pitches
3. **pitch monitoring**: the ability to hear and focus on one's own vocal pitch
4. **motivation to sing**: having the desire and positive self-esteem to sing with others

All of these behaviours play important roles in the child's success at learning to sing accurately, and indeed, several are still in the process of development at age five when children enter Kindergarten (Davidson and Scripp, 1988). Careful planning by the elementary music teacher to incorporate classroom games and activities that will facilitate positive growth in each of these areas will be beneficial to children's singing development.

Kindergarten to Grade 3 are critical years for helping children to move towards positive singing in tune.

Following is a list of eleven classroom strategies recommended by the author for helping children move towards singing in tune. Most are intended for use with children at the critical stage in their singing development (Kindergarten–Grade 3) when such intervention will have a significant and positive affect on their ability to sing in tune. This is not meant to imply that these strategies should not be used with older elementary school children. Experience indicates, however, that children who have not achieved accurate singing by Grade 4 lose so much self-esteem that their subsequent desire to sing after that is significantly reduced. The majority of children who find themselves in this unfortunate position do so because of a lack of knowledge by the child's elementary music teacher for finding the right teaching strategy, not from any lack of singing ability by the student. Thus, carefully planned teacher input in the Kindergarten–Grade 3 years can be critical for helping children make a positive transition into accurate singing.

Teachers may utilize any or all of the following strategies with elementary school children (especially Kindergarten–Grade 3 music classes) to help facilitate positive development of accurate singing.

1. *Always use the criteria listed in Table 4.1 to select songs for the classroom.* This will go a long way towards making sure class content matches the vocal developmental level of the students. These criteria are especially important for beginning singers (Kindergarten–Grade 2) who need a great deal of practice with the head voice. Thus, it is recommended that notes for songs in these grade levels should fall only in the upper range of the child's voice:

Research indicates that boys and girls share the same voice ranges until puberty (Brown, 1988; Goetze et al., 1990; Cooper, 1992) so boys do not need to have the pitch lowered for them in the early-middle elementary music classroom.

2. *Always sing the starting pitch and tempo for students before asking them to sing any song.* Teachers might use a tuning fork, a quietly tapped xylophone, or a quietly played recorder note to give themselves the correct beginning note for the song. However, the teacher's voice should then be used as the model to give the children their starting pitch before singing (male teachers might use another child's voice or the recorder, if necessary, to give the pitch to the class).

3. *Use a unique concrete motivator with each classroom song.* If consistently utilized during lessons where a particular song is used, children will begin to associate the notes of the song itself with that motivator. That means when teachers show a particular object, article of clothing, or picture at the beginning of each lesson, the children will already be hearing the melody of the song in their heads before they sing. Thus, the children get the benefit of a mini-rehearsal before they even open their mouths to sing!

See-Saw model to use with the song *See-Saw*

4. *Help children (especially Kindergarten–Grade 1) to explore the differences between each of the* **four voices:** *the talking voice, the whispering voice, the shouting or playground voice, and the singing voice.* As mentioned earlier in this chapter, many children enter Kindergarten with an aural concept of the low adult chest voice as being a proper singing voice. Some may never have heard or physically experienced a child's natural singing voice—the *head* voice—in their home environment. The *talking voice* and *whispering voice* should be introduced into Kindergarten–Grade 1 music classroom repertoire in order to allow children to consciously experience and practise the differences between these three voices. Here are four ways this might be done this in a lesson:

(a) Juxtapose a rhyme with a song. Use a puppet to guide the children towards the use of their talking voice or their whispering voice with the rhyme and their singing voice with the song. (Ask the children to use the same voice as the puppet.) A puppet whose mouth opens wide, as in speaking or singing, is helpful.

Five Little Pumpkins and *Pumpkin, Pumpkin* make an excellent rhyme-and-song combination for a Grade 1 lesson in the Halloween season.

Sophie bird puppet

Five Little Pumpkins

Traditional

Five little pumpkins sitting on a gate,

The first one said, "Oh, my it's getting late!"

The second one said, "There are witches in the air!"

The third one said, "But I don't care."

The fourth one said, "Let's run and run and run!"

The fifth one said, "Let's go and have some fun!"

Ooooo went the wind and out went the light,

And all the little pumpkins rolled out of sight!

Pumpkin, Pumpkin

Traditional Halloween song

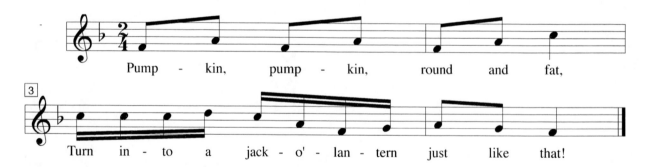

Pump - kin, pump - kin, round and fat,

Turn in - to a jack - o' - lan - tern just like that!

Game: Ask one child to imagine they are a pumpkin. This child faces away from the other children. After all the children sing the song, the child who is playing the pumpkin role chooses an expression (sad, happy, surprised, etc.), pretends to become a jack-o'-lantern, and turns around to face the rest of the class. The children try to name the expression on the "jack-o'-lantern." Then the game begins again with another child playing the pumpkin role.

(b) Tell the children a story that requires a sound effect such as a train whistle, a fire engine siren, or ghost noises. Ask children to create these special sound effects; this will automatically throw their voices up into the head-voice range.

(c) Use a story songbook such as *Row, Row, Row Your Boat* (Muller, 1993) that alternates between telling a story (where the teacher uses a talking voice) and singing a song (where children can use their singing voices). Here the children may be asked to monitor the use of their singing voice at the correct time.

(d) Use a song such as *One, Two, Tie My Shoe*, which requires the use of both the singing voice and (for small sections) the talking voice. Again, a puppet can be a helpful prop to encourage the children to use the proper voice at the correct time.

One, Two, Tie My Shoe

Traditional call-and-response song

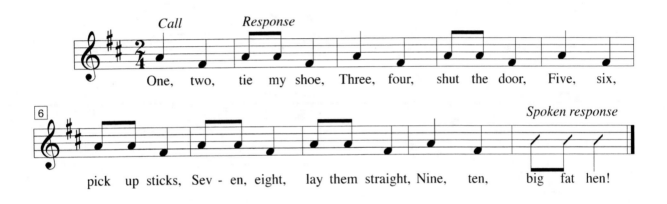

5. *As children become more comfortable with their singing voices, introduce* **fill-in-the-blank songs** *(songs in which the teacher sings most of the song and the children sing only a small part indicated by a blank line in the music). Usually the teacher begins the song and the children's part comes later. This means that the children hear the correct vocal model first, and have a greater likelihood of matching the model when their turn comes. Three excellent examples of fill-in-the-blank songs are* Bought Me a Cat *(for Grade 1),* There Was an Old Woman *(for Grade 2), and* Who's Got a Fish Pole? *(for Grade 3).*

Bought Me a Cat

Traditional fill-in-the-blank song

Note: This song can continue indefinitely with new soloists adding new animal names to extend the song.

There Was an Old Woman

Traditional Halloween fill-in-the-blank song

Solo
Group

1. There was an old wom-an all skin and bones, Ooo! _____

2. She lived down by the old graveyard, Ooo!

3. One night she thought she'd take a walk, Ooo!

4. She walked down by the old graveyard, Ooo!

5. She saw the bones a-layin' a-round, Ooo!

6. She went to her closet to get a broom, Ooo!

7. She opened the door and BOO!!

Who's Got a Fish Pole

Traditional fill-in-the-blank song

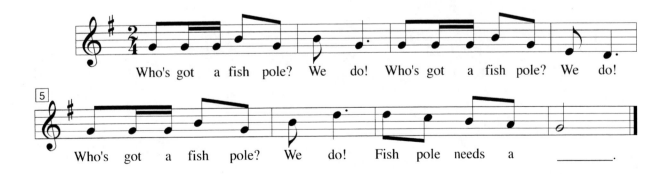

Who's got a fish pole? We do! Who's got a fish pole? We do!

Who's got a fish pole? We do! Fish pole needs a _____.

6. *Research indicates the importance of providing developing young singers (Kindergarten–Grade 2) with an opportunity to experience* **individual singing** *so that they can learn to monitor their own voices* (Goetze, 1985; Clayton, 1986; Smale, 1988; Cooper, 1992; Rutkowski, 1996). Group singing makes it difficult for many children to hear their own voice as distinct from those around them. In addition, teachers need to hear children singing individually in order to give appropriate feedback needed to develop the skill of singing in tune. Most importantly, activities for individual singing need to be non-threatening and inviting so that the children will be motivated to want to sing by themselves. Here are a few suggestions in this regard:

(a) In the early elementary grades, establish individual singing as a regular part of every elementary music lesson, starting as soon as kindergarten. Children who begin to feel comfortable with this kind of activity when they are quite young will continue to look forward to it again in Grades 1 and 2. If class sizes are large, have about ten children sing individually during the beginning of each lesson, with the goal to have all the children participate in individual singing at least once a week.

(b) Use puppets for individual question-and-answer or **call-and-response** singing between teacher and student. Teachers can use a puppet to invite the child's puppet (rather than the child herself or himself) to sing back. For many students, this puppet game seems to depersonalize solo singing and makes it feel "safer" to sing alone. Of course the children know that they create the voice of their puppets, but the fact that they can pretend that the puppet is singing helps them feel more comfortable with the process of individual singing. Three excellent examples of songs that work well in this regard for Kindergarten–Grade 1 are *Colour Song*, *Cuckoo*, and *Doggie, Doggie*.

Colour Song

Traditional call-and-response song

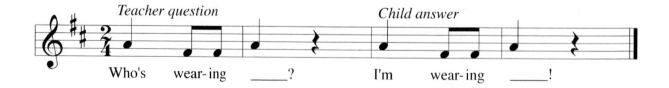

Cuckoo

Traditional chant

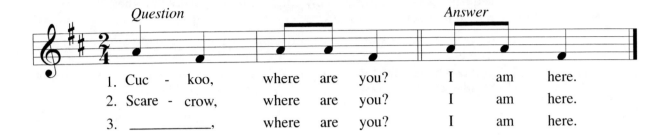

1. Cuc - koo, where are you? I am here.
2. Scare - crow, where are you? I am here.
3. _____, where are you? I am here.

Doggie, Doggie

Traditional chant

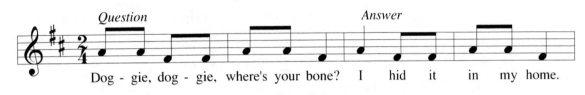

Dog - gie, dog - gie, where's your bone? I hid it in my home.

Where did you hide it? I hid it in my ____.

(c) The journey towards success with individual question-and-answer singing is gradual (it may take many weeks or even months!) and teachers should not expect every child to match pitch accurately the very first time. Instead, any response—including a simple wave back from the child's puppet, or use of the talking voice—can make an excellent beginning. At subsequent lessons the growth process can be continued by helping the child progressively bring his or her voice closer to the proper vocal model. Since most children will sing back at a lower pitch, teachers should use techniques that will help the child to learn how to raise her or his singing voice to the same pitch level as theirs. One strategy that works well is to echo back the child's response at whatever pitch level the child has sung; then, sing the question part of the phrase again, at a slightly higher pitch than the child's and invite the child to sing his or her

answer at this new pitch. Any raise in pitch from the child's initial response can be complimented with such statements as "Great, you were able to raise your voice a little bit higher!" Avoid generalized statements (for example, "Great job") since the child might assume that they were successful at matching the original pitch. Repeated use of such strategies over a number of subsequent lessons will help many children to eventually find their head voices and match exact pitch levels.

(d) Use singing games that have individual singing embedded within the game. The fun of the game will distract most children from realizing that they are actually being asked to sing by themselves. Two excellent examples of this for Grades 1 and 2 are *We Are Dancing in the Forest* and *Are You My Children?*

We Are Dancing in the Forest

Traditional call-and-response singing game

Game: The child selected to play the role of the wolf stands in the "den" area. The rest of the children form into groups of four or five in the "forest" area of the room; they hold hands and skip around in circles while singing the song. At the end of the song ("... at our play.") one child sings the solo question, asking the wolf what she or he is doing. The "wolf" sings the solo answer, then runs about trying to catch the children as they scamper for safety out of the forest. Any children who are caught join the wolf for the next round of the game and help the wolf with his or her duties. The game continues until all the children are captured. *Please note that this game requires a large area for running to be played safely.*

Are You My Children?

Traditional call-and-response singing game

Witch, witch, could-n't sew a stitch, Picked up a pen-ny and thought she was rich!

Are you my child-ren? Yes mamm! Are you my child-ren? No you old witch!

Game: The children sit on the floor in a circle. One child, who is selected to play the role of the witch, sits in the middle. The children in the circle sing the "group" parts of the song, and the "witch" sings and speaks the "solo" parts. At the end of the song, the teacher selects a new child to play the witch and the game begins again.

(e) When the children become fairly successful with call-and-response songs in which the teacher is the leader, introduce songs that switch roles and let a single child sing the question part while another child or a group of children sing the solo answer. Excellent examples of such singing games are: *Hey Hey* (for Grade 1), *Who's That?* (for Grade 2), and *Charlie over the Ocean* (for Grade 3).

Hey, Hey

Traditional chant

Hey hey, look at me, I am ____ you can see!

Game: The children stand in a circle. One child sings the whole song through, filling in the blanks with words such as "smiling," "singing," or "playing." On the repeat, all the children echo back the solo part and act out the word supplied by the soloist (for example, big smiles on their faces for "smiling"). Then the song begins again with a different child leading the class.

Who's That?

Traditional singing game

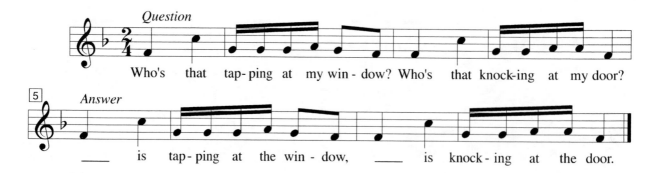

Game: The children sit in pairs on the floor with one child directly behind the other. The child sitting in the front of each pair sings the question, then the child in the back sings the answer, filling in the blank with her or his name. To add a rhythmic and timbral focus, have the children play the "tapping" and "knocking" rhythms on wood blocks or rhythm sticks.

Charlie over the Ocean

Traditional call-and-response singing game

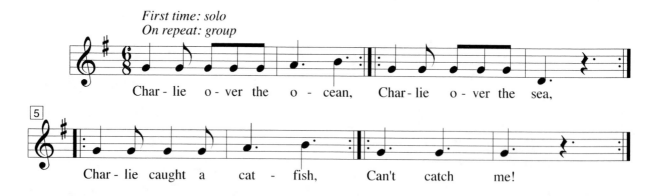

Game: The children sit in a circle on the floor with their eyes closed. The child selected by the teacher to play the role of "Charlie" stands outside the circle. "Charlie" sings the solo parts of the song while skipping around the outside of the circle, with the group echoing on the repeats. When the song is finished, the children try to guess which one of their classmates is playing the part of Charlie. Whoever Charlie is standing behind at the end of the song becomes the new "Charlie" and the game begins again.

7. *Songs for beginning instruction should have small ranges (three to four notes) in order to facilitate accurate singing.* Some research suggests initial songs might best contain some descending **minor 3rd patterns** (for example, *soh–mi*), as younger children find these some of the easiest patterns to sing (Sinor, 1985). Other researchers have determined that instruction that includes singing both **pentatonic patterns** (*melodic patterns that are based on a five-note scale containing no half steps*) and **diatonic patterns** (*melodic patterns that are based on an eight-note scale containing some half steps*) is most effective (Jarjisan, 1983). Research also suggests that younger children find songs with unique melodies easier to learn than "piggy-back songs" (songs that combine a familiar melody—such as *Twinkle Twinkle Little Star*—with new words) (Feierabend et al., 1998). Younger children also seem to find songs with actions easier to learn, as they can associate the melodic content of each phrase with a unique movement. *Teddy Bear* is an excellent example of a Kindergarten–Grade 1 song that fits all of these criteria.

Teddy Bear

Traditional singing game

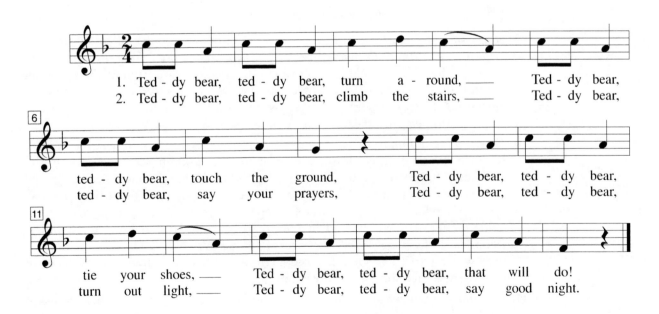

Activity: Invite the children to stand in their own space on the floor and perform the various actions ("turn around," "touch the ground," etc.) as they sing the words.

8. *Songs presented in other formats—such as* **story songbook** *form—can be useful in helping develop children's ability to sing in tune.* Here the children listen while the teacher leisurely sings the song and shows pictures from the book; this provides the children with a precious opportunity for aural review of the song without the need to use their singing voices. As the children become more familiar with the song, they may wish to join the teacher by singing certain sections. Story songbooks can be a powerful way to close a Kindergarten–Grade 2 lesson and provide another means for experiencing the melody of a song. Here is a list of excellent *story songbooks* to try.

All the Pretty Little Horses (Saport, 1999)
Big Fat Hen (Baker, 1994)
Brown Bear, Brown Bear, What Do You See (Martin and Carle, 1992)
Deck the Hall (Long, 2000)
Fiddle-I-Fee (Sweet, 1992)
Hush Little Baby (Long, 1997)
Itsy Bitsy Spider (Trapani, 1993)
London Bridge Is Falling Down! (Spier, 1967)
Mary Had a Little Lamb (de Paola, 1984)
Over in the Meadow (Carter, 1992)
Teddy Bear (Hague, 1993)
This Old Man (Adams, 1974)
Twinkle, Twinkle, Little Star (Moroney, 1994)

9. *Songs should initially be taught to children without accompaniment in order to help them monitor their own voices without the distraction of another timbre.* As soon as the song is learned, accompaniment—on **non-pitched percussion** (hand drums, wood blocks, triangles, etc.) or **pitched percussion** (xylophones, glockenspiels, etc)—might be added, as unlike the piano, these instruments can be played in beautiful balance with children's voices.

10. *Repetition is an important element in the process of learning to sing in tune.* Repeat songs in several different lessons in order to give children adequate opportunity to practise the correct notes. Don't be afraid that the children will become bored with such repetition, as "children are often spontaneously repetitive in many aspects of behaviour and the urge for repetition may well be part of the natural tendency which has survived in part because it is so beneficial to learning" (Sloboda, 1985, p. 225). Teachers are, of course, well advised to vary the activity used with a particular song in subsequent lessons (for example, adding different actions, accompaniment, or movement).

11. *Experiment with kinesthetic aids.* For example, teachers might use their hands to trace the melodic contour (the rise and fall of the melody) in the air while the children are singing. Another option is to use **hand signs** to indicate individual pitches (a system initially developed by Sarah Glover and John Curwen in England in the 1870s, see Chapter 9), which can be very helpful to young singers in feeling the highness or lowness of the pitch. Such tools may be eliminated in further repetitions of a song, once children have learned to accurately sing the correct pitches.

Tonal Memory Games

All of the above strategies may prove to be helpful to the teacher in facilitating growth in pitch accuracy. Once children start developing the ability to sing back short songs, games such as Inside-Outside Voice and Mystery Tune can be added in the classroom to help facilitate children's further development of tonal memory.

In the Inside-Outside game, teachers use an object such as a **cone puppet** (a puppet that can pop its head in and out of a cone-shaped barrel) or a **reversible sign with a face** (a double-sided sign showing a face with an open mouth on one side and a closed mouth on the other) to signal the children when to sing out loud and when to continue singing the song silently in their heads. By alternating the singing of phrases in this way, children are required to keep the pitch going in their heads in order to be able to come back in on the correct note when the puppet or reversible sign directs them to sing out loud again. This kind of game is enjoyed by older elementary grade children as well, and can be used effectively through Grade 6 with the more complicated songs sung by the children at this level.

Cone puppet

The Mystery Tune game may also be used from Kindergarten through to Grade 6. In this game the teacher asks the children to guess the name of a familiar song after the melody has been hummed, sung on a neutral syllable (such as "loo"), or played on a recorder by the teacher. For younger students, possible song choices might be listed on the board either by title or with felt pictures that represent the songs iconically (for example, a felt engine for a train song).

Learning to sing accurately in tune can be a positive experience for children in the elementary grades if the teacher plans the instruction carefully. Although singing in every music class is important for such development, it is the choice of music and the presentation of those songs that will prove to be the key to success.

Facilitating the Development of Part-Singing

Once children are comfortable with singing a wide variety of **monophonic songs** *(songs with only one voice part)*, they are ready to begin exploration of the exciting world of singing in harmony. For most children, this comes in Grades 2–3. Successful two-part singing should begin either with song arrangements in which the second vocal line is a **melodic *ostinato*** *(a short melodic phrase repeated over and over)* or with simple **rounds** *(short songs in which two or more voices sing the same melody starting one after the other)*.

Melodic Ostinato

Any simple melodic fragment that produces acceptable harmony when repeatedly sung as an accompaniment throughout an entire song can be sung as a melodic *ostinato*. Children should have experience in the classroom at singing both parts, but initial learning of the song should precede the addition of the *ostinato* vocal line. In the following arrangement of *Canoe Song*, the lower part is an example of a melodic *ostinato*.

Canoe Song

Traditional Canadian camp song
Arranged by A. Montgomery

Rounds

Simple rounds for two or three voices may also provide successful early part-singing experiences for Grades 2–3 children when taught in the correct manner. No attempt should be made to sing the song in more than one vocal part until the song itself has been learned securely by the children. As a first step, the children start the song while the teacher sings the second voice of the round alone (starting at the "*2" in the music). The children will need several repetitions in this manner before they are ready to divide into two groups to sing the song in a round without the teacher's help. Three parts should only be undertaken once the children can successfully sing the round with two voice parts.

Excellent examples of rounds appropriate for Grades 2–3 include *London's Burning, Laugh Ha Ha!, Christmas Is Coming,* and *Hey-Ho.*

London's Burning

Traditional English round

Lon-don's burn - ing, Lon-don's burn - ing, Fetch the en - gines, fetch the en - gines, Fire, fire! Fire, fire! Pour on wa - ter, pour on wa - ter!

Laugh Ha Ha!

Traditional English round

Laugh ha ha! Here's a mer - ry jest, But if you will laugh last, You will laugh best!

Christmas Is Coming

Traditional English round

Christ - mas is com- ing, The goose is get - ting fat.

Please to put a pen - ney in the old man's hat,

Please to put a pen - ney in the old man's hat.

Hey-Ho

17th-century round

Hey - ho, no - bo - dy at home, Meat nor drink nor mon - ey have I none,

Yet will I be mer - ry, — Hey - ho, no - bo - dy at home.

Partner Songs

Teachers might also use **partner songs** (*two songs that produce acceptable harmony when sung simultaneously*) to help children develop the ability to hold on to their own part. Have the children learn both parts separately before they divide into groups to sing the two songs together. The following arrangement, which combines *Frère Jacques* and *London Bridge* is an example of such partner songs.

Frère Jacques–London Bridge Partner Song

Traditional rounds
Arranged by A. Montgomery

Descants and Countermelodies

The choices available for two-part singing in Grades 3–4 also include descants and countermelodies, both of which are excellent for this age group. A **descant** is *an independent melody that is written above the main melody*; its chief purpose is to provide harmony but some descants are also ornamental. A **countermelody** is *an independent melody written below the main melody*. The main function of a countermelody is to provide harmony for the tune of the song, but like descants, countermelodies have an independent character, and the contrast between the two enriches the song.

Again, all the children should learn to sing both voice parts, beginning with song tune first. Many examples of this kind of appropriate two-part arrangements may be purchased from leading choral publishers across the country.

Advanced Rounds and Canons

Grade 4 students should also extend their part-singing experience to include longer rounds and **canons** (*polyphonic pieces for voices or instruments, in which all parts perform the same melody, where each voice enters after a specific time interval, and imitates exactly the melody sung of played by the first voice*). The simpler canons suggested for the upper elementary grades are much like rounds. Excellent examples of such rounds and canons are *Music Alone Shall Live, Oh How Lovely Is The Evening, Viva la musica*, and *Entendez-vous sur l'ormeau*.

Music Alone Shall Live

Traditional German round

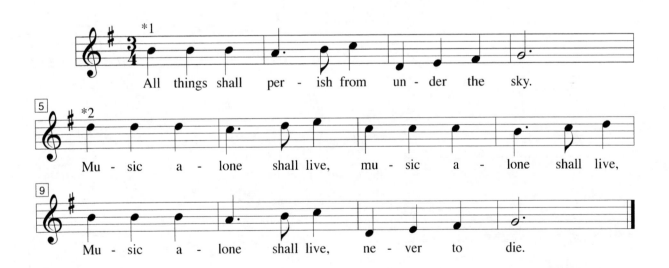

Oh How Lovely Is the Evening

Traditional German round

Oh how love-ly is the ev-en-ing, is the ev-en-ing,

When the bells are sweet-ly ring-ing, sweet-ly ring-ing,

Ding, dong! Ding, dong! Ding, dong!

Viva la musica

canon for three voices
Michael Praetorius (1571–1621)

Vi - va vi - va la mus - i - ca, Vi - va vi - va la

mus - i - ca, Vi - va la mus - i - ca.

Entendez-vous sur l'ormeau

Traditional French round

Students in Grades 5 and 6 will then be ready to try more difficult canons and rounds such as *The Ghost of John, C-o-f-f-e-e Canon, Shalom Chaverim,* and *Toembai.*

The Ghost of John

Traditional round

C-o-f-f-e-e Canon

Karl Gottlieb Hering (1765–1853)
English text by A. Montgomery

C - O - F - F - E - E don't drink that much — cof - fee, Not for a - ny one is this — brown — drink, Makes you ner- vous pale and out — of — sync, Don't let your caf - feine make you feel not in the pink!

Shalom Chaverim

Traditional Hebrew round
Engish text by A. Montgomery

Sha - lom cha - ver - im, sha - lom cha - ver - im, Sha -
Have peace my ___ friend, have peace my ___ friend, Have

lom, sha - lom, L' - hit - ra - ot, l' -
peace, have peace, Till we meet a - gain, till

hit - ra - ot, Sha - lom, sha - lom.
we meet a - gain, Have peace, have ___ peace.

Toembai

Israeli nonsense round

Toem-bai, toem-bai, toem-bai, toem-bai, toem-bai, toem-bai, toem - bai.

Tra la la, la la la la la, la la la la la la.

Tra la la la la, la la la la la, la la la la la la.

Choral Arrangements

Part-singing in Grades 5 and 6 may also be expanded to include music with three independent melodic lines. Arrangements that feature **polyphonic** writing (*distinct voice parts that are independent melodically and rhythmically*) rather than **homophonic** writing (*voice parts that share the same rhythm and usually move together in 3rds or 6ths*) are most successful with this age group. Children love these experiences with harmony that provide them with wonderful opportunities to enjoy the world's music.

Children's Choirs

Children's choirs may be used to provide additional singing experience beyond the elementary music classroom.

Children who are interested in extending their singing time beyond the regular elementary music classroom might be interested in joining an extracurricular elementary school choir. Traditionally such choirs meet during lunchtime or after school and are divided up into junior (Grades 3–4) and senior (Grades 5–6) levels. Children are sometimes expected to audition for such groups in order for the conductor to ascertain their vocal strengths, but the choir should be accessible to any child interested in participating.

Children that sing in school choirs may share the results of their hard work during rehearsals at such events as school concerts, visits to hospitals or senior citizens' homes, or regional music festivals. Resources for teachers interested in finding out more about running a school choir include texts such as *Lifeline for Children's Choir Directors* (Bartle, 1988), or *Directing the Children's Choir* (McRae, 1991).

Questions for Discussion and Practice

1. Why is singing considered natural to the child? Describe an excellent teacher vocal model for children's singing.

2. What is meant by the head voice? List a variety of classroom strategies useful for helping beginning singers to become comfortable with using this voice.

3. Discuss the criteria for selecting songs for the elementary music classroom. Pick one age group and list six songs found in other chapters of this textbook that fit the appropriate parameters. Be prepared to justify your choices.

4. Describe the two different approaches for teaching a song by rote in the classroom. How do these approaches differ from teaching a song using the note method? Choose one approach and practice it by teaching a new song to your peers.

5. Discuss the development of two- and three-part singing. What types of songs are used at the beginning, middle, and later stages of this development process? Visit your nearest music library or store and make a list of *two* pieces of music that would work well with elementary school children at each of these *three* levels.

References

Adams, P. (1974). *This Old Man*. Singapore: Child's Play International

Baker, K. (1994). *Big Fat Hen*. New York: Harcourt Brace.

Bartle, J. (1988). *Lifeline for Children's Choir Directors*. Toronto: Gordon V. Thompson.

Carter, D. (1992). *Over in the Meadow*. New York: Scholastic.

Clayton, L. (1986). *An investigation of the effect of a simultaneous pitch stimulus on vocal pitch accuracy*. Unpublished master's thesis, Indiana University, Bloomington.

Cooper, N. (1992). *Selected factors related to children's singing accuracy*. Unpublished doctoral dissertation, Indiana University, Bloomington.

Davidson, L. (1985). Tonal structures of children's early songs. *Music Perception 2(3),* 361–74.

Davidson, L. and Scripp, L. (1988). Young children's musical representations: Windows on music cognition. In John Sloboda (Ed.) *Generative Processes in Music*. New York: Oxford University Press.

De Paola, T. (1984). *Mary Had a Little Lamb*. New York: Holiday House.

Dowling, W. (1984). Development of musical schemata in children's spontaneous singing. In W. Crozier and A. Chapman (Eds.), *Cognitive Processes in the Perception of Art*. Amsterdam: North Holland Press.

Dowling, W. (1988). Tonal structure and children's early learning of music. In John Sloboda (Ed.), *Generative Processes in Music*. New York: Oxford University Press.

Feierabend, J., Saunders, C., Holahan, J, and Getnik, P. (1998). Song recognition among preschool age children: An investigation of words and music. *Journal of Research in Music Education, 46(3),* 351–9.

Goetze, M. (1985). *Factors affecting accuracy in children's singing*. Unpublished doctoral dissertation, University of Colorado, Boulder.

Goetze, M., Cooper, N., and Brown, C. (1990). Recent research on singing in the general music classroom. *Bulletin of the Council for Research in Music Education, 104,* 16–37.

Green, G. (1987). *The effect of vocal modeling on pitch-matching accuracy of children in grades one through six*. Unpublished Doctoral Dissertation, Louisiana State University and Agricultural and Mechanical College.

Hargreaves, D. (1986). *The Developmental Psychology of Music*. New York: Cambridge University Press.

Hague, M. (1993). *Teddy Bear, Teddy Bear*. New York: Morrow Junior Books.

Jarjisan, C. (1983). Pitch pattern instruction and the singing achievement of young children. *Psychology of Music, 11(1),* 19–25.

Klinger, R; Campbell, P., and Goolsby, T. (1998). Approaches to children's song acquisition: Immersion and phrase-by-phrase. *Journal of Research in Music Education, 46,* 24–34.

Long, S. (1997). *Hush Little Baby*. San Francisco: Chronicle Books.

Long, S. (2000). *Deck the Hall*. San Francisco: Chronicle Books.

Martin Jr., B., and Carle, E. (1992). *Brown Bear, Brown Bear, What Do You See?* New York: Henry Holt.

Moore, R., Brotons, M., Fyk, J., and Castillo, A. (1997). Effects of culture, age, gender, and repeated trials on rote song learning skills of children 6–9 years old from England, Panama, Poland, and the United States. *Bulletin of the Council for Research in Music Education, 133,* 83–8.

Moroney, T. (1994). *Twinkle, Twinkle, Little Star*. Westport, CT: Joshua Morris.

Muller, R. (1993). *Row, Row, Row Your Boat*. Richmond Hill, ON: Scholastic Canada.

Rutowski, J. (1996). The effectiveness of individual/small-group singing activities on kindergartner's use of singing voice and developmental music aptitude. *Journal of Research in Music Education, 44(4),* 358–68.

Saport, L. (1999). *All the Pretty Little Horses*. New York: Clarion.

Sims, W., Moore, R., and Kuhn, T. (1982). Effects of female and male vocal stimuli, tonal pattern length and age on the vocal pitch-matching abilities of young children from England and the United States. *Psychology of Music,* Special Issue: Proceedings of the IX International Seminar on Research in Music Education, 104–108.

Sinor, J. (1985). *The singing of selected tonal patterns by pre-school children*. Unpublished doctoral dissertation, Indiana University, Bloomington.

Sloboda, J. (1985). *The Musical Mind*. Oxford: Clarendon Press.

Smale, M. (1988). *An investigation of pitch-accuracy of four and five-year-old singers*. Unpublished doctoral dissertation, University of Minnesota, Minneapolis.

Spier, P. (1967). *London Bridge Is Falling Down!* New York: Doubleday.

Stadler, S. (1990). Vocal pitch-matching ability in children between 4–9 years of age. *European Journal of High Ability, 1*, 33–41.

Sweet, M. (1992). *Fiddle-I-Fee*. New York: Little, Brown.

Trapani, I. (1993). *Itsy Bitsy Spider*. Danvers, MA: Whispering Coyote Press.

Veenker, R. (1999). *Children's short term memory processing of melody, rhythm, and text reproduction of song*. Unpublished doctoral dissertation, University of Minnesota, Minneapolis.

Yarborough, C., Bowers, J., and Benson, W. (1992). The effect of vibrato on the pitch-matching accuracy of certain and uncertain singers. *Journal of Research in Music Education, 40(1)*, 30–38.

CHAPTER 5

Playing Classroom Instruments

SYNOPSIS

Chapter 5 discusses the role of classroom instruments in the elementary school, and includes sections specific to body percussion, non-pitched percussion instruments, pitched percussion instruments, and the recorder. Pictures of the instruments, descriptions of proper playing technique, and sample activities are provided for each of the four different instrumental groups. Information on playing the recorder also includes repertoire for use by beginning teachers and/or elementary school children.

Introduction

Playing classroom instruments is a favourite activity of children in the elementary music class.

Playing musical instruments is a natural part of childhood. During pre-school years, young children are eager to make music with anything they can find around the house, including plastic boxes, pots and pans, spoons, or pairs of shoes. This love for making music with "objects" continues well into the elementary grades, and research indicates that playing instruments remains the most favoured music classroom activity at all grade levels (Bowles, 1998). Campbell (1998) suggests that children enjoy being able to see as well as hear the sound being produced when they play an instrument—thus musical instruments are a significant symbol of music-making for many children.

Instruments commonly utilized by children in the elementary music classroom include:

1. **Body percussion**: *use of the body as an instrument to make sounds such as snapping, clapping, or stamping*

2. **Non-pitched percussion instruments**: *percussion instruments that sound on only one pitch, such as finger cymbals, claves, or sand blocks*

3. **Pitched percussion instruments**: *multi-barred instruments that produce thirteen different pitches (such as glockenspiels, xylophones, and metallophones), or single bass bars that sound only one pitch*

4. **Recorders**: *small flute-like instruments belonging to the woodwind family*

The piano, although present in many elementary music classrooms, is generally used by teachers to play accompaniments for the children and therefore will not be discussed in the context of this chapter on children's performance. Other instruments—such as the guitar, the **ukulele** (*a small four-string instrument belonging to the guitar family*), the **autoharp** (*a box-shaped string instrument with chord-buttons*), or **handbells** (*sets of small bells of varying sizes, which together cover a range of notes*)—may also be found in a small number of schools across the country. Resources such as Carlin (1982) or Snyder (1976) are excellent for teachers interested in learning more about any of these instruments.

Playing classroom instruments enhances the development of a child's personal musical understanding by giving her or him an opportunity to experience the structure of music in a concrete way. Through this kind of musical experience, children "bring music to life" on an instrument, thus gaining the physical sensation of musical concepts such as *forte* and *piano*, melodic contour, rhythmic patterning, ABA form, and timbral colour. When reflection time is included in these instrumental activities, children have the added opportunity of bringing these physical sensations to cognitive consciousness. In other words, playing instruments combined with active reflection on the various musical components in a performance helps children work on the process of interpreting their growing knowledge of musical structure.

Playing classroom instruments also provides elementary school children with access to a much wider range of pitch levels than that available to them with their singing voices. This makes playing instruments an ideal vehicle for experiencing improvisation and composition. In addition, the combination of classroom instruments with singing allows children to have the truly exhilarating experience of making both the "tune" (the song) and the "harmony" (the accompaniment) of the music. These can be powerful moments for children, moving them one step closer towards musical independence.

Playing classroom instruments can help to make musical concepts concrete for children.

Elementary school children enjoy taking responsibility for playing accompaniments for their singing.

Matching Instruments to Children's Developmental Levels

Children's success with playing classroom instruments is closely connected to their physical development. Certain non-pitched percussion instruments are easier for early elementary school-aged children to play because of the relationship between the size of the instrument and the size of their hands. For example, a **tone block** (*a hollow, tubular piece of wood open at one end with a small handle*

a **mallet** (*a wooden stick with a small round tip made of wood, plastic, felt, wound yarn, or cloth*). Younger children may find a **wood block** (*a solid or slightly hollow chunk of wood*)—which must be balanced on the palm of the hand while striking with a mallet—more difficult to cope with.

There is a similar difference with barred instruments. Both the **xylophone** and the **glockenspiel** are played by striking individual bars that are laid across a frame with a mallet. However, the bars of a **xylophone** are 6 cm wide while those of the glockenspiel are only 2 cm wide. Thus, the xylophone is most often used in Grades 1–2 because of its larger striking surface. Another example, the **recorder** is generally not introduced to elementary school children until Grade 4 (or sometimes late Grade 3), when most children's hands are big enough to cover the holes successfully. As a result, teachers should be aware that creating a learner-centred environment with classroom instruments should include careful consideration as to the size of an instrument and the proper playing technique, combined with the knowledge of a variety of activities appropriate for utilizing the instrument during music making.

Creating a learner-centred environment is important when using classroom instruments.

Body Percussion

Body percussion is used as a first instrumental experience in the elementary grades.

The body can be a used as a wonderful "first" musical instrument experience for children in the elementary grades. Whether young or old, children love to use their bodies to make clapping, snapping, ***patsching*** (*patting the thighs*), and stamping sounds. Children might first be encouraged to utilize their bodies in this way through **simultaneous imitation**: while keeping a steady beat, *teachers continuously model snapping, tapping, etc. on various parts of the body while the children simultaneously copy the movements as quickly and accurately as possible.* When they are comfortable following the teacher's motions, children can take over the leadership role for such body-percussion activities, thus gaining valuable experience in the art of improvisation with their peers.

Body percussion can also be used to help children gain beginning experiences in **timbre exploration**. Encourage children to explore the many different kinds of tone colours that can be produced with the body and to determine appropriate sounds to accompany the chanting of a rhyme or a poem. *Two Little Sausages* is a good example of a rhyme for which body percussion could be used in Grade 1 to help illustrate the sounds of the underlined words in the rhyme. There are many "answers" to this challenge and children should be encouraged to experiment with a variety of body sounds until they find the one that has the most personal meaning to them for a particular line of text. Each child might then be asked to perform her or his unique version for the rest of the class.

Two Little Sausages   Traditional

Two little sausages <u>frying</u> in a pan,

One went <u>sizzle</u> and the other went <u>bam!</u>

Body percussion is also used in the elementary classroom to help children gain initial instrumental ensemble experiences. Children can learn short body-percussion pieces, such as *Body Fun*, by imitating the teacher, and then perform them as a group. Children can also compose their own body percussion pieces using iconic representations of the various sounds to write down the music. Such experiences lay an important foundation for composing and performing activities with non-pitched and pitched percussion instruments.

Body Fun

A. Montgomery

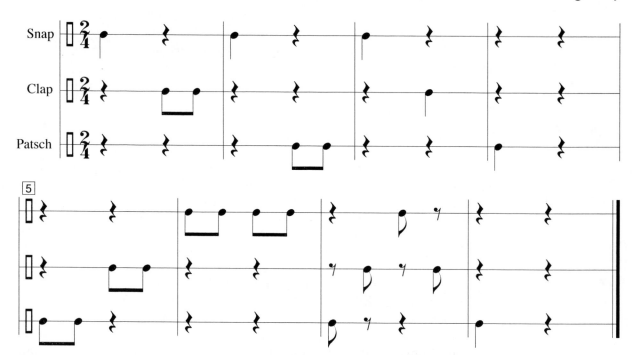

Non–Pitched Percussion Instruments

Non-pitched percussion instruments used in the elementary music classroom are generally divided into three categories, based on the material used in their construction. These are:

metal instruments (finger cymbals, triangles, cowbell, sleigh bells, etc)

wood instruments (rhythm sticks, claves, woodblock, guiro, maracas, etc.)

skin or membrane instruments (hand drums, bongo drums, conga drum, etc.)

These percussion instruments originate from all over the world (for example, the **guiro** comes from Latin America, the finger cymbals from the Middle East, the gong from Asia, and the **cabaça** from Africa) and they provide opportunities for utilizing authentic sounds when singing music from a variety of cultures.

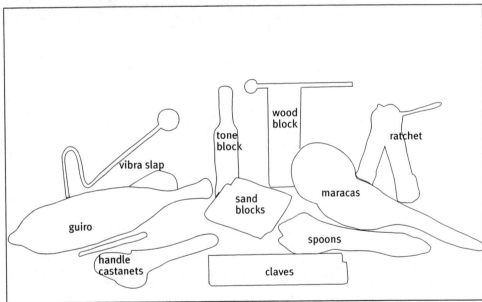

Non-pitched woods

Labels in diagram: vibra slap, tone block, wood block, ratchet, guiro, sand blocks, maracas, handle castanets, spoons, claves

Individual instruments should be introduced into the classroom one at a time so that children have an opportunity to become familiar with the name, the unique timbre, and the proper playing technique of each instrument in turn.

This is especially important in the younger grades, where children may be learning how to play an instrument for the first time. This might mean, for example, using the tone blocks to keep the beat while singing in one lesson, the hand drum in the next lesson, and the finger cymbals in a third lesson. On the fourth lesson, all three instruments could be brought back for review by the children using a **timbre discrimination** game such as *Hicketty Picketty*.

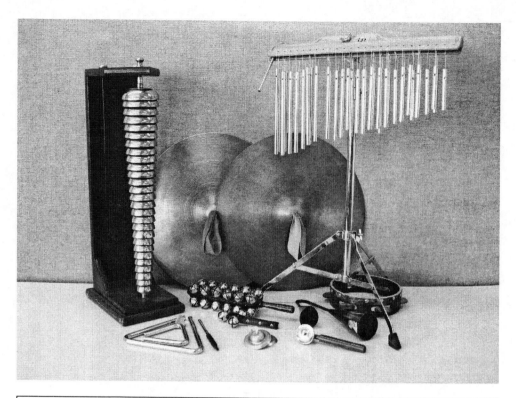

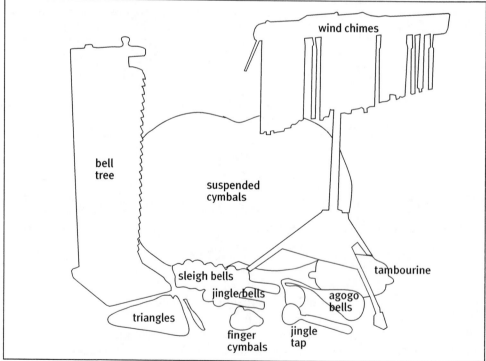

wind chimes

bell
tree

suspended
cymbals

tambourine

sleigh bells

jingle bells

agogo
bells

triangles

finger
cymbals

jingle
tap

Non-pitched metals

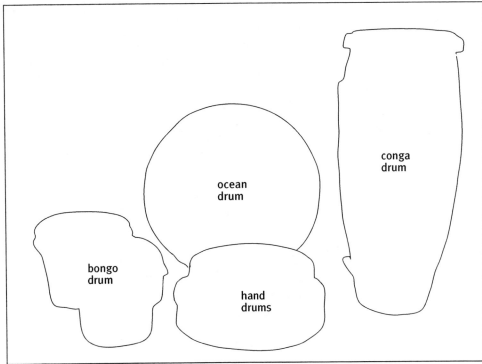

Non-pitched skins

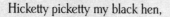

Hicketty Picketty

Traditional

Hicketty picketty my black hen,

She lays eggs in a great big pen,

Boys and girls come everyday,

To see what my black hen did lay.

Game: The children sit in a circle. In the centre of the circle there is a covered basket containing a variety of non-pitched percussion instruments. While the children chant the rhyme and *patsch* the beat, one child walks around the outside of the circle keeping the beat with his or her feet. At the end of the rhyme, the child goes into the centre of the circle, reaches inside the basket without lifting the cover, and plays one of the instruments. The children try to guess the name of the instrument belonging to the "mystery" timbre. The child takes his or her selected instrument out of the basket and returns to the circle, ready to play the beat. The game continues with another child walking outside the circle.

In subsequent lessons, the teacher could continue to introduce individual instruments from each of the three categories; children will then begin to develop a solid repertoire of instrumental timbres from which to select during later classroom instrumental activities.

Non-pitched percussion instruments are frequently used in the classroom, with or without pitched instruments, to accompany children's singing or chanting of rhymes, stories, and poetry. In the younger grades (Kindergarten–Grade 2), children might be asked either to play these instruments on the beat or to emphasize a particular rhythmic pattern. Two examples include *Doctor Foster* (playing on the beat) and *Jingle at the Window* (playing a specific rhythm).

Doctor Foster

Traditional rhyme

Doctor Foster went to Gloucester,

In a shower of rain,

She stepped in a puddle right up to her middle,

And never went there again!

Activity: Invite the children to keep the beat using the swishing sounds of the sand blocks to represent stepping in the watery mud puddles.

Jingle at the Windows

Traditional singing game

Pass one win-dow, ti - de - o, Pass two win-dows, ti - de - o.

Pass three win-dows, ti - de - o, Jin-gle at the win-dows ti - de - o.

Game: The children stand in a circle while singing the song. One child skips around the outside of the circle carrying a jingle bell. At m. 7 the child outside the circle taps the rhythm of the words "Jingle at the windows, tideo" lightly on the back shoulder of the closest child in the circle. The game begins again with the child who was tapped skipping outside the circle.

Non-pitched percussion instruments can also be used with younger students to provide sound to illustrate certain words in a rhyme (for example, the underlined words in *The Loose Tooth*, for Grade 1), or to heighten the expressive quality of a poem or a story (as in *The Lion and The Mouse*, for Grade 2).

The Loose Tooth

Traditional

I had a <u>loose</u> tooth, a <u>wiggly</u>, <u>jiggly</u> loose tooth,

I had a <u>loose</u> tooth hanging by a thread.

I pulled my <u>loose</u> tooth, my <u>wiggly</u>, <u>jiggly</u> loose tooth,

And put it 'neath my pillow and went to bed.

The fairy took my <u>loose</u> tooth, my <u>wiggly</u>, <u>jiggly</u> loose tooth,

So now I have a loonie and a <u>hole</u> in my head

Activity: Invite the children to choose non-pitched percussion instruments to help express the meaning of the underlined words. Instruct the children to play their instruments when they say these words or to substitute the instrument sounds for the words when they chant the rhyme.

The Lion and the Mouse
(an adaptation of an Aesop fable)

Once upon a time there was a lion sleeping soundly in his den. He had fallen asleep with a piece of food still clenched in his paw. As he slept, a tiny mouse crept softly into his lair. The mouse stopped and stared at the lion's paw. "I am so hungry," thought the mouse to himself. "Do I dare reach for it?" After a minute or two, he reached over gently towards the food. Just at that moment, the lion woke up and slapped his paw down firmly on the little mouse. "A-ha! I have you now!" roared the lion. "I am going to eat you for supper!" "Oh dear," cried the little mouse. "Please have mercy on me. You deserve a much bigger mouthful than a tiny mouse!" The lion yawned, thought for a moment, and then set the mouse free. The mouse scampered quickly away and the lion fell lazily back to sleep.

An hour or two later, three hunters walked into the forest and found the sleeping lion. They were very excited at their luck and immediately threw a net over the sleeping lion. The lion awoke with a start and tried to escape but the net only wound tighter and tighter around his legs. The lion roared ferociously! The hunters ran back to the village for extra hands to carry the lion.

Meanwhile, the trapped lion called out "Help! Help!" and who should hear him but the tiny mouse. Into the lair he ran. "Oh little mouse, thank goodness you are here" cried the lion. "Look at the mess I am in. I can't get loose from this awful net the hunters cast over me. What shall I do?" "I can help you!" cried the little mouse who got busy gnawing a big hole in the net right away. After several minutes, the lion was able to wiggle around and escape from the net. "Oh thank you, thank you!" cried the lion. The mouse smiled, waved good-bye, and scampered quickly away. The lion learned a good lesson that day: sometimes good things come in small packages!

Activity: Invite the children to choose a variety of non-pitched percussion instruments that can be used to create sound effects when re-telling the story.

In Grades 3–6, non-pitched percussion instruments are often used, with or without pitched percussion, to play **rhythmic *ostinati*** (*short rhythmic patterns repeated over and over as an accompaniment to a rhyme or song*) or to play at selected moments during a song to add tone colour for expression of the text. Teachers are cautioned, however, not to add so much accompaniment that the sound becomes too "thick" and overpowering for the children's voices. A combination of one instrument each from the wood, skin, and metal groups, plus one or two pitched percussion instruments, is generally enough to beautifully support children's singing.

The following arrangement of *My Bark Canoe* is an example of a simple accompaniment for the middle elementary grades that involves only non-pitched percussion instruments.

My Bark Canoe

Traditional Ojibwa song
English text and arrangement by A. Montgomery

The following arrangement of *Land of the Silver Birch* includes both non-pitched and pitched percussion instruments.

Land of the Silver Birch

Traditional Canadian camp song, ca 1920
Arrangement by A. Montgomery

Activity: Invite children to choose non-pitched percussion instruments to play the rhythms of the words in italics (silver birch, beaver, etc.) when they sing the song. This percussion accompaniment will enhance the expressive power of the text.

Music written solely for a non-pitched percussion ensemble is also fun for elementary school children to perform. The body-percussion pieces discussed earlier in this chapter can be logical stepping stones to new non-pitched percussion compositions: snapping finger parts can be played on finger cymbals, clapping parts can be transferred to wood blocks, and *patsching* parts can become drum parts, thereby allowing easy learning of the same rhythmic motives for both performing experiences. The following re-orchestration of *Body Fun* for non-pitched percussion—retitled *Percussion Fun*—illustrates this.

Percussion Fun

A. Montgomery

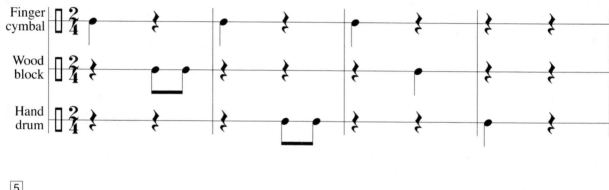

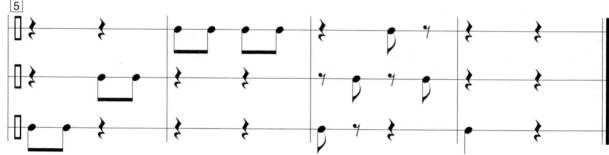

Further examples of these kinds of classroom activities with non-pitched percussion can be found in Chapters 10–15.

Metal Non-pitched Percussion Instruments

Here are some of the non-pitched percussion instruments of the *metal* family that might be found in the elementary classroom (see photograph on p. 70).

Finger cymbals—The player suspends both cymbals horizontally, and lightly strikes the rim of one cymbal with the other in a slight downward motion. Finger cymbals produce a lovely ringing sound. They are excellent for older children, and can add interesting colour to an accompaniment.

Triangle—The player suspends the instrument from a string and strikes the edge with a metal beater. The triangle produces a lovely, bright ringing tone and is excellent for keeping the beat. Children in the early elementary grades will have greater success when playing smaller triangles (about 10 to 15 cm per side).

Jingle bells or sleigh bells—These bells come in sets attached to a handle, and can be played by either gently shaking the bells in the air, or by holding the bells in an upside-down position with a clenched fist and gently tapping the top of the fist to make the bells ring. Jingle bells usually have three or four bells on a short handle, and are easier for younger elementary students to play. Sleigh bells are larger, with 15 to 20 bells on a long handle, and can be quite heavy to hold and manipulate. Both types of bells produce a pleasing ringing sound and are a wonderful addition for accompanying seasonal music.

Cowbell—The player holds the top of the bell with one hand and strikes the edge near the opening with a wooden or metal-tipped mallet. The cowbell produces a low, muffled ring and is useful for creating metallic sound effects with rhymes, poetry, or stories.

Suspended cymbal—The player suspends the cymbal horizontally and strikes the top edge with a metal, wooden, or yarn-tipped mallet. The suspended cymbal produces a long, resonant ringing sound that can be altered by the choice of mallet. It is excellent for creating special effects with rhymes, stories, poetry, or music. Younger children may need to play the instrument in pairs: one holds the cymbal while the other strikes it.

Cabaça—The player holds the instrument by the handle while gently rolling the beads back and forth with the palm of the other hand. These Latin American and African instruments produce a scraping or rattling sound and work well with older children for keeping the beat or for playing a rhythmic *ostinato*.

Tambourine—The player either holds the instrument horizontally while tapping the rim, or strikes the instrument firmly against the side of the body. The tambourine produces a metallic, jingling sound and is useful for keeping the beat or for playing a rhythmic *ostinato*.

Gong (or **Tam Tam**)—The player strikes the suspended gong about half-way between the centre and the edge with a rubberized or padded mallet. This instrument, originally from the Far East, produces an impressive, long sustained sound and is excellent for creating dramatic sound effects with rhymes, poetry, or stories.

Bell Tree—The player holds the instrument in an upright position and gently pulls a metal-tipped mallet down across the bells. The bell tree is originally from the Far East; it produces a pleasing series of ringing sounds from lower to higher notes and is excellent for illustrating special words in a rhyme or song (for example, it might be used to suggest the sun rising)

Wind chimes—The player gently pulls a metal-tipped mallet across the hanging cylinders. Wind chimes produce a lighter series of ringing sounds than the bell tree, and are also excellent for illustrating special words in a rhyme or song (for example, the wind blowing).

Agogo Bells—The player holds the instrument upright and strikes one or both of the bells with a wooden-tipped mallet. This West African or Latin American instrument produces two metallic notes, one slightly higher than the other, and is excellent for providing culturally appropriate timbral colour with songs from West Africa or Latin America.

Wooden Non-pitched Percussion Instruments

Here are some of the non-pitched percussion instruments of the wood family that might be found in the elementary classroom (see photograph on p. 69).

Rhythm sticks—The player strikes one stick against the middle of the other stick; the bottom stick is held firmly in place in a horizontal position to the body. Rhythm sticks come in different lengths (20 cm is about the right length for younger children). They produce a light tapping sound and are excellent for playing a variety of rhythmic patterns

Claves—The player rests one clave gently on the fingernails of a curled-up hand and strikes it in the middle with the other clave. This Latin American instrument, often made of rosewood, produces a resonant knocking sound and is wonderful for older children, either for keeping the beat or for playing rhythmic *ostinati*.

Wood Block—The player balances the wood block lightly on the palm of the hand and strikes it firmly with a wooden-tipped mallet. The wood block produces a vibrant knocking sound and is excellent for older children either for keeping the beat or for playing rhythmic *ostinati*.

Tone block—The player holds the tone bock upright with the handle, and strikes it firmly with a wooden-tipped mallet. A variation of the wood block, the tone block produces a mellower knocking sound and is useful for younger children for keeping the beat, or for playing rhythms and rhythmic *ostinati*.

Guiro—The player holds the "tail" of the instrument and scrapes a small stick across the serrated surface. This Latin American instrument produces a unique, scratchy sound that is excellent for playing rhythmic *ostinati* or for creating sound effects with rhymes, stories, poetry, or songs.

Sand blocks—The player rubs one block against the other. The sand block produces a swishing sound that is excellent for younger children for keeping the beat or for creating special sound effects in rhymes, stories, poetry, or songs.

Maracas—The player can either shake both maracas in the air or tap one maraca gently against the palm of the hand. This Latin American instrument produces a wonderful rattling sound and is excellent for keeping the beat, for playing rhythmic *ostinati*, or for creating interesting sound effects with rhymes, poetry, stories or songs.

Handle castanets—The player either taps the instrument against the palm of the hand, or shakes it lightly in the air. Handle castanets are a modified classroom version of the more traditional Spanish finger castanets. They produce a light, clicking sound and are great for keeping the beat or for creating special sound effects for rhymes, poetry, stories, or songs.

Spoons—The player strikes the handle against the thigh or palm of the hand. This instrument of European ancestry produces a clicking sound that has become a traditional timbre for keeping the beat with a variety of French Canadian or Newfoundland folk songs.

Temple blocks—The player strikes the top of the blocks with rubber tipped mallets. This instrument from the Far East produces a resonant tick-tock sound and is excellent for older children for playing rhythmic *ostinati* or for creating sound effects such as horse-hooves for rhymes, poetry, stories, or songs.

Skin or Membrane Non-pitched Percussion Instruments

Here are some of the non-pitched percussion instruments of the *skin* family that might be found in the elementary classroom (see photograph on p. 71).

Hand drum—The player holds the drum by the rim and gently taps the skin side with the fingertips, the ball of the hand, or (in later grades) the side of the thumb. The hand drum produces a light, patting sound and is excellent for keeping the beat, for playing rhythmic patterns, or for playing rhythmic *ostinati*.

Bongo drum—The player holds the drum between the legs or in the crook of the arm, or places it on the floor, and taps the skin side with the fingertips or the whole hand. This Latin American instrument produces a hollow, pitter-patter sound and is excellent for older children for keeping the beat, for playing a rhythmic pattern, or for playing rhythmic *ostinati*.

Conga drum—The player hits the skin of the drum with the whole hand, fingertips, heel of the hand, or knuckles. This African and Latin American instrument can produce a variety of resonant, drumming sounds depending on how and where (close to the edge or in the middle) the player hits the skin. With practice, older children will have success using the conga drum to play assorted rhythmic patterns or rhythmic *ostinati*.

Bass drum—The player uses a padded beater to strike the middle of the skin with a glancing blow. The bass drum produces a low, resonant, booming sound and is best used for creating special sound effects with rhymes, poetry, stories or songs.

Collecting Non-pitched Percussion Instruments

Non-pitched percussion instruments are available for purchase from a variety of music stores across Canada. Teachers making initial purchases for their classrooms are urged to buy multiples of a few typical instruments from each of the three groups, and add further instruments from each group as budgets permit at a later date. For example, an initial purchase of finger cymbals, triangles, and jingle bells (from *metals*), rhythm sticks, wood blocks, sand blocks, and maracas (from *woods*), and hand drums and a conga drum (from *skins*) would make an excellent classroom start. Increase the quantities of each of these instruments little by little until there are enough for one-third of the class (approximately ten) to play any one instrument at a time. This is especially important in the younger grades where children often find it difficult to wait their turn to play an instrument.

Well-constructed instruments will promote artistic performance.

Although some *wood* instruments can be easily hand-made by students or parents (for example, rhythm sticks can be made out of hardwood dowels, sand blocks out of small chunks of wood and sandpaper, and maracas out of plastic containers filled with dried beans or corn), teachers are encouraged to purchase the best quality instruments they can afford, especially from the *metal* and *skin* categories. Sound quality can make a tremendous difference to the children, and the attractive timbres that are possible with well-constructed, non-pitched percussion instruments will motivate them to give their very best performance.

Pitched Percussion Instruments

Pitched percussion instruments commonly found in elementary music classrooms include multi-barred instruments—such as the **glockenspiel**, **xylophone**, and the **metallophone**—as well as large, **single bass bars** that sound only one note. These instruments were originally developed in the mid-twentieth century under the guidance of German composer and music educator Carl Orff (1895–1982), and are used today by elementary school children throughout Canada to play melodies and harmonic accompaniments.

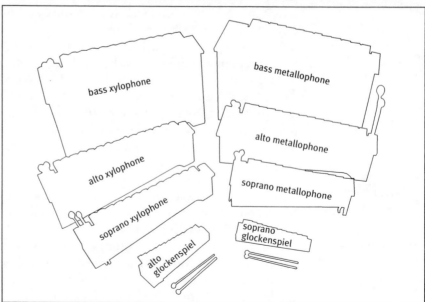

Mixed pitched percussion

The Orff-inspired versions of the xylophone, glockenspiel, and metallophone consist of 13 removable bars that sit over a wooden frame: the xylophone has wooden bars, the glockenspiel has short thin metal bars, and the metallophone has thick metal bars. The individual bars on each instrument play one note when struck with a mallet. Music for these barred instruments is always notated on the **treble clef** between middle C and A above the staff.

but the instruments sound in different **octaves**, depending on their size. The glockenspiel is usually played with a wooden, plastic, or rubber tipped mallet and comes in two sizes: the **soprano glockenspiel** (SG) and the **alto glockenspiel** (AG). They sound in the following ranges:

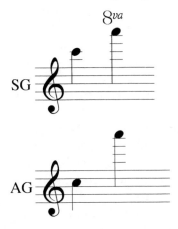

The xylophone and metallophone are frequently played with wool-, yarn-, felt-, or rubber-tipped mallets, and come in three sizes: **soprano xylophone** (SX) or **soprano metallophone** (SM), **alto xylophone** (AX) or **alto metallophone** (AM); **bass xylophone** (BX) or **bass metallophone** (BM). They sound in the following ranges:

Any bar not in use for a particular accompaniment can be removed, thereby making it easier for students to successfully strike the correct notes. (For example, if only the notes C and G are needed to play a particular accompaniment, all the other bars can be removed.) Barred instruments also come with additional bars for notes with **accidentals** (such as F♯ and B♭) that can be substituted for the F and/or B bars when needed for a particular song or to accompany music with key signature that requires these notes. (For example, the F♯ bar can be substituted for the F bar, to accompany music in G major; the B♭ bar can replace the B bar for songs in F major).

The glockenspiel produces a bright, tinkling sound that can easily be heard above the other instruments in an ensemble. The xylophone has a resonant, mellow tone that is lovely for accompanying children's voices. The metallophone produces a thick, resonant, ringing sound that, if played too loudly, can sometimes overwhelm young voices. All three instruments are extremely attractive to children and provide a wealth of timbres for students to play accompaniments, melodies, and improvisations, or to create special sound effects for rhymes, stories, poetry, and singing. Barred instruments are especially useful for helping children to experience a variety of melodic and harmonic aspects of musical structure.

Working with Barred Instruments in the Classroom

Barred instruments are placed on the floor or on a low table or stand. Children sit, kneel, or stand depending on the height at which the instrument is placed. Children should hold the mallets as if they were holding on to their bicycle handles, with the elbows relaxed but bent and held slightly away from the body (see photograph). Young children may need to grasp the mallet closer to the middle of the stick. At the beginning, ask the children to pretend the bars are like a "hot stove" so that they remember to lift the mallet back off the instrument quickly each time they strike a bar in order to let the bar resonate fully.

Xylophone mallet
position

Children in the early grades generally begin their experiences with barred instruments using the xylophone rather than the glockenspiel, because the larger bars are easier for younger children to strike. Children should learn the proper technique for playing the xylophone before they ever sit down in front of an instrument. This means asking the students to "rehearse" the notes they are going to play ahead of time by *patsching* the rhythm of the repeated melodic pattern on their legs (using the left hand for the low note and the right hand for the high note). Melodies with more than two different notes are best played with alternating hands (Grades 4–6) and will require some thinking through by students ahead of time. This "pre-practice" is very helpful and enables successful playing experiences for children of all ages.

One of the powerful benefits of using barred instruments in the elementary music classroom is their potential for opening up the world of musical accompaniment to children. If piano accompaniments are always used for singing in the elementary grades, the teacher usually takes the responsibility for playing the accompaniment while the children only participate as singers. Although this is appropriate for some choral arrangements in the later grades, use of piano in the early to middle elementary grades as an accompaniment instrument is not conducive to facilitating singing in tune: children have more success singing in tune when they sing **a cappella** (*without instruments*) or with only a light accompaniment. In addition, piano accompaniments do not provide children with a truly complete musical experience. Having elementary school children use barred instruments for playing lightly orchestrated accompaniments with singing not only provides a beautiful tonal blend with the children's voices but also gives the students a wonderful opportunity to be responsible for the whole music experience—both tune and harmony.

Barred instruments enable children to play the accompaniment for their singing.

Harmonic Accompaniments on the Xylophone

Teachers outfitting their classrooms with barred instruments for the first time should seriously consider a *bass xylophone* as their initial purchase. This instrument works well both because of its size (it is large enough for Grade 1 students to play) and its range. Because the range of the bass xylophone includes notes that are lower than the children's voices, it can provide a lovely tonal support for singing when playing harmonic accompaniments such as **pedal tones** or **drones**, **borduns**, and I–V or I–IV–V patterns.

Pedal Tones or Drones

Pedal tones or **drones** consist of a single note—usually the **tonic** (I) note of the **key** of the song—played as an ostinato. Pedal tones are used to accompany simple **pentatonic songs** (*songs that are based on a five-note scale*). The most common **pentatonic scale** is made up of the first (*doh*), second (*re*), third (*mi*), fifth (*soh*), and sixth (*lah*) notes in the key of a song (in any order); the fourth (*fa*) and seventh (*ti*) notes are missing (unless present in the melody as passing tones). Simple pentatonic songs can be accompanied effectively using only the tonic (I) note.

The following arrangement of *Ickle Ockle,* a simple pentatonic song for Grade 1, illustrates a pedal tone accompaniment appropriate for playing by young elementary school children.

Ickle Ockle

Traditional singing game
Arranged by A. Montgomery

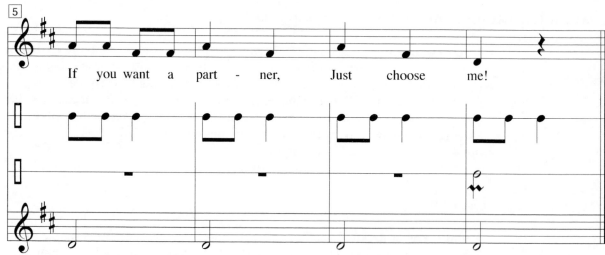

Game: The children sing the song while keeping the beat with their feet as they walk around in a circle. At the end of the song, the children run into the middle of the circle, choose a partner, and return to the circle, standing beside their partner. Holding hands, the children skip around the circle in pairs while they sing the song for a second time. The game begins again with everyone choosing a new partner.

Borduns

The second type of accompaniment frequently played on the bass xylophone by elementary school students is called a **bordun**. A *bordun* consists of *two notes— usually the tonic (I) and the* **dominant** *(V) notes of the key of the song—that are played as an ostinato.* For example, the *bordun* notes for C major would be C and G. Like pedal tones, *borduns* can be used to support the tonal centre of pentatonic songs in a non-functional way. For example, the following arrangement of *À la claire fontaine* has a G–D *bordun* accompaniment played on the bass xylophone.

À la claire fontaine

Traditional French Canadian folk song
English text by A. Montgomery

*Bordun*s can be used as accompaniments for children's pentatonic songs in a variety of *ostinato* patterns. These include:

1. *simple or chordal bordun*: both notes of the *bordun* are played simultaneously on the strong beats.

2. *broken bordun*: the two notes of the *bordun* are played in alternation.

3. *level bordun*: both notes of the *bordun* are played simultaneously on the beat in alternating registers. (This is often done using a bass barred instrument to play the lower pair of notes and an alto barred instrument to play the upper pair.)

4. *arpeggiated bordun*: the two notes of a broken *bordun* are repeated an octave higher in an arpeggiated fashion.

Simple and broken *borduns* are accessible for Grade 2–3 students, while level and arpeggiated *borduns* are more appropriate for students in Grades 3–6.

I, IV, and V Chord Notes

The third type of accompaniment—based on the notes of **I, IV, or V chords**—is used with **diatonic songs** (*songs that use notes from the major or minor scale*). These three chords are based on the first, fourth, and fifth notes of the scale of the key of the song. Each chord consists of that note, plus the two notes that are a 3rd and a 5th above that note.

> *I (tonic) chord*: This chord is built on the first degree of the scale. For example, in G major the I (tonic) chord would be G (the first scale degree), B (a 3rd above) and D (a 5th above)
>
> *IV (subdominant) chord*: This chord is built on the fourth degree of the scale. (For example, in G major, the IV (subdominant) chord is C (the fourth scale degree), E (a 3rd above) and G (a 5th above)
>
> *V (dominant) chord*: This chord is built on the fifth degree of the scale. For example, in G major, the V (dominant) chord is D (the fifth scale degree), F♯ (a 3rd above) and A (a 5th above)

Because diatonic songs use any of the eight notes in a major or minor scale, these melodies sound best when accompanied by chord progressions such as I–V or I–IV–V. These accompaniment patterns consist of various notes from the I, IV, and/or V chords of the key of the song and are usually played on several different barred instruments (for example, bass xylophone, alto xylophone, and alto glockenspiel). The following arrangement of *I'se the B'y* is a classroom example of a I–V accompaniment appropriate for students in Grades 3–4.

I'se the B'y

Traditional Newfoundland folk song
Arranged by Robert de Frece

I'se the b'y that builds the boat, and I'se the b'y that sails her,

I'se the b'y that catch-es the fish and brings 'em home to Li - za.

I'se the B'y (PEA 5, no. 3, CMC Archives) was collected by Kenneth Peacock,
and is used by courtesy of the Canadian Museum of Civilization.
The arrangement by Dr. Robert de Frece is used by permission.

The higher barred instruments (such as glockenspiels and the soprano xylophone) are also useful for playing descants, countermelodies, and short melodic *ostinati* with children's singing. These instruments sound quite beautiful when used in conjunction with a recorder melody and/or a simple *bordun* accompaniment played on bass barred instruments. The following arrangement of *Un canadien errant* is an example of an accompaniment that incorporates several barred instruments together with recorder in a lovely singing arrangement for Grade 5–6 students.

Un canadien errant

Traditional French Canadian folk song
English text by Edith Fowke
Arrangement by Robert de Frece

The different kinds of accompaniments played on barred instruments require varying degrees of skill and coordination on the part of children. Since certain patterns are easier to play than others, accompaniment patterns should be taught in a logical order for ease of learning. (For example, *bordun*s with notes played together are easier than broken or arpeggiated *bordun*s.) Further advice on such sequencing, along with information on orchestrating accompaniments for barred instruments can be found in resources such as Frazee (1987) and Warner (1991). Canadian sources that contain excellent orchestrations designed to accompany children's songs and rhymes include Otto and Asplund (1990), Wuytach and Sills (1994), Birkenshaw-Fleming (1996), Shieron (1997), Sills (1999), and de Frece (2000).

Teachers will find that barred instruments are also excellent tools for use during improvisation experiences in the classroom. For example, teachers might try a *question-answer improvisation* in which the teacher plays a short melodic "question" on the xylophone and the children improvise a melodic "answer" on the metallophone. Or, an **ABA (ternary) form**—*consisting of two contrasting sections (A and B) with a return of the first (A) section at the end*—can be built using melodic phrases improvised by the children on the glockenspiel. The barred instruments provide a wonderful extension to vocal improvisation because of the large range of pitches available. More detailed discussion of specific activities for instrumental improvisation with elementary school children can be found in Chapter 6.

The Recorder

Recorders are used in the elementary music classroom to give children their first experience with playing a wind instrument. Very accessible to beginners, this flute-like instrument dates back to the Renaissance and Baroque periods, and wind music that could be played by the instrument appeared as early as the late fifteenth century. One source suggests the word "recorder" means to warble or sing like a bird, which is a good description of the clear, singing-like tone produced on the instrument.

The Recorder Family

Recorders come in five different sizes, ranging from the very high **sopranino recorder** (about 23 cm long) to the low **bass recorder** (about 88 cm long). The **soprano recorder** (about 33 cm long), is the second highest of the five. Students in Grade 4 are generally considered to be ready, in terms of physical development (hand size, finger dexterity, and breathing) to begin playing the recorder, and they usually start with the **soprano** recorder. The range of this instrument

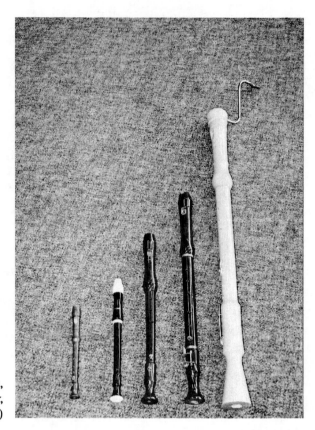

Recorders (left to right: sopranino, soprano, alto, tenor, and bass)

is similar to that of children's voices and thus it blends beautifully when playing a melody, melodic *ostinato*, descant, or countermelody as an accompaniment for singing. For children who are interested in learning to play other sizes of recorders, teachers usually add the **alto** (about 50 cm long), followed by the **tenor** (about 65 cm long) or the sopranino. The bass recorder is generally too long for even Grade 6 children to reach the finger holes.

Many elementary music teachers also find that the soprano recorder or the alto recorder are the most comfortable for beginning their own personal recorder experience. Both can be useful tools for a variety of teacher activities, such as modelling the melody of a song or playing the beginning motive of an improvisation fragment to the children.

Fingering

Recorders are made with one of two fingering systems. **Baroque fingering** (also called English fingering) is modelled on fingering systems that were used in the sixteenth century. **German fingering** is an early twentieth-century invention that was developed as an attempt to simplify the instrument for beginners. In reality, this simplification is minimal (you can play F with one finger of the right hand instead of using a forked fingering involving two fingers), while the trade-off in intonation is considerable.

Most teachers choose to use recorders that are built for playing with the Baroque (or English) fingering (see Table 5.1), as these instruments will allow the children to play with better octave and chromatic intonation. Good quality plastic models of these traditionally wooden instruments are available at reasonable prices from music stores across Canada.

Care of the Recorder

Learning to care for the recorder is an important part of the instructional process.

Elementary school children should be taught how to care for their recorders from the first time the instruments are used in the classroom. Encourage children to warm their instruments to room temperature before playing by holding them under their armpits for a minute or two. The connecting joints between the two or three sections of the instrument (mouthpiece, body, foot) should be kept lubricated on a regular basis with a commercially made grease manufactured specifically for this purpose. Teach children how to put their recorders together properly—by twisting the parts slowly in place rather than shoving them directly into each other. The body and the foot sections of the recorder need to be cleaned out gently with a lint free swab after every use. Moisture in the mouthpiece can be removed by blowing into it while completely covering the hole on the top with the hand. Plastic recorders can be washed periodically in mild soap and warm water, then rinsed and put away. For storage, a vertical position in a cloth bag or plastic case is desirable.

Playing the Recorder

When playing the recorder, remember the importance of good posture and breathing. The brief discussion in Chapter 4 on diaphragm breathing (see p. 27) is also relevant here, since the recorder requires a steady flow of air to make the instrument "sing." Encourage children to sit on the front edge of their seats with their feet flat on the floor, leaning slightly forward over their knees. Their chins should be level with the floor (encourage children to look straight ahead rather than bending their heads down), with the recorder brought up to their mouths and held at about a 45-degree angle. The elbows should be relaxed but held slightly away from the body (see photograph on p. 98).

In fingering, the left thumb covers the back hole on the recorder. The first three holes on the top are covered by the index, middle, and ring finger of the left hand. The thumb of the right hand sits gently on the back of the recorder behind the fourth or fifth hole to help support the weight of the instrument. The bottom four holes of the recorder are covered with the fingers of the right hand. The fingers should rest gently on the instrument, and the pads of the fingers rather than the tips should be used to cover the holes.

For ease of instruction, fingers on the hand are usually labelled "thumb–1–2–3–4" (the index finger is "1" and the pinky finger is "4"). This makes talking about fingering quite simple. In the classroom, when a teacher calls out, "G is fingered with thumb, left fingers 1, 2, and 3," the children should be able to quickly determine the correct placement of their fingers.

Correct hand position
for playing the recorder

The recorder is placed lightly between the lips in front of the teeth, and the corners of the mouth are brought gently around the mouthpiece to close off any air leakage. Initially, children might be asked to say the word "poo" and freeze their mouths in this position while gently placing the recorder in the open space. This can help to give the students an approximate sense of how the proper **embouchure** (*the shape of the mouth when playing a wind instrument*) should look and feel. Children should be instructed to blow gently, but with enough force to produce a warm, steady tone. Initially, if students blow too hard they will produce a high, squeaky tone; an inadequate supply of air will result in a shaky rise and fall of pitch. Students will need to experiment a bit in order to find the right amount of air needed to sustain a steady sound.

After initial experimentation, children may be taught how to **articulate**— that is, how to *start the sound properly with the tongue*. Instructing them to begin each note as if they were saying "du" seems to give them a good idea of how to start a note. Tonguing on the recorder involves placing the tongue above the teeth against the palate, without touching either the teeth or the recorder mouthpiece, just before releasing the air. Children will need considerable practice with this in order to become comfortable with starting each note properly.

Playing Different Notes

Most teachers recommend starting the children with the note G and adding new notes gradually as the students become accustomed to moving their fingers efficiently between pitches. **Echo games**—*where the teacher plays a short motive using the new note and the children echo the same passage back*—can be useful in helping children to practise new notes. Generally the progression of instruction continues from the note G to A, B, C, etc. as illustrated below.

Recommended order for teaching new notes on the soprano recorder

Table 5.1

Soprano Recorder Fingerings

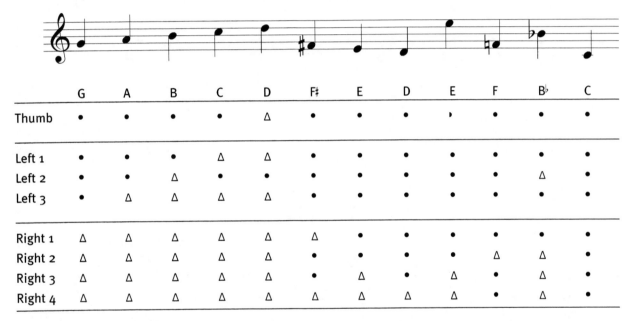

	G	A	B	C	D	F#	E	D	E	F	B♭	C
Thumb	•	•	•	•	Δ	•	•	•	›	•	•	•
Left 1	•	•	•	Δ	Δ	•	•	•	•	•	•	•
Left 2	•	•	Δ	•	•	•	•	•	•	•	Δ	•
Left 3	•	Δ	Δ	Δ	Δ	•	•	•	•	•	•	•
Right 1	Δ	Δ	Δ	Δ	Δ	Δ	•	•	•	•	•	•
Right 2	Δ	Δ	Δ	Δ	Δ	•	•	•	•	Δ	Δ	•
Right 3	Δ	Δ	Δ	Δ	Δ	•	Δ	•	Δ	•	Δ	•
Right 4	Δ	Δ	Δ	Δ	Δ	Δ	Δ	Δ	Δ	•	Δ	•

• covered hole

Δ open hole

› partially covered hole (the left thumb covers only half of the hole)

Examples of music appropriate for teachers and children learning the notes G, A, and B include *Merrily We Roll Along*, *Hot Cross Buns*, and *Grandma Grunts*. (Please note that the "apostrophe" symbols in the music indicate breathing places.)

Merrily We Roll Along

Traditional

Hot Cross Buns

Traditional

Grandma Grunts

Traditional American folk song

Examples of music appropriate for learning the note C include *Bransle, La capucine,* and *Les cloches.*

Bransle

Claude Gervaise (fl. Paris 1540–1560)

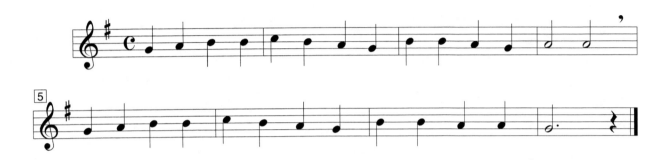

La capucine

Traditional

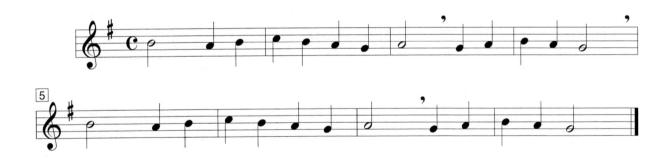

Les cloches

17th-century French round

Examples of music appropriate for learning the note D include *À Saint-Malo, beau port de mer, À la claire fontaine,* and *The May Song.*

À Saint-Malo, beau port de mer

Traditional French Canadian folk song

À la claire fontaine

Traditional French Canadian folk song

The May Song

Traditional English tune

Examples of music appropriate for learning the note F♯ include *A Little Melody, Gagliarda,* and *Gilotte.*

A Little Melody

Tylman Susato (ca 1510–1570 or later)

Gagliarda

Fabrito Caroso (ca 1527-32–after 1605)

Gilotte

Michael Praetorius (1571–1621)

Examples of music appropriate for learning low D and E include *Inuit Lullaby, Au clair de la lune,* and *Good King Wenceslas.*

Inuit Lullaby

Traditional Inuit melody

Au clair de la lune

Traditional French folk song

Good King Wenceslas

Traditional Bohemian tune from Piae Cantiones (1582)

106   Part Two   Authentic Musical Experiences

Examples of music appropriate for learning the note high E include *My Bark Canoe, Nun komm der Heiden Heiland,* and *Gavotte.*

My Bark Canoe

Traditional Ojibwa melody

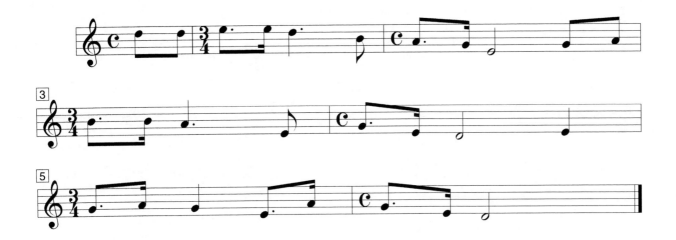

Nun komm der Heiden Heiland

Johann Walter (1496–1570)

Gavotte

George Frideric Handel
(1685–1759)

Source: Sonata no. 2 in D major, HWCV 397

Examples of music appropriate for learning the notes F and B♭ include *O du Liebe*, *Alleluia Canon*, and *Les petites marionettes*.

O du Liebe

18th-century Swiss melody

Alleluia Canon

Attributed to Wolfgang Amadeus Mozart (1756–1791)

Les petites marionettes

Traditional French children's song

Examples of music appropriate for learning low C include two French rounds: *Entendez-vous sur l'ormeau* and *Le coq est mort*.

Entendez-vous sur l'ormeau

French Canadian round

Le coq est mort

Traditional French round

Teachers can find additional music in any of the many excellent recorder methods currently available including Orr (1961), Burakoff and Hettrick (1980), King (1985), and Kulich and Beraducci (1993).

Using the recorder for a few minutes each week over an entire year rather than doing an isolated unit (for example, ten consecutive lessons) once a year seems to be well suited for the elementary grades. This spacing of instruction over time not only allows for longer sustained practice, but also enables the children to use the recorder to further their musical understanding. Playing the recorder can provide elementary school students with a wealth of opportunities for experiencing many musical concepts including those from pitch, texture and harmony, dynamics, and tempo. Children can use the recorder to play familiar songs, learn about music from a variety of cultures, play ensemble music from the sixteenth and seventeenth centuries, accompany their singing, practise reading staff notation, improvise melodic conversations, or write musical compositions. Such broad experiences, accessible through playing the recorder, will continue to help children build their knowledge of musical structure thereby leading to further growth in musical understanding. Specific examples of classroom activities are included in Chapters 10–15.

Questions for Discussion and Practice

1. Briefly discuss a variety of benefits of using classroom instruments in the elementary grades.

2. What is meant by body percussion? Give examples of appropriate activities for the elementary music class using this instrument. Compose a three-part body percussion piece suitable for use with Grade 2 students. Re-arrange it for three non-pitched percussion instruments.

3. Why are barred instruments a good choice for accompanying children's singing? Find a pentatonic song appropriate for Grade 3 students and write an accompaniment that includes one of the *bordun* patterns described in this chapter. Add non-pitched percussion instruments to the accompaniment to provide extra colour.

4. Create another arrangement as described in question 3, this time suitable for Grade 5–6 students.

5. Why is recorder an excellent choice as a melody instrument for the upper grades? Outline what you might teach children during their first lesson with the recorder?

References

Birkenshaw-Fleming, L. (Ed.) (1999). *An Orff Mosaic*. New York: Schott.

Bowles, C. (1998). Music activity preferences of elementary students. *Journal of Research in Music Education, 46*, 193–207.

Burakoff, G., and Hettrick, W. (1980). *The Sweet Pipes Recorder Book*. Livittown, NY: Sweet Pipes Inc.

Campbell, P. (1998). *Songs in Their Heads*. New York: Oxford University Press.

Carlin R. (1982). *How to Play Autoharp*. New York: Music Sales.

De Frece, R. (2000). *Hooray for Singing! Part-Singing Adventures for Upper Elementary and Middle School*. Florida: Warner Bros.

Frazee, J. (1987). *Discovering Orff*. New York: Schott.

King, C. (1985). *Recorder Routes*. Memphis: Memphis Musicraft Publications.

Kulich, B., and Beraducci, J. (1993). *Windsong Series*. Vancouver, BC: Empire Music.

Orff, C., and Keetman, G. (1956–61). *Music for Children*, Eds. D. Hall and A. Walter, vols. I–V. Mainz, Germany: Schott.

Orr, H. (1961). *Basic Recorder Technique*. Toronto: Berandol Music Canada.

Otto, D., and Asplund, D.(1990). *Let's Do It Again*. Vols. I–III. Memphis: Memphis Musicraft Publications.

Shieron, D. (1997). *Let's Sing and Dance Today*. Edmonton: Black Cat Productions.

Sills, J. (1999). *A Musical Treat That's Fun to Beat*. Edmonton: Black Cat Productions.

Snyder, J. (1976). *Teacher's Guide to the Guitar Class*. New York: Charles Hansen Educational Music and Books.

Warner, B. (1991). *Orff Schulwerk: Applications for the Classroom*. Englewood Cliffs, New Jersey: Prentice Hall.

Wuytach, J., and Sills, J. (1994). *Music Activa*. New York: Schott Music.

CHAPTER 6

Improvising and Composing

SYNOPSIS

Chapter 6 discusses the process of music creativity, setting standards for promoting artistic creation in the elementary music classroom. Examples of specific classroom activities for both improvising and composing are included, with grade level recommendations for each.

Introduction

Creativity in music takes many forms. Both the *process* of creation and the *product* created are significant in relation to children's development of musical understanding. As Aiello (1994) states, "in order to learn to create music, children abstract some of the rules [syntax] of their musical culture and use them creatively" (p. 66). Barret (1996) goes on to say that

> A composition is demonstrative of thought within the art form of music, and the ways in which the techniques of the discipline have been used within that composition are as indicative of the child's musical thinking as any linguistically expressed statement. (p. 43)

Thus, *the process of creating music requires thoughtful manipulation of the structural properties of music by the child, with the product being an excellent representation of the child's understanding of how these musical properties may be put together.*

According to Eisner (2000), "Creation in music, as in the other arts, is vitally important in promoting forms of thinking that demand attention to the ways in which sound or other qualities are modulated and organized" (p. 10). Given the power of creative activities for facilitating such musical understanding, it is interesting that, according to research, elementary music teachers spent on

Children learn from both the process and the product of artistic creation.

average less than ten percent of their curricular time involving children in music creation (Montgomery, 1990). It may be that these teachers were drawn to spend less time in this area of music making because of their greater familiarity with the process of developing other musical modes, such as performance. Teachers should be encouraged, however, to make the authentic process of music creativity an important cornerstone of the elementary school music curriculum. The rewards for children are tremendous: they gain a more comprehensive understanding of music while engaged in the process of artistic creation.

Creativity in music traditionally takes two forms:

1. **improvising**: *the immediate extemporization of new musical material using the voice or an instrument*

2. **composing**: *the thoughtful writing down of new musical material with the opportunity to re-work several times if desired*

In the elementary grades, musical creation also includes *movement* or *artwork* as additional tools through which children can express or accompany their impression of musical sounds. For purposes of clarity, this chapter will describe activities for musical improvisation and composition. Discussion of creative strategies regarding music with movement may be found in Chapter 8, and activities that combine art with music are included in Chapters 10–15.

The question of developmental appropriateness surrounds both improvisation and composition. Which is easier for children and thus, should potentially come first? Unfortunately, no easy answers apply, since children vary greatly in their inclination towards creating new music. Although there is a logical increase in children's sophistication at inventing new music in the years between Kindergarten and Grade 6 (Davidson and Scripp, 1988), it seems likely that early experiences in both types of music creativity are desirable.

Initial experiences in the elementary grades should involve creation of short motives or parts of music, whether improvised or composed. Later experiences may involve children taking responsibility for writing out an entire musical composition including text, rhythm, melody, harmony, and theatre accompaniment (for example, movement and costumes). Regardless of the type of creative activity, recording the product on videotape for later student reflection is worthwhile. Written reflections, along with the composition itself and/or a videotape of the improvisation or compositional performance, can become a part of the student's **music class portfolio** (*a collection of a student's work, reflections, self-assessments, journal entries, and videotapes of performances that records the student's growth in musical understanding*—see Chapter 17).

Children flourish creatively in a music classroom that is relaxed and accepting of individual response. Teachers must promote an environment that encourages children to try novel ideas, that respects their attempts at individuality, and that helps them to explore a variety of options available to them in the creative process. Such activities should be included in the elementary music curriculum as early as Kindergarten, thereby establishing creative activity as a normal and natural occurrence in the music lesson. Reflection should play an important role in the creative process as well, since children learn a great deal by engaging in discussion of the various choices available to them in musical construction. Thus, musical creativity, when facilitated by a thoughtful teacher, can be a significant mode of musical expression for children.

Improvisation

Improvisation requires children to invent an immediate response to a particular musical situation.

Structure gives children the freedom to create with confidence.

Improvisation in music requires children to explore or invent an immediate response to a particular musical situation. This improvised response is traditionally either oral (for example, chanting or singing) or instrumental (for example, playing a non-pitched or a pitched percussion instrument or a recorder).

Children generally respond most positively when their first attempts at improvisation are embedded within a safety net of some kind of structure. For example, Chapter 4 described an vocal improvisation activity for Kindergarten and Grade 1 children using simple question-and-answer songs such as *Doggie, Doggie* (p. 45) or *We Are Dancing in the Forest* (p. 46). When children are ready to move to more abstract question-and-answer improvisations, such as in *rhythmic or melodic conversations* (Grade 2), you might initially specify the length of the improvisation, the rhythmic values (for example, quarter notes and eight notes), or the notes for melodies (for example, *mi–re–doh*) to be used in the conversation. This imposed structure will give children a sense of security within which they can feel free to explore a wealth of creative alternatives.

Improvisation in music may be grouped under five categories:

1. word improvisation
2. timbre improvisation
3. rhythmic improvisation
4. melodic improvisation
5. form improvisation

Sample activities for each category are given below, and additional strategies can be found throughout Chapters 10–15.

Word Improvisation

Example 1: Substituting new word(s) for a selected portion of the text of a rhyme or song (Kindergarten–Grade 4)

Here the children learn a song (for example, *Great Big House* for children in Grades 3–4). Then, individual children are invited to improvise a new word or phrase to fill in the blanks each time the song is sung.

Great Big House

Traditional fill-in-the-blank song

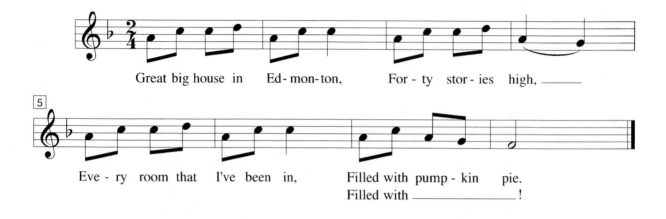

Great big house in Ed - mon - ton, For - ty stor - ies high, _____

Eve - ry room that I've been in, Filled with pump - kin pie.
Filled with _____ !

Example 2: Improvising new words to a familiar melody (Grades 1–4)

Children are invited to improvise new words to a familiar melody such as in *Here We Go Looby Loo*. Students especially enjoy this kind of improvisation during holiday seasons. For example, around Halloween, when they can improvise words about trick-or-treating, pumpkins, or decorating cookies.

Example 3: Improvising a verse of rap (Grades 4–6)

Children are invited to select a topic of interest for the text of their rap, such as eating lunch in the cafeteria or taking a dog for a walk. Individual children are then asked to vocally improvise words in a specified rap format, such as in four lines of four beats each. Children might work in small groups of three to four, alternating between chanting their rap words and improvising accompaniments for the rap on non-pitched percussion instruments.

Timbre Improvisation

Example 1: Telling a story with an instrument (Kindergarten–Grade 3)

With the help of a teacher, children discuss a variety of actions they do on a daily basis, such as riding the bus to school, playing outside at recess, or doing their homework. Next, individual children select one action and use either body percussion or a non-pitched percussion instrument to "play the story." Set a time limit (for example, one minute), and invite the children, one by one, to "play" the actions of their stories on their instruments, using as many different sounds as needed to convey the meaning.

Example 2: Finishing an improvisation in a similar style (Grades 2–4)

Here the teacher plays an un-pitched percussion instrument (such as a hand drum) for 30 seconds, performing in a particular style, such as *legato* and *piano* (smooth and soft) or *staccato* and *forte* (detached and loud). Then the teacher invites a child to "finish" the piece using the same instrument and playing in a similar style. Children must listen carefully to the model in order to get a "feel" for the style of the music. A child might also serve as the model.

Rhythmic Improvisation

Example 1: Improvise the missing measure (Grades 2–4)

This activity is based on a rhythmic pattern of a specified length and metre—for example, a four-measure rhythm in 4/4 metre. The teacher writes three measures of the rhythmic pattern on the board and leaves the last measure blank. The whole class reads the first three measures, immediately followed by an individual child who improvises a rhythm for the blank measure, either clapping or playing a non-pitched percussion instrument. The only restriction given may be the number of beats to be filled in; alternatively, the teacher could specify the rhythmic values (for example, quarter notes, eighth notes, and quarter rests) that may be used.

Whole class — *Individual student improvises the missing bar*

Example 2: Rhythmic conversations (Grades 2–6)

Here, the teacher invites a child to have a rhythmic conversation. The child listens while the teacher claps (or plays using body percussion or a non-pitched percussion instrument) a four-beat rhythmic pattern. Ideally, the child responds with an four-beat improvised rhythmic answer of his or her own without missing a beat. With more experience, older children might improvise rhythms of eight or even sixteen beats. Again, the structure can simply involve a set number of beats, or the teacher can specify the rhythmic values from which the child may select. Children may also serve as the initiators for such rhythmic conversations.

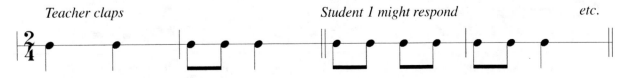

Teacher claps — *Student 1 might respond* — *etc.*

Example 3: Rhythmic snake (Grades 3–5)

In this activity a child claps a four-beat rhythm to her or his neighbour while keeping a steady tempo. The second child repeats the original rhythm and goes on to clap a new four-beat rhythm to a third child. This process is repeated around the room until each child has had a chance to repeat a four-beat rhythm and then invent a new one. Ideally, the "snake" should be continuous, with no extra beats between one child's improvisation and the next child's clap back.

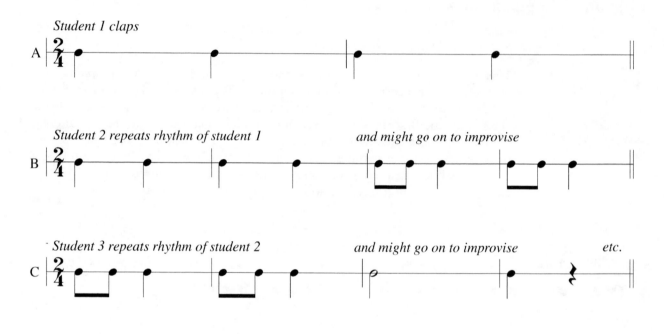

Melodic Improvisation

Example 1: Question and answer melodies (Kindergarten–Grade 2)

The teacher sings a question to the child, and then invites him or her to sing back an answer. This kind of improvisation is considered delightful play by most children and works well in the early grades.

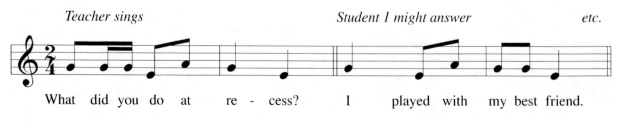

Example 2: Melodic conversations (Grades 2–6)

This activity is more abstract than Example 1, and is identical to the rhythmic conversations except for the addition of pitch. Teachers and children might improvise such conversations with their voices, on pitched percussion instruments (for example, xylophones), or on recorders. As children get more sophisticated at improvising short melodies, they might be instructed to finish their improvisations with an "ending" tone (such as *doh*) to give closure to the conversation.

Example 3: Melodic snake (Grades 3–5)

This activity is similar to the rhythmic snake, with the addition of pitch. Again, children might experience the improvisation through use of voices, pitched percussion instruments, or recorders.

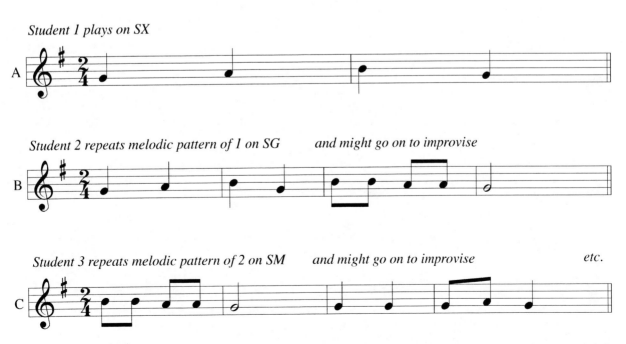

Example 4: Melodic improvisation over a chord structure (Grades 4–6)

In this fairly sophisticated improvisation activity, children are asked to improvise a melody (on the recorder or a pitched percussion instrument) over a specific chord pattern that is played by another child on the bass xylophone. The chord pattern might be as simple as a I–IV–V–I progression or as complex as a **twelve-measure blues pattern**: I–I–I–I⁷–IV–IV–I–I–V⁷–V⁷–I–I. Older children enjoy this kind of improvisation because it leads them towards experimentation with **non-chord tones** (*notes that are not part of the harmony—i.e. the chord—at the moment they occur*) such as **neighbour tones** (or auxiliary tones; *non-chord tones positioned above or below a chord tone that are approached and left by step*) and **passing tones** (*non-chord tones that are positioned a step between two different chord tones, as in a scale*).

Student 1 might improvise this melody on the soprano recorder

A chord pattern played by student 2 and 3 on the AX and BX

Form Improvisation

....

Example 1: Improvising a piece in rondo form (Grades 3–6)

In this activity, children experience the process of improvising short motives that can be combined to build a composition that is constructed using a traditional form such as **rondo (ABACA) form**—*a form that organizes music into three (or more) contrasting sections; the first (A) section returns after each contrasting (B or C) section resulting in an ABACA structure.* Children might use the first eight measures of a song such as *Donkey Riding* (see next page) as the A section. Individual children would then be asked to improvise short melodies for the B and C sections on the recorder or a pitched percussion instrument. The B and C sections should match the A section in key, metre, and length (in this case, F major, 2/4 time, and eight measures—or sixteen beats).

This kind of activity can be repeated any number of times, using other known songs as the A section, and it also works well with other forms, including:

binary (AB) form—*music that is organized into two sections (A and B)*

ternary (ABA) form—*music that is organized into two sections (A and B) with a return of the first (A) section at the end*

theme and variations form—*music that is organized into several sections: a theme (melody), followed by several variations, in which the original theme is altered in one or more ways through different compositional techniques*

Donkey Riding

Traditional Canadian folk song

1. Were you ev-er in Que-bec, Stow-ing tim-ber on a deck, Where there's a king with a gol-den crown, Rid-ing on a don-key.

Refrain
Hey ho, a-way she goes, Don-key ri-ding, don-key ri-ding, Hey-ho, a-way she goes, Rid-ing on a don-key.

2. Were you ever in Cardiff Bay,
   Where the folks all shout Hooray,
   Here comes John with his three months pay,
   Riding on a donkey!
   Refrain

Example of rondo form improvisation using *Donkey Riding* as the A section

Section A: 8 bars of Donkey Riding

Were you ev-er in Que-bec, Stow-ing tim-ber on a deck, Where there's a king with a gol-den crown, Rid-ing on a don-key.

Composing

Composing—the writing down of new musical ideas—provides the child with an opportunity for a longer construction time during the creative process. Here, the child has the opportunity to

1. take time to plan out the composition;
2. sketch a variety of musical ideas using concrete manipulatives (for example popsicle sticks and round wooden disks), large poster paper and markers, pencil and paper, or computer notation software;
3. try out these written sketches on an appropriate instrument;
4. re-craft the work as necessary to create a meaningful musical composition; and
5. listen to the final work performed by others.

The teacher's role is similar to the one played during improvisation activities in that he or she provides a safety net of structural limits within which the children work freely to construct their new compositions. For example, the teacher might specify a form and ask the children to write a rhythm and melody within that form. In addition, teachers will need to provide guidance to the self-assessment process once the composition is complete.

Activities appropriate for beginning the compositional process in the elementary music class focus children's attention on writing only one or two aspects of music. For example, children might write a four-beat rhythmic *ostinato* to accompany a pre-existing melody. Or the teacher may provide a rhythmic phrase and ask the children to add pitches to turn the rhythm into a melody. These initial experiences provide important practise for the child in constructing *individual* components of a musical composition, thereby paving the way towards later composing an entire piece of music (words, rhythm, pitch, harmony, theatre accompaniment).

Composing with music may be grouped under five broad categories:

1. composition involving timbre construction
2. composition involving rhythmic construction
3. composition involving melodic construction
4. composition involving harmonic construction
5. total composition involving all aspects of the music

Sample activities for each category are given below, and additional strategies can be found throughout Chapters 10–15.

Composition Involving Timbre Construction

Example 1: Adding instruments to heighten the expressive power of a rhyme, poem, story, or song (Grades 1–3)

This activity is similar to an improvisational experience mentioned in Chapter 5 in reference to the rhyme *The Loose Tooth* (p. 73), the story *The Lion and the Mouse* (p. 74), and the song *Land of the Silver Birch* (p. 76). Here, however, the children are asked to invent their own graphic or iconic notation in order to write down the instrumental parts that accompany a piece of poetry or a song. By doing so, the accompaniment becomes permanently recorded so that it can be brought back and performed again at a later date by the children.

Example 2: Sound walk (Grades 3–6)

This activity builds on the experiences of Example 1. The children are divided into small groups of five to seven, and invited to take a sound walk together along a predetermined route in or around the school. Each group is directed to listen for and attempt to remember as many sounds as they can while on their walk. When the children return to the classroom, they are asked to reflect on and write down all the sounds they heard, in the order that they heard them. Each group then writes a composition on poster paper, using graphic notation to illustrate their individual sound walk. The compositions are performed by each group using either body percussion or various non-pitched and pitched percussion instruments.

Example 3: Musique concrète

Musique concrète is a form of musical composition that was developed in Paris in the late 1940s; it involved assembling tape recordings of both environmental sounds (such as screeching tires, dripping faucets, rain falling, horns blowing) and newly created sounds. In the studio, composers manipulated these reel-to-reel tape recordings (for example, editing them, splicing them together, playing them at different speeds, or playing them backwards) and recorded the result as a new composition.

Modern technology permits students to revamp this interesting compositional technique. Here, the children are asked to collect a variety of sounds they hear in their environment using a portable tape or CD recorder. Back in the classroom, these recorded sounds are re-sampled into a synthesizer or recorded directly into a computer. The child is then asked to edit these sounds and arrange them into a meaningful compositional order on the synthesizer or computer for playback. The completed composition can be burned on to a CD for a permanent record. This activity is an excellent individual or small-group project for the upper grades and can yield extremely interesting musical results. (Grades 5–6)

Composition Involving Rhythmic Construction

Example 1: Writing rhythmic ostinati for accompaniment of rhymes or songs (Grades 1–6)

Children are invited to write a short rhythmic *ostinato* pattern (about four beats) to be played on a non-pitched percussion instrument as an accompaniment to a song. Students might be asked to consider the "harmonic" implications of their *ostinato* by making sure that the *ostinato* rhythm is **complementary** to the rhythm of the song—that is, *it sounds like an independent accompaniment part rather than just an imitation of the rhythms sung by the voice.*

Older children might also be asked to transfer their written *ostinato* to a full score including both song and accompaniment—either on the board or on paper. This will allow the children to visualize how the two parts (melody and *ostinato* accompaniment) are written together. In the following example, *Sakura* is written in full score form with a four-beat complementary *ostinato* accompaniment.

Sakura (Cherry Blossoms)

Traditional Japanese folk song
English text by A. Montgomery

....

Example 2: Writing a short rhythm (Grades 3–4)

In this activity, children are asked to write a short rhythm (about four measures) using a metre (for example, 6/8) and note values (for example, quarter notes, eighth notes, and dotted quarter notes) specified by the teacher. The rhythm can be written either with concrete manipulatives or with pencil and paper. In order for the activity to have musical context, rather than be simply perceived as an isolated exercise, children could be invited to perform their rhythms on non-pitched percussion instruments as part of a performance of a favourite song. Individual rhythms might serve either as an **introduction** (*a brief section that precedes the main body of a piece of music, serving as a prologue*) or a **coda** (*a brief section that follows the main body of a piece of music to bring it to a close*). (Grades 1–6). The following arrangement of *Bonavist' Harbour* has an added rhythmic introduction and *coda*.

Bonavist' Harbour

Newfoundland folk song

Student 1 might write this short rhythm to be used as the INTRODUCTION

Oh! there's lots of fish in Bo-na-vist' har-bour,

Lots of fish right in a-round here, Boys and girls are fish-ing to-geth-er,

For-ty-five from Car-bon-ear. ——— Oh!

Catch-a-hold this one, catch-a-hold that one, Swing a-round this one, dance a-round she.

Catch-a-hold this one, catch-a-hold that one, Did-dle-dum this one, did-dle-dum dee!

Student 2 might write this short rhythm to be used as a CODA

Bonavist' Harbour (PEA 5, no. 3, CMC Archives) was collected by Kenneth Peacock and is used by courtesy of the Canadian Museum of Civilization.

Example 3: Writing a rhythm to a given set of pitches (Grades 1–6)

Here, children are presented with a set of pitches and invited to add note values to the pitches so as to turn them into a melody. The structure given by the teacher might also include the specific note values from which the students might select, as in this example (eighth notes, quarter notes, and half notes). This new melody could be either sung or played by the children on pitched percussion instruments or recorder.

A set of pitches given to the students by the teacher

Student 1 might add rhythm to the set of pitches to create this melody

etc.

Composition Involving Melodic Construction

Example 1: Adding pitches to a given rhythm (Grades 1–4)

This activity is the opposite of the previous one. Here the children are presented with a short rhythm and invited to add pitches so as to turn the rhythm into a melody. The structure given by the teacher might include a tone set from which students could select their notes (for example, *doh* to *doh* in G major). This new melody should be either sung or played on pitched percussion instruments or recorders.

A rhythm given to the students by the teacher

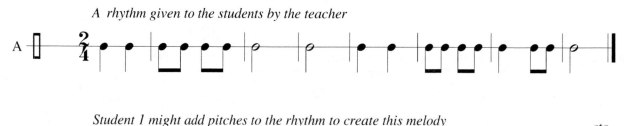

Student 1 might add pitches to the rhythm to create this melody

etc.

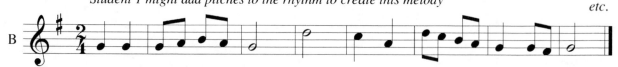

Example 2: Adding pitches to the words of a rhyme (Grades 1–4)

Children are asked to write a melody to go with the words of a familiar rhyme—for example, *Jelly in a Bowl*. Because the rhyme is chanted with a particular rhythm, this activity is similar to example 1; the child only has to add pitches in order to "sing" the rhyme as a song.

Jelly in a Bowl

Traditional rhyme

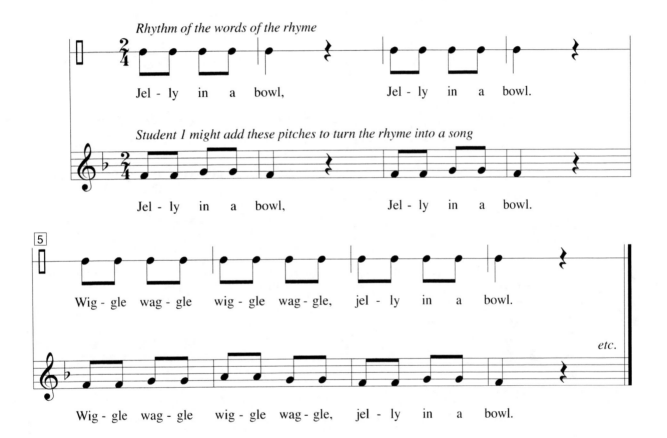

Example 3: Writing a short melody (Grades 1–6)

Children are asked to write a short melody (about two to four measures) using notes (for example, *doh*, *re*, and *mi*) specified by the teacher. The melody can be written using either concrete manipulatives or pencil and paper. Again, such melodies can be sung or played by the children on pitched percussion instruments or recorders, and used as introductions or *codas* to familiar songs sung in class.

Composition Involving Harmonic Construction

Example: Writing a bordun pattern to accompany a song

Ask the children to write a *bordun* pattern appropriate for accompanying a pentatonic song on a pitched percussion instrument. Again, as with composing a rhythmic *ostinato*, children should be asked to write their composition in full score form so that they can visualize how the song and the accompaniment are put together. Children in music classes with access to computers could use music notation software to orchestrate the songs with both the *bordun* and the *ostinato* accompaniments (Grades 3–6). In the following example, *Ah! les jolis papillons* is written in full score form with a *bordun* accompaniment. (Grade 3).

Ah! Les jolis papillons

Une mission folklorique aux Îles Saint-Pierre et Miquelon

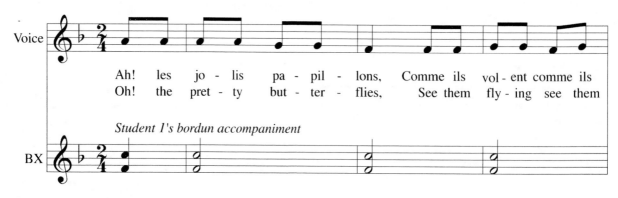

Ah! Les jolis papillons was collected by Carmen Roy and published in the National Museum of Man Bulletin 182, 1962. *It is used here by courtesy of the Canadian Museum of Civilization.*

Composition Involving Form

Example 1: Constructing a theme and variations form using an existing melody (Grades 4–6)

The children are presented with a known melody, such as *Twinkle, Twinkle, Little Star*, and asked to compose a series of variations it. This activity gives children an opportunity to practise a variety of compositional techniques used to alter a melody. These might include:

1. altering a melody by changing the tempo or the dynamics;

2. altering a melody by changing the rhythmic structure;

3. altering a melody by adding non-chord tones such as passing tones or neighbour (auxiliary) tones;

4. altering a melody by changing the key from major to minor (or from minor to major);

5. altering a melody by adding an instrumental accompaniment (or altering an existing accompaniment);

6. altering the rhythm of a melody through **augmentation** : *increasing all the note values of the rhythm by the same proportion* (for example the eighth notes become quarters, the quarter notes become half notes, etc.);

7. altering the rhythm of a melody through **diminution**: *decreasing all the note values of the rhythm by the same proportion* (for example the quarter notes become eighths, the half notes become quarters, etc.);

8. adding a second (and even a third) voice through use of a canon.

The following example illustrates four of these techniques applied to the first line of *Twinkle, Twinkle, Little Star.*

Twinkle, Twinkle, Little Star

Theme

Twin - kle, twin - kle, lit - tle star, How I won - der what you are.

Variation 1: altering the rhythm

continued

Variation 2: adding passing tones

Twin-kle, twin-kle, lit - tle_ star, How I won-der what_ you_ are.

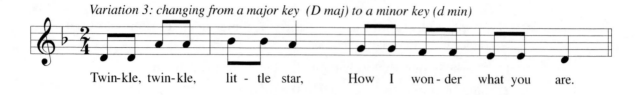

Variation 3: changing from a major key (D maj) to a minor key (d min)

Twin-kle, twin-kle, lit - tle star, How I won-der what you are.

Variation 4: augmentation

etc.

Twin - kle, twin - kle, lit - tle star,

Practice with these kinds of sophisticated compositional techniques will help children to develop a variety of approaches to draw on when they write their own compositions.

Example 2: Writing a complete composition including text and movement (Grades 5–6)

Here children are invited to write a poem, set this text to a rhythm and a melody, orchestrate this new song with accompaniment utilizing non-pitched and pitched percussion and/or a recorder, add movement and/or costumes, rehearse the work, and finally record it as a music video. This activity may take the form of an individual or a small group project requiring several weeks to complete. The results can be stunning, and the children will gain an incredible sense of pride in their growing understanding of how music is put together! (Grades 5–6)

In summary, improvising and composing activities in the elementary music class place the child in the centre of the learning process. Both activities provide the child with an opportunity to manipulate the vocabulary and syntax of music in a personal and meaningful way. During beginning creative experiences, students need basic musical guidelines within which to experience the flexibility of the creative process. Such "restrictions" free children to create with confidence. Both the process and product of music creativity are important in the development of children's ability to think, act flexibly, and bring personal intervention to the music experience.

Questions for Discussion and Practice

1. Does participation in music creativity promote the development of children's musical understanding? Why or why not?

2. Discuss the difference between improvising and composing? Give an example of both an improvising and a composing activity appropriate for the early elementary grades. Now, give one for each category for the later grades.

3. Describe a classroom environment designed for successful participation by children in composing and improvising. What role does the teacher play?

4. Describe a variety of improvising and composing activities appropriate for practicing artistic creation with rhythm.

5. What kinds of classroom management strategies should a teacher consider when planning for small-group composing activities in the elementary music class?

References

Aiello, R. (1994). Musical perceptions. In R. Aiello and J. Sloboda. (Eds.), *Music and Language*. Oxford: Oxford University Press.

Barret, M. (1996). An analysis of children's musical discourse as composers. *International Society for Music Education Journal, 27,* 40–48.

Davidson, L., and Scripp, L. (1988). Young children's musical representations: Windows on music cognition. In J. Sloboda (Ed.), *Generative Processes in Music*. New York: Oxford University Press.

Eisner, E. (2000). Music education six months after the turn of the century. Unpublished paper presented at the 24th Biennial World Conference of the International Society for Music Education, Edmonton, Alberta, 1–15.

Montgomery, A. (1990). The effect of selected factors on the use of instructional time by elementary music specialists in Atlantic Canada. *Canadian Journal of Research in Music Education, 32(3),* 48–61.

CHAPTER 7

Listening to Music

SYNOPSIS

Chapter 7 discusses the role of listening in the elementary music classroom. Advice on planning for listening experiences is included, followed by a list of recorded music examples useful for highlighting a variety of musical concepts with elementary school children.

Introduction

Listening is the predominant vehicle through which adults experience music.

The quality and richness of a child's future listening experience is the concern of the elementary school music educator.

Music listening is a lifelong activity. In fact, listening to music performed by others—rather than performing or composing one's own music—tends to become the predominant vehicle through which many adults encounter music in their lives. Whether hearing recorded music while shopping at the mall, listening to a new song on the radio, watching a favourite video, or attending a local concert, adults have the opportunity to listen to a tremendous amount of music on a daily basis.

The quality and richness of these future listening experiences is the concern of the elementary school music educator. Although some music is obviously meant to be in the background (for example, the recorded music one hears while eating in a restaurant), other music listening experiences, such as relaxing by the fire with a favourite CD, can be powerful musical moments within a person's life.

This second kind of adult music listening experience can become more meaningful if music teachers in the elementary grades carefully orchestrate children's entrance into the world of **active listening**. This means planning for effective listening lessons that will help children learn how *to focus on and respond to the music they hear*—that is, *to aurally interact with the structural properties embedded within that music.*

Music listening lessons help elementary-age children learn how to focus on and respond to music.

As stated in Chapter 1, *people make sense of the music they listen to through musical cognition of the structural components in that music combined with the social, emotional and spiritual background they bring to the listening experience.* Although teachers have no control over the personal background that individual children bring to music listening in the classroom, they can have a significant impact on a child's growing sophistication at perceiving a variety of structural components in music. A heightened aural sensitivity to the manipulation of these musical properties, gained through developmentally appropriate listening lessons in the elementary school, will help children enjoy more powerful and personally meaningful experiences when listening to music. Through such pedagogy, children gain the capacity to have richer and more intense listening experiences with any kind of music they might encounter later in their world.

Planning for Listening Experiences in Elementary Music Lessons

Teachers need to consider a number of variables when planning to engage children in listening experiences during music lessons in the elementary classroom. Here are some of the most important variables:

1. *the style and performance medium of the music example used in the listening experience*: for example, styles such as classical, rock, or jazz, and performance mediums such as instrumental or vocal

2. *the structural properties of the music example*: properties such as the tempo or the type of melodic activity

3. *the length of the music example*

4. *the manner in which the music example is presented*: live performers in the classroom or recorded music on CDs or audio tape

5. *the structural aspect of the music that is specifically highlighted:* for example, the beat, the metre, or the form

6. *the performing or composing experience that is used in the lesson just prior to the listening experience*: the activity used to provide a bridge to link the highlighted musical concept to the listening piece (for example, singing a song with the same rhythmic pattern as in the listening piece)

7. *the classroom activity in which the children participate during the listening portion of the lesson*: the activity in which the children are involved—for example, raising their hands when they hear a particular motive, following a **call chart** (*a chart outlining various aspects of the music, such as the themes*), clapping the *ostinati* pattern, or using movement to reflect the style of the music—in order to help them to stay focused on the music.

Each of these important points will be addressed separately.

Style and Performance Medium

Music listening in the elementary grades should expand children's musical horizons.

When making decisions about which musical styles to utilize during listening experiences, teachers should first consider musical styles and genres to which the child has little access to in other situations. For the same reason that a language arts teacher may feature Shakespeare in a reading class, the elementary music teacher should feel justified in expanding children's listening horizons by exposing them to less familiar styles such as:

1. Western art music of previous centuries (for example, music from the Baroque, Classical, and Romantic periods)
2. different styles of jazz (for example, Dixieland, bebop, or swing)
3. music of Inuit and First Nations peoples (such as round dances, ceremonial music, throat singing)
4. music from other parts and other cultures of the world.

This is not to imply that more "popular" styles—such as rock, pop, hip hop, rap, or country—should not be used during classroom listening, but rather that listening lessons provide a golden opportunity to expand children's musical experience beyond their normally restricted diet of popular music. As Kodály (1974) stated, "often a single experience will open the young soul to music for a whole life time. This experience cannot be left to chance, it is the duty of the school to provide it" (p. 120). Thus, the wealth of beautiful music that children generally have little exposure to should be of prime concern to the elementary music educator.

This also means that teachers might choose instrumental music selections rather than vocal music for use during listening lessons, since elementary school children's opportunities for experience with orchestral, band, and chamber music are limited because of their developmental non-readiness for playing in such instrumental ensembles. Thus, carefully selected listening examples will provide a window of opportunity through which children may gain exposure both to new musical styles and to instrumental genres that they normally would neither hear nor be able to perform.

Structural Properties

Young children like music that has a lively tempo, active melodic rhythms, dynamic contrasts, and interesting timbral colours.

After selecting the musical style to be featured in the listening experience, the next consideration is the structural properties of the particular musical example being used. Some research suggests that music containing certain structural characteristics may be more appealing to children. For example, according to the results of musical preference research involving tempo, middle to upper elementary school children (generally Grades 2 and up) prefer music with faster tempos or music that they perceive as being fast because of the presence of active melodic rhythms (Montgomery, 1998). This seems to be true regardless of musical style, according to research involving jazz (Burnstead and Price, 1987; LeBlanc and Cote, 1983;

LeBlanc and McCrary, 1983; LeBlanc, et al., 1988), piano music from the Classical period (Burnstead and Price, 1987; Sims, 1987), Hap Palmer music (Burnstead and Price, 1987), and orchestral selections from early Romantic operas (Montgomery, 1996). As a result, beginning with music that has faster tempos or active melodic rhythms may help motivate children towards being more receptive to new musical styles that are introduced through listening lessons. Other structural characteristics in music that seem to appeal to children include dynamic contrasts and the use of interesting timbral colours. All of these characteristics may be found in music from a variety of styles.

Length

The third variable to consider when planning for listening experiences involves finding musical selections that are an appropriate length for classroom listening. Shorter examples or excerpts from longer works are most effective with younger elementary school children. This also holds true when working with students in the upper grades who may be new to focused listening. Examples that are approximately one and a half to two and a half minutes long work well (perhaps because of the children's familiarity with listening to popular music played on the radio, where the average length of a song is two minutes and six seconds).

Listening to a piece more than once can lead to a greater appreciation of the music.

Pieces used in listening lessons should be made available for individual revisiting by students at a listening centre in the regular classroom. As described in Chapter 3, this centre should consist of a table and chairs with a CD player (and/or a computer) and headphones. Individual listening experiences provide the children with opportunities to hear complete performances of longer works during their free times. In addition, repeated hearings of shorter pieces can lead children towards a new appreciation of music they might initially have considered unattractive after only one hearing (Moskovitz, 1992; Perry and Perry, 1986; Shehan, 1985).

Manner of Presentation

Live performances make the listening activity a more three-dimensional experience.

The manner in which the music is presented to children during listening experiences also merits careful consideration. The majority of music used during listening experiences must of course, for practical reasons, be recorded music. However, short pieces either sung or played on the recorder, guitar, piano, or other instrument by the teacher are especially motivating for children in the younger grades. These "live" performances help to make the listening activity a more three-dimensional experience. Guest musicians can also be invited to give live performances in the elementary music classroom. Parents, community musicians, local junior or senior high school bands, or music education students from a nearby university are excellent sources for these kinds of live listening experiences.

Highlighting a Structural Aspect of the Music

Since most of the music examples used during listening experiences will be recorded, teachers need to consider various strategies for keeping children's focus on the music itself. The key to success here lies in directing students to listen for a particular structural element that is embedded within the music (for example, the beat and metre, a rhythmic motive, the tempo, or the dynamics). Research (Sims, 1995) suggests younger children have greater success when instructed to listen for only one musical characteristic at a time. Multiple repetitions of a music example either in the same lesson or in subsequent lessons later in the year can provide further opportunities for pulling out various layers of musical patterning in the music (Montgomery, 1991). Ideally, the more structural properties the children are eventually able to aurally interact with and respond to in a particular piece of music, the richer their listening experience will be.

Musical concepts selected by the teacher for highlighting during any listening activity should correlate with those already being experienced in the performing and creating activities for the grade level. As discussed in Chapter 2, these musical concepts are sequenced in an easy-to-complex teaching order that is based on the profession's growing knowledge of how children learn music. Thus, Grade 2 students might be directed to listen for the beat, tempo, dynamics, or an easy rhythmic pattern in a listening example, while Grade 5 students might be directed to listen for more sophisticated musical manipulations such as ABA form, a particular melodic motive, or a texture involving a rhythmic *ostinato*. With carefully planned listening lessons, children's sophistication at perceiving such musical patterning will grow throughout the elementary grades, and contribute to the further development of the child's musical understanding. (See Chapter 2, pp. 12–13 for recommended sequencing of concepts.)

Performing or Composing Activities prior to Listening Lessons

The next variable to be considered when planning for listening experiences involves the performing or composing activities utilized in the lesson just prior to the actual listening experience. The purpose of these activities is to set the stage for the listening example by bringing to consciousness the musical concepts under consideration. For example, the listening selection for a Grade 2 class might be the opening of the second movement of Symphony no. 7 by Ludwig van Beethoven (1770–1827). The teacher could direct the children's attention to the rhythmic motive that is repeated throughout the movement:

In order to set the stage for listening for this structural pattern in Beethoven's symphony movement, the teacher might initially invite Grade 2 children to sing and play *Bluebird*, which uses the same rhythmic pattern in the first four measures of the song. Children could also be asked to clap the rhythm as an *ostinato* to accompany their singing, further emphasizing the rhythm that will be subsequently re-discovered in Beethoven's music.

Bluebird

Traditional singing game

Game: The children stand in a circle, leaving about a metre of space between each child. While everyone sings the first eight measures, one child skips in and out of the circle through these spaces. At the words "Take a little partner . . ." the child joins hands with the nearest child in the circle, and the two continue the skipping pattern until the end of the song. The game begins again with a new child, chosen by the teacher, skipping alone.

Another example, this time for the upper grades, focuses on *Newfoundland Rhapsody* by Canadian composer Howard Cable. Here, the musical structure being highlighted in the listening activity would be the use of a folk song as melodic material for a new instrumental composition. Cable uses several Canadian folk songs in *Newfoundland Rhapsody* including *The Petty Harbour Bait Skiff*. In the part of the lesson that precedes the listening experience, students might be asked to compose rhythmic *ostinati* to accompany their singing of *The Petty Harbour Bait Skiff*. The students would then be asked to listen to and compare the kinds of accompaniment Cable wrote to go with his setting of the melody in *Newfoundland Rhapsody*.

The Petty Harbour Bait Skiff

Newfoundland folk song

Good peo - ple all both great and small I —
hope you will at - tend. And lis - ten to these
ver - ses — few that — I have late - ly penned, And
I'll re - late the hard - ships — great that —
fish - er - men must stand, While fight - ing for a
live - li - hood on the coast of New - found - land!

G.S. Doyle (Ed.). (1966). From Old-Time Songs and Poetry of Newfoundland: Songs of the People from the Days of Our Forefathers (4th ed.). Reprinted with the permission of the Doyle family.

Linkages of this kind between performing or composing activities and listening experiences in an elementary music lesson not only promote more focused listening but also contribute to a broader understanding of how music is put together. A successful listening lesson always includes both, thereby making the listening experience as rich as possible.

Classroom Activities during a Listening Experience

The final variable to consider when planning for the listening lesson involves the classroom strategy employed by the teacher to keep the children focused during the listening activity itself. Simply listening for a particular musical concept in a piece of music is often not enough to keep children focused on the music for any length of time. Directing children to identify when the structural element (musical concept) occurs—using activities that involve moving, reading, or writing—while they are listening is usually more effective. Here are some examples of activities that will focus children's attention on the music they are listening to.

Structural element—tempo: Ask the children to pass a small ball around a circle; the ball should change direction whenever the children hear a tempo change in the music.

Structural element—ostinato: Direct the children to clap lightly along with the music whenever they hear a previously identified rhythmic *ostinato* being played.

Structural element—canon: Instruct the children to raise their hands every time they hear a previously identified melody start again, as in a canon.

Structural element—metre: Invite the children to "conduct the orchestra" as they listen to the music, changing conducting patterns whenever they hear a change of metre.

Structural element—timbre (brass instruments): Direct the children to pretend to play the trumpet every time they hear this instrument.

Structural element—I–IV–V chords: Give the children cards that read "I," "IV," or "V," and instruct them to hold up the appropriate card every time they hear the a chord change in the music.

Structural element—phrases: Invite the children to "draw" the phrases of the melody in the air using a rainbow shape, starting new rainbows every time they hear a new phrase beginning.

Structural element—melodic contour: Instruct the children to use a piece of yarn to "draw" the melodic contour of a repeated melodic motive they hear in the music.

Structural element—timbre (brass instruments): Direct the children to answer written questions about the music while they listen (for example, "Which instrument plays the melody the first time you hear it in this piece: the trumpet or the trombone?).

Structural element—melody: Invite the children to follow the music along in the score with their fingers while they listen.

Further examples of moving, reading, and writing activities for use during listening to music can be found in Chapters 10–15.

Recorded Music Examples

Building a Collection of Recorded Music

Recorded music that is useful for classroom listening experiences is available for purchase by teachers from various sources. Elementary music textbook series often include listening CDs to accompany songbooks. The National Film Board of Canada (**www.nfb.ca**) has produced a number of interesting videos featuring Canadian artists and their music, such as *Celtic Spirits* (fiddlers from Cape Breton), *In the Key of Oscar* (jazz pianist Oscar Peterson), and *Weinzweig's World* (Canadian composer John Weinzweig). In addition, CDs featuring art music by Canadian composers can be purchased through the Canadian Music Centre (**www.musiccentre.ca**). Special CD collections, such as the *Bowmar Records Series* (1981), include excellent examples of Western art music for children's listening. Single CDs or CD sets featuring "The best of. . ." (*The Best of Baroque Music*, *The Best of Music from China*, etc.) are usually available at local music stores and can be another affordable option when starting a classroom collection. Quality is of utmost importance: teachers should look for excellent performances that are well recorded, whatever musical style they wish to feature during classroom listening experiences.

Choosing Music that Features a Particular Characteristic

When looking for listening examples that highlight particular structural characteristics, teachers are cautioned to select music by listening to a variety of selections rather than by examining the printed scores. For example, if you want to find music that contains a rhythmic *ostinato*, you should listen to several pieces, and choose the one that *clearly* exhibits a repeated pattern. If you look at the score while you listen to the music, you may notice structural characteristics that are actually too subtle or too deeply embedded in the music for children to hear what is happening. Thus, initial listening experiences with elementary school children should include music that contains easily heard manipulations of particular musical characteristics

The following list of music is useful for this purpose. These excellent examples are classified according to specific prominent structural characteristics that can easily be heard by elementary school children. All the examples can also be used during repeated listening experiences with children for the purpose of delving more deeply into the music in order to identify other musical characteristics. A variety of CDs containing these selections should be available for purchase at most local music stores or over the Internet.

Recorded Music to Highlight Specific Musical Characteristics

A Steady Beat

"Procession of the Nobles" from the opera *Mlada* by Nikolai Rimsky-Korsakov (1844–1908)

"Badinerie," the final movement of the Orchestral Suite no. 2 in B minor, BWV 1067, by Johann Sebastian Bach (1685–1750)

Teddy Bears' Picnic by John Bratton (1867–1947)

"Ritual Fire Dance" from the opera *El amor brujo* by Manuel de Falla (1876–1946)

"The Imperial March" from the film score for *Star Wars* by John Williams (born 1932)

Tempo

Adagio—Irish Tune from County Derry (Danny Boy) by Percy Grainger (1882–1961)

Allegro—"The Dance" from *Atayoskewin Suite,* for orchestra by Malcolm Forsyth (born 1936)

Tempo changes—"Russian Sailors Dance" from the ballet *The Red Poppy* by Reinhold Glière (1875–1956)

Tempo changes—second movement of the Concerto Grosso in A major, op. 2, no. 6 by Francesco Geminani (1687–1762)

Tempo changes—third movement from the Concerto Grosso in G minor, op. 6, no. 8 ("Christmas Concerto") by Arcangelo Corelli (1653–1713)

Metre

3/4 metre—"Laurentide Waltz" from the *Canadiana Suite* by Oscar Peterson (born 1925)

4/4 metre—"Romance" from the *Lieutenant Kije Suite* by Sergei Prokofiev (1891–1953)

6/8 metre—"Barcarole" from *The Tales of Hoffman* by Jacques Offenbach (1819–1880)

5/4 metre—*Take Five* by Dave Brubeck (born 1920)

Metre changes (3/4 to 6/8)—*Slavonic Dance,* op. 46, no. 1 in C major by Antonín Dvořák (1841–1904)

Dynamics—*Forte-Piano* Contrasts

Allegro movement from *Spring*, the first concerto of *The Four Seasons* by Antonio Vivaldi (1678–1741)

Now Is the Month of Maying, by Thomas Morley (1557-8–1602)

fourth movement from Symphony no. 39 in E flat major, K 543, by Wolfgang Amadeus Mozart (1756–1791)

Marche militaire, op. 51, no. 1 in D major by Franz Schubert (1797–1828)

Joyeuse marche (*Joyous March*) by Emmanuel Chabrier (1841–1894)

Rhythm

The first theme of the second movement of the Symphony no. 7 in A major, op. 92, by Ludwig van Beethoven (1770–1827) emphasizes this rhythm:

The first theme of the second movement of the Symphony no. 94 in G major ("Surprise") by Joseph Haydn (1732–1809) has the following rhythmic pattern:

The melody of "In the Hall of the Mountain King" from the *Peer Gynt Suite* no. 1, op. 46 by Edvard Grieg (1843–1907) has the following rhythmic pattern:

The melody in the "Finale" of the *Overture to William Tell* by Gioachino Rossini (1792–1868) emphasizes this rhythm:

The melody in "Galop" from the ballet *La boutique fantastique* by Ottorino Respighi (1879–1936) emphasizes the following rhythm:

Melody

Melody in a minor mode—"The Old Castle" from *Pictures at an Exhibition* by Modest Mussorgsky (1839–1881)

Melodies in major and minor modes—"Minuet" of the Suite in F major, HWV 348, from *Water Music* by George Frideric Handel (1685–1759)

Canadian folksong melody (À *la claire fontaine*) used in a new composition—"The Contented House" from *Canadian Mosaic* by Jean Coulthard (1908–2000)

À la claire fontaine

Traditional French Canadian folk song

À la clai - re fon - tai - ne, M'en al - lant pro - me - ner,

J'ai trou - vé l'eau si bel - le, Que je m'y suis bai - gné.

Lui y'a long - temps que je t'ai - me, Ja - mais je ne t'ou - blie - rai.

Caribbean folksong melody used in a new composition—"Mango Walk" from *Jamaican Rumba* by Arthur Benjamin (1893–1960)

Mango Walk

Traditional Jamaican folk song

My moth-er did - a tell me that you go man - go walk, You

go man-go walk, you go man - go walk. My moth - er did - a tell me that you

go man - go walk, and find all the num - ber 'lev - en.

Russian folksong melody (*The Birch Tree*) used in a new composition—the fourth movment from the Symphony no. 4 in F minor, op. 36, by Pyotr Il'yich Tchaikowsky (1840–1893)

The Birch Tree

Russian folk song
English text by A. Montgomery

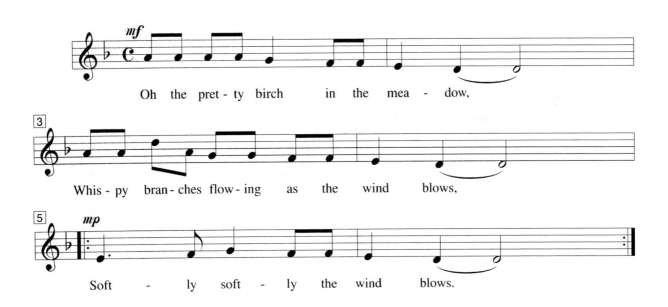

Oh the pret-ty birch in the mea-dow,

Whis-py bran-ches flow-ing as the wind blows,

Soft - ly soft - ly the wind blows.

Instrumental timbres

Brass—*Fanfare for the Common Man* by Aaron Copland (1900–1990)

Strings—*Adagio for Strings* by Samuel Barber (1910–1981)

Woodwinds— "Polovtsian Dances" from *Prince Igor* by Alexander Borodin (1833–1887)

Percussion— "Samba no. 1" from the suite from the ballet *Oiseaux exotiques* by Harry Freedman (born 1922)

Double Bass—"The Elephants" from *Carnival of the Animals* by Camille Saint-Saëns (1835–1921)

Form

Ternary (ABA) form—"En bateau" (In a Boat) from *Petite suite* by Claude Debussy (1862–1918)

Rondo (ABACA) form—"The Viennese Musical Clock" from the *Háry János Suite* by Zoltán Kodály (1880–1967)

Fugue—Little Fugue in G minor, BWV 578, by Johann Sebastian Bach (1685–1750)

Theme and variations form—the final movement (air and variations, "The Harmonious Blacksmith") from the Suite no. 5 in E major, HWV 430 by George Frideric Handel (1685–1759)

Canon—third movement from the *Canon mélodieux* (Canonic Sonata) no. 1 in G major, TWV 40: 118 by Georg Philipp Telemann (1681–1767)

Expression

Pizzicato—Plink, Plank, Plunk! by Leroy Anderson (1908–1975)

Pizzicato—third movement from the Symphony no. 4 in F minor, op. 36, by Pyotr Il'yich Tchaikowsky (1840–1893)

Pizzicato—Holiday for Strings by David Rose (1910–1990)

Staccato—"Polka" from the ballet *The Golden Age* by Dmitri Shostakovich (1906–1975)

Staccato vs. *legato—Danse macabre* by Camile Saint-Saëns (1835–1921)

Texture and Harmony

Ostinato in bass—*Berceuse* by Igor Stravinsky (1882–1971)

Ostinato in bass—"Pavanne" from Symphonette No. 1 (American Symphonette) by Morton Gould (1913–1996).

Ostinato in bass—"March Past of the Kitchen Utensils" from *The Wasps, Aristophanic Suite* by Ralph Vaughan Williams (1872–1958)

Ostinato in bass—"Mars" from *The Planets* by Gustav Holst (1874–1934)

I–IV–V chord pattern repeated in bass—*Watermelon Man* by Herbie Hancock (born 1940)

Additional examples of excellent recorded music suitable for use during listening experiences in the elementary grades can be found throughout Chapters 10–15.

Questions for Discussion and Practice

1. Make a list of the times you heard music today. Were any of these "active" listening experiences? Why or why not?

2. How do well-planned listening experiences in the elementary general music classroom lead children towards achieving richer music listening experiences in the future?

3. What variables should teachers consider when planning for effective listening experiences with children? Discuss one of these variables in detail.

4. Using the criteria discussed in this chapter, give an example of a performing or composing activity that could be used at the beginning of a lesson to help to bring to consciousness a musical concept that will be highlighted later during the listening portion of the lesson.

5. Using the criteria discussed in this chapter, choose ten examples of recorded music that illustrate at least one musical concept from each of the ten elements of music.

References

Bowmar (1981). *The Bowmar Records Series on CD*. Florida: C.P. Belwin; Warner Bros.

Burnstead, V., and Price, H. (1987). The effect of traditional music class versus repeated listening on the music preferences of kindergarten and primary grade children. *Missouri Journal of Research in Music Education, V(5),* 26–38.

Kodály, Z. (1974). *The Selected Writings of Zoltán Kodály*. London: Boosey and Hawkes.

LeBlanc, A., and Cote, R. (1983). Effect of tempo and performing medium on children's music preference. *Journal of Research in Music Education, 31,* 57–66.

LeBlanc, A., and McCrary, J. (1983). Effect of tempo on children's musical preference. *Journal of Research in Music Education, 31,* 283–94.

LeBlanc, A., Colman, J., McCrary, J., Sherril, C., and Malin, S. (1998). Tempo preferences of different age listeners. *Journal of Research in Music Education, 44,* 49–59.

Montgomery, A. (1998). Tempo, melodic rhythm, tempo perception and the music preferences of elementary school children. *Canadian Journal of Research in Music Education, 39(4),* 17–23.

Montgomery, A.P. (1996). The effect of tempo on the musical preferences of elementary and middle school children. *Journal of Research in Music Education, 42(3),* 119–28.

Montgomery, A.P. (1991). Listening in the elementary grades: Current research from a Canadian perspective. Unpublished paper presented at the Conference of the International Kodály Society, Calgary, Alberta.

Moskovitz, E. (1992). The effect of repetition on tempo preferences of elementary children. *Journal of Research in Music Education, 40(3),* 193–203.

Perry, J., and Perry, I. (1986). Effects of exposure to classical music on the musical preferences of pre-school children. *Journal of Research in Music Education, 31(1),* 24–33.

Shehan, P. (1985). Transfer of preference from taught to untaught pieces of non-western music genres. In C. Madsen and C. Prickett (Eds.), *Applications of Research in Music Behavior*. Tuscaloosa: University of Alabama Press.

Sims, W. (1987). Effect of tempo on music preference of pre-school through fourth grade children. In C. Madsen and C. Prickett (Eds.), *Applications of Research in Music Behavior*. Tuscaloosa: University of Alabama Press.

Sims, W. (1995). Children's Ability to demonstrate music concept discrimination in listening. *Journal of Research in Music Education, 43(3).* 204–21.

CHAPTER 8

Moving with Music

SYNOPSIS

Chapter 8 discusses the power of accompanying music with movement in the elementary grades. Strategies for facilitating positive movement experiences are given, with suggestions for managing classroom behaviour and establishing a movement vocabulary through the initial use of exploratory movement experiences. Music-movement activities for the elementary music classroom are grouped into three distinct categories with specific examples and grade level recommendations given for each.

Introduction

Children and movement are natural partners.

Music heightens children's desire to move their bodies.

Children and movement are natural partners. From birth, humans learn about their world through kinesthetic and tactile experiences. This exploration continues throughout childhood with physical action becoming an important part of children's daily lives (Stinson, 1990).

Music heightens children's desire to move their bodies. Indeed, it is difficult to imagine music in the elementary grades without seeing some kind of movement Although music is structurally an aural art, most children believe that the movement that accompanies music—as in a singing game—is as significant as the sounds themselves. Many of the world's cultures consider music and movement as synonymous; one rarely exists without the intertwining of the other (Campbell, 1991). As children grow beyond the singing games of childhood and become more deeply involved in North American popular culture, movement continues to be an integral part of their music experiences, as is evident in music videos and live pop or rock concerts.

Human movement can be grouped in two distinct categories:

1. **non-locomotor** or **axial movement:** *movement that is performed in a stationary position* (for example, stretching the arms upward, bending at the waist, swaying back and forth)

2. **locomotor movement:** *movement that involves travelling from one space to another* (for example, walking, skipping, running)

Both types figure prominently in movement activities utilized with children in the elementary grades.

Planning for Positive Movement Experiences

Movement should be an integral part of the elementary school music class.

Teachers planning for elementary school music-movement activities must consider several variables. As described in Chapter 3, space is the first and foremost consideration; movement requires an area that is obstacle-free and is preferably carpeted, if the movement involves sitting on the floor. Teachers working in classrooms where children must sit at tables or desks may still incorporate movement activities, but for the sake of safety, they should consider focusing on axial or non-locomotor forms of movement. Relocating to the gymnasium is worth considering, but unfortunately this option implies that movement-music activities should be saved for "special" lessons (i.e., when the gym is free). Ideally, movement should be an integral part of the elementary music class and should somehow be included in every lesson.

Teachers need to manage the traffic flow and noise that naturally bubbles forth when using movement with children.

The next consideration is how to "manage" the traffic and noise level that naturally bubbles forth when children are involved in making music and movement. Teachers need to devise procedures that will help to move children efficiently from their desks to the movement spaces in the room and re-gain their attention when instructions need to be given to the whole class. One way to facilitate this, when using prescribed movement activities such as in dances, is to begin by using a small group of students at the front of the room to demonstrate the movements of the dance for the rest of the students. Once all the children are up and ready to sing and move, you can use a pair of claves, lightly tapped, as a signal to capture the children's attention for further instructions.

The third consideration is the children's emotional comfort level during movement activities. At first, some children may feel shy about expressing themselves during creative movement activities. Directing the children to shut their eyes during non-locomotor experiences may encourage some children to feel safer at moving their bodies differently from others. Props such as scarves, streamers, and hoops may also help children to feel less self-conscious during creative, locomotor movement activities.

Teachers should be sensitive to children's emotional comfort level when introducing movements.

Other issues—for example, "not wanting to hold hands"—may emerge in the middle-elementary grades. One solution is to use a piece of rope or thick yarn (about 25 cm long) to "connect" individual students to each other without actually requiring them to touch each other. Students can also link by touching elbows or by standing with their legs spread apart so that the sides of their feet touch their neighbours'. Movement that requires partners can also present a challenge for classes with uneven numbers of boys and girls, and for those children who always seem to be the last to be picked by their peers. A sensitive teacher will devise an objective, non-threatening way in which to select partners for music-movement activities (for example, "numbering off" 1–2, 1–2, etc.) so that all children will feel valued.

In addition, teachers will need to devise a system (such as a checkmark in the grade book) to keep track of those children who have had an opportunity to play the role of "leader" or "special character" in a singing game (such as "Mary" in *Mary Had a Little Lamb*, see p. 209). Although singing games are often repeated multiple times during a lesson, it may take several lessons before all the children will have had an opportunity to take their turn as leader.

Teachers should also keep in mind the powerful, aesthetic nature of the music and movement experience for the child. When students are playing a singing game such as *Lucy Locket,* each is involved in the joyful activity of childhood play.

Lucy Locket

Traditional singing game

Game: The children sing the song seated in a circle. One child skips around the outside of the circle, carrying a beanbag. At the end of the song, she or he drops the beanbag behind the nearest child in the circle and continues around the circle at a quick walk. Meanwhile, the child in the circle grabs the beanbag from behind, stands up, and begins to walk quickly around the outside of the circle in the opposite direction. When the two children meet, they must stop and shake hands before continuing around the circle. Then, whichever child reaches the empty spot in the circle first gets to sit down. The game begins again with the other child skipping around the circle with the beanbag.

Singing games offer glorious opportunity for bringing children's natural play into the music class.

As Rodgers and Sawyers (1988) state, "Play is central to what it means [for the child] to be alive." Singing games offer glorious opportunity for bringing natural play into the music classroom, and consequently provide for authentic moments of childhood music-making. As a result, elementary music teachers are encouraged to refrain from interrupting the children in order to correct oral qualities of the music (such as the rhythm or singing in tune) while a singing game is being played in a music lesson. Such unbroken music-making will allow the aesthetic power of combining music and movement to bear fruit naturally in the child's musical soul.

Establishing a Movement Vocabulary

Successfully using movement requires the development of a flexible movement vocabulary.

Using movement successfully requires the development of a flexible movement vocabulary. Children may need opportunities to try out this vocabulary first, through *exploratory movement activities* in the elementary classroom. The following activities might take place *before a* music class or be used as a *warm-up* for music-movement activities in a music lesson. Each will help children to gain the confidence to use movement more freely.

1. **Spatial awareness activities**: movement activities that explore moving the body within personal space and through space at different levels and on different pathways

2. **Body awareness activities**: movement activities that explore different ways to move various body parts

3. **Energy and time awareness activities**: movement activities that explore the amount of force, speed, and weight that various movements take

Examples of Exploratory Activities That Encourage Spatial Awareness

1. Awareness of personal space.
   The teacher helps each child to find a space of his or her own on the floor. Individual spaces can be delineated by an object such as a hula hoop. The teacher then plays music, and invites the children to pose as a different statue every time the music stops. Encourage the children to use the *low* (lying on the floor), *middle* (sitting position), and *high* (standing) levels in their spaces when creating their statues.

2. Awareness of the personal space of others.
   The children sit in their personal spaces and wave to someone in a space next to them. Then the children toss an imaginary ball back and forth with this person while listening to a piece of music. When the music is temporarily turned off, children trade places with their next-door neighbours. When the music resumes, they carry on with their imaginary ball toss in the new space with a new neighbour. For this activity, choose music that has an obvious, steady beat and a medium tempo—for example, *Molly on the Shore* by Percy Grainger.

3. Awareness of direction when travelling to different spaces.
   The children walk around the room while the teacher plays lightly on a non-pitched percussion instrument. Whenever the rhythm stops, the children stop. If the teacher resumes playing with a different instrument, the children change direction. Children begin and end this activity in their own personal place on the floor.

4. Awareness of pathway.
   The children are divided into groups of four to six, and asked to use all of their bodies to make a shape using straight lines (a triangle or a square) or curved lines (a circle or a crescent moon). When the children hear the teacher play a rhythm on the drum, they all walk the shape their group has just made by moving along its imaginary outside lines.

Examples of Exploratory Activities that Encourage Body Awareness

1. Invite the children to think of a variety of images that involve motion—for example, jumping over a puddle on the way home from school, digging a hole in the ground, or a bird flying through the sky—then ask the children to act out these images in their personal spaces.

2. The children sit in their personal spaces while music is played. The teacher keeps the beat using a variety of body actions (for example, tapping their shoulders or moving one finger), and the children imitate the teacher's actions. Children can also serve as the leaders for this activity.

3. The teacher stretches a piece of rope (about 3 to 4 metres long) across the floor. The children are invited to start at one end and demonstrate how many different ways—such as crawling, skipping, leaping, sliding—they can use to travel from one end of the rope to the other.

Examples of Exploratory Activities that Encourage Energy and Time Awareness

1. In their own personal spaces, the children are invited to use movement to portray a variety of contrasting images—such as a feather floating to the ground, a roller coaster going around a corner, a mother rocking a baby gently in her arms, or a piece of toast popping out of the toaster. Reflection should include discussion of the differing amounts of energy used to convey the different kinds of movements.

2. The children are divided into pairs, and invited to throw imaginary round objects—such as a balloon, a tennis ball, a soccer ball, or a bowling ball—to their partner, demonstrating the differing amounts of energy each of the objects might take.

All of these exploratory movement activities contribute to the children's flexibility and confidence at moving their bodies, and thereby provide an excellent way to set the stage for using music with movement during a music lesson.

Music and Movement in the Elementary Music Classroom

Classroom experiences involving movement during the music lesson may be organized into three broad groups:

1. *Prescribed or creative movements that naturally accompany music*: finger plays, action songs, clapping games, singing games, and dances

2. *Prescribed or creative movements that are used by teachers or students to accompany music for the purpose of highlighting musical structure by helping children to kinesthetically feel the manipulation of particular musical concept(s) in the music*: for example, using *patsching* to feel the beat, using large arm movements to indicate *forte* and *piano*, or using a change in locomotor direction to illustrate ABA form

3. *Creative movement that accompanies a piece of music in order to dramatize the mood, expression, or story of the music*

All three of these types of movement activities can play a significant role in the development of children's musical understanding.

Finger Plays, Action Songs, Singing Games, and Dances

Music and movement in this category plays a large role in the elementary music class. These "games" are natural childhood expressions of musical play and can shift easily back and forth between the music room and the playground. Children enjoy the act of moving in time with music. Kindergarten–Grade 1 classes can begin with finger plays and action songs. Children in Grades 1–4 can progress to clapping games and singing games (for example, circle games, chasing games), and passing games work well beginning in Grades 3–4. Students in Grades 4–6 are ready for line games and dances.

For the most part, the song should be taught before any movement is added. The only exception to this is for finger plays and action songs, which generally involve only non-locomotor movements. These kinds of songs are suitable and quite motivating for younger students when the music and the finger or body actions are taught simultaneously.

After a song has been learned, the movements for the singing game or dance should be broken down into segments for teaching purposes. This might need to be done a lesson or two later, so as to give the children time to really learn how to sing the song. In the following example, the movements for *Bow Wow Wow* are broken down so that they can be taught using a phrase-by-phrase approach.

Bow Wow Wow

Traditional singing game

Bow, wow, wow, Who's dog art thou?

Lit - tle Tom - my Tuck - er's dog, Bow, wow, wow. WOOF!

Game: The children stand in a circle, and every second child turns around to face backwards, thereby creating a series of partners within the circle. As the children sing the song, they make the following movements

phrase 1 (mm. 1–2): With hands on hips the children face their partners and stamp their feet to the rhythm of the words.

phrase 2 (*mm*. 3–4): With the right elbow cradled in the left hand, the children shake their right index fingers at their partner, to the rhythm of the words

phrase 3 (*mm*. 5–6): The children join hands with their partners, and walking to the beat, switch places.

phrase 4 (*mm*. 7–8): Repeat actions of phrase 1. On the "Woof," each child spins around with a jump to face their new partner, and the game begins again . . . and again . . . and again . . . !

Rules regarding safety, honouring personal space, and valuing individual response may need to be reinforced on a regular basis before beginning a singing game. Indeed, non-musical side benefits, such as cooperation and teamwork, can be gained during such music-movement activities.

Children must know classroom rules regarding personal space and safety during music-movement activities.

Finger Plays

Two examples of a finger plays appropriate for Kindergarten–Grade 1 are *Open Them, Shut Them* and *A Skeleton Jiggles His Bones*.

Open Them, Shut Them

Traditional

Open them, shut them, open them, shut them,
Give them a little clap,
Open them, shut them, open them, shut them,
Fold them in your lap.
Creep them, creep them, creep them, creep them,
Up to your little chin,
Open up your little mouth (pause),
But don't let them in! (said quickly)

Actions:

line 1: hold hands up in the air; open and shut fingers as directed by the text

line 2: clap twice after the word "clap"

line 3: repeat action from line 1

line 4: fold hands slowly in the lap

line 5: walk fingers of one hand up the other arm

line 6: walk fingers from the arm to the chin

line 7: slowly open the mouth wide pretending to stop the fingers from falling in the mouth

line 8: quickly hide both hands behind the back

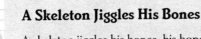

A Skeleton Jiggles His Bones

Traditional

A skeleton jiggles his bones, his bones,
A skeleton jiggles his bones,
A leg goes up, an arm comes down,
Jigglety jagglety Jones.

Actions:

lines 1 *and* 2: Shake body like a skeleton with jiggly bones

line 3: Push leg up and arm down

line 4: Repeat actions of lines 1 and 2

Further finger play examples included in other sections of this textbook are *Criss Cross* (see p. 218), *Slowly, Slowly* (see p. 194), and *Engine, Engine* (see p. 192).

Action Songs

An example of an action song for Kindergarten–Grade 1 is *Sleep, Baby, Sleep*.

Sleep, Baby, Sleep

Traditional lullaby

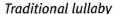

Action: *The children pretend to rock a baby back and forth to the beat of the music.*

Further examples of action songs in other sections of this textbook include *Hey, Hey* (p. 47), *Savez-vous planter des choux?* (p. 31), *Teddy Bear* (p. 49), *Johnny Works with One Hammer* (p. 193), *See-Saw* (p. 191), *Jolly Old St. Nicholas* (p. 223), *Hey Betty Martin* (p. 202), and *Hop Old Squirrel* (p. 217).

Clapping Games

Bingo is an example of an clapping game appropriate for Grades 1–2, and *A Sailor Went to Sea* is appropriate for Grades 3–4.

Bingo

Traditional clapping game

Game (as taught to the author by Dianne Edwards, Toronto, Ontario): The children stand in a circle holding hands. During mm. 1–4 they walk around the circle to the beat. At "B" in m. 5, they drop hands and face into the centre of the circle to sing the rest of the song. At the end of the song, the children grab hands again and slowly creep into the middle of the circle, quietly chanting "B...I...N...G...O." On "O" they scurry backwards, still holding hands, to reform the circle. The entire process is repeated five times: on the second repetition, a clap is substituted for "B" in m. 5; on the third repetition, claps are substituted for "B" and "I," and so on, until there are five claps.

A Sailor Went to Sea

Traditional clapping game

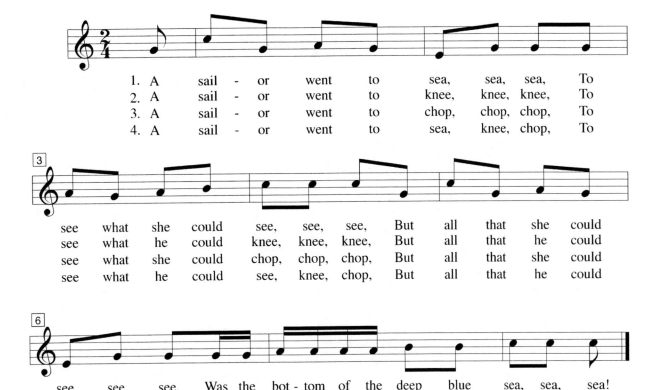

1. A sail - or went to sea, sea, sea, To
2. A sail - or went to knee, knee, knee, To
3. A sail - or went to chop, chop, chop, To
4. A sail - or went to sea, knee, chop, To

see what she could see, see, see, But all that she could
see what he could knee, knee, knee, But all that he could
see what she could chop, chop, chop, But all that she could
see what he could see, knee, chop, But all that he could

see, see, see, Was the bot - tom of the deep blue sea, sea, sea!
knee, knee, knee, Was the bot - tom of the deep blue knee, knee, knee!
chop, chop, chop, Was the bot - tom of the deep blue chop, chop, chop!
see, knee, chop, Was the bot - tom of the deep blue sea, knee, chop!

Game: In this game, the children combine a clapping pattern with the actions. The children stand in pairs facing one another. The *clapping pattern* is used for the five eighth notes that go with the phrases "A sailor went to," "To see what she could," and "But all that she could."

1. hit own thighs with both hands
2. clap own hands together
3. clap right hands with partner
4. clap own hands together
5. clap left hands with partner

The actions are used for the three eighth notes that go with the words "sea, sea, sea." In the first verse the children mime looking out to sea three times. In the second verse ("knee, knee, knee") they tap their knee three times. In the third verse ("chop, chop, chop"), they pretend to chop their arm three times. In the last verse, they do the appropriate motions for all three words ("sea, knee, chop").

Circle Games

Jingle Bells is an example of a circle game appropriate for Grades 2–3. *Great Big House* is excellent for Grades 3–4, and *Circle 'round the Zero* works well with Grades 4–5.

Jingle Bells

James Pierpont (1822–1893)

Game: The children stand in pairs in a circle, facing their partners, and perform the following actions:

mm. 1–2: tap the rhythm of the words on own thighs

mm. 3–4: clap partners' hands on the beat (i.e., clap quarter notes)

mm. 5–8: link arms with partner and skip around in a small circle

These actions are repeated in the second half of the song, but in mm. 13–16 the children skip in the opposite direction.

Great Big House

Traditional singing game

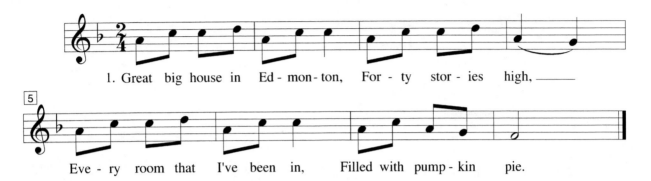

1. Great big house in Ed-mon-ton, For-ty stor-ies high, _____
Eve-ry room that I've been in, Filled with pump-kin pie.

2. Went down to the old mill stream,
   To fetch a pail of water,
   Put one arm around my wife,
   The other 'round my daughter.

3. Fare thee well my darlin' girl,
   Fare thee well my darlin',
   Fare thee well my darlin' girl,
   With the golden slippers on her!

Game: The children form small groups of six, eight, or ten. Each group stands in a circle and the children number off (1–2, 1–2, etc.).

verse 1: all hold hands and skip around in a circle to the beat; change direction at m. 5.

verse 2: mm. 1–2: "1s" join hands to make a small circle inside the "2s"

mm. 3–4: "2s" join hands and reach arms over heads of "1s" (as if fetching a pail of water from a well)

mm. 5–6: "2s" pull their joined hands back over heads of "1s" and hold their arms slightly behind the backs of "1s"

mm. 7–8: "1s" lift their joined hands over heads of "2s", so that all are interwoven in one circle (as in a grapevine)

verse 3: all move in clockwise direction with a sliding step (left foot step, right foot slide)

Chapter Eight   Moving with Music   **163**

Circle 'round the Zero

Traditional American singing game

Game: The children stand in a circle facing their partners, and perform the following actions.

mm. 1–4:   link arms with partner and skip around in a small circle to the beat

mm. 5–8:   change arms and skip around with partner in opposite direction

mm. 9–10:   face away from partner and touch back of shoulders together to the beat

mm. 11–12: stand beside partner and tap hips together to the beat

mm. 13–14: turn to face partner and clap partner's hands to the beat

mm. 15–16: step back into circle, on the opposite side of partner so that the game can begin again with new partners

Examples of circle games for Grades 1–2 in other sections of this textbook include *Ickle Ockle* (p. 86), *Jingle at the Windows* (p. 73), *Pease Porridge Hot* (p. 222), *Lucy Locket* (p. 154), *All around the Buttercup* (p. 200), *Closet Key* (p. 266), *Diddle Diddle Dumpling* (p. 285), *The Bridge at Avignon/Sur le pont d'Avignon* (p. 289), and *Bluebird* (p. 141). Other circle games for Grades 3–4 include *Weevily Wheat* (p. 290), and *Draw a Bucket of Water* (p. 224).

Chasing Games

Built My Lady a Fine Brick House is an example of a chasing game that works well with Grades 3–4 when played outside or in a gym where there is plenty of safe room to run between the "houses."

Built My Lady a Fine Brick House

Traditional singing game

Built my la - dy a fine brick house,

Built it in a gar - den, She jumped in but

then jumped out, So fare thee well my dar - lin'!

Game: The children number off 1–2–3; two or three additional children become "4s". The "1s" and "2s" become partners and stand facing each other; holding hands, they raise their arms to form the "roof" of a house. The "3s" choose a house to stand inside. All the children sing the song. During the singing the "1s" and "2s" sway gently to the beat, gently rocking the "3s" inside the houses. Meanwhile the "4s" play the role of house shoppers, strolling around the room looking at various houses to buy. At the end of the song, the houses open up, allowing the "3s" to jump out and run to a different house, and the "4s" join in the race to find accommodation. The children left outside become house shoppers for the next repetition.

Further examples of chasing games for Grades 1–2 are *We Are Dancing in the Forest* (p. 46) and *Mary Had a Little Lamb* (p. 209).

Passing Games

Passing games that are appropriate for Grade 3 and up include such favourites as *Al citron.*

Al citron

Traditional Latin American passing game

Game: The children sit in a circle, each with a stone or a small object in their hand. On the pickup beat, they tap their stone once on the floor. On the first beat of m. 1, they set their stones on a point on the floor in front of the child to their right; on the second beat of m. 1, they pick up the stone that has been placed in front of them (by the child to the left); and so on. This pick-up-and-pass routine continues through the rest of the song, and the children sing as many repetitions as needed for their stones to travel all the way around the circle.

Further examples of passing games for Grades 3–4 include *Obwisana* (p. 198) and *Guessing Game* (p. 195).

Dances

A line dance that is enjoyed by Grade 4–5 students is *Willoughbee*.

Willoughbee

Traditional singing game

This way we wil - lough - bee, —— wil - lough - bee, ——

wil - lough - bee, —— This way we wil - lough - bee, ——

all the way home. Oh, —— Dan - cing down the

al - ley, —— al - ley, —— al - ley, ——

Dan - cing down the al - ley, —— all the way home.

Game: The children stand in two parallel lines, facing their partners in the opposite line. During the first half of the song (mm. 1–8) the children join hands with their partners and make some kind of motion to show the beat of the music. On "Oh" (m. 9) they back away from each other, making an "alley" about two metres wide between the two lines. The couple at the head of the line proceeds down the alley in a beat motion of their choice, while the rest of the children sing the second half of the song. This sequence is repeated until all the couples have had a chance to move down the alley in their chosen method of beat locomotion. Creativity is needed since no two couples are allowed to move the same way!

Children in Grades 4–6 are ready to progress from movements learned in circle and line games to **circle dances**: *folk-like dances done in a circle and accompanied by the dancers' own singing.* Stinson (1990) states, "Dance has the appeal and creativeness necessary to evoke the joy of movement . . . Its problem solving potential for exploratory learning and skill development is not limited to psychomotor but includes cognitive and affective enhancement as well" (p. 4). Examples include *I'se the B'y, Ah! si mon moine voulait danser,* and *Bonavist' Harbour.*

I'se the B'y

Traditional Newfoundland folk song

1. I'se the b'y that builds the boat, And I'se the b'y that sails her,

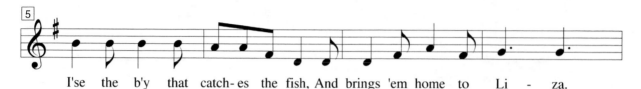

I'se the b'y that catch-es the fish, And brings 'em home to Li - za.

Refrain

Hip yer part - ner Sa - ly Tib - bo, Hip yer part - ner Sal - ly Brown!

Fo - go, Twil - lin - gate, Mor - ton's Har - bour, all a - round the cir - cle.

2. Sods and rinds to cover your flake,
And cake and tea for supper,
Cod fish in the spring of the year,
And fried in maggoty butter!
Refrain

3. I don't want your maggoty fish,
That's no good for winter,
I could buy as good as that,
Down in Bonavista!
Refrain

4. I took Lizer to a dance,
And faith but she could travel,
And every step that she did take,
Was up to her knees in gravel.
Refrain

5. Susan White, she's out of sight,
Her petticoat wants a border,
Old Sam Oliver, in the dark,
He kissed her in the corner.
Refrain

I'se the B'y (PEA 5, no. 3, CMC Archives) was collected by Kenneth Peacock,
and is used by courtesy of the Canadian Museum of Civilization.

Circle dance: The children stand in a circle next to their partners. All the dance steps are done to the beat.

mm. 1–4:	turn to face partner, link arms, and skip around in small circle.
mm. 5–8:	change arms and skip around in opposite direction.
mm. 9–10:	stand facing into the circle and bump hips with partner twice
mm. 11–12:	bump hips with person on other side twice
mm. 13–16:	face partner, link arms, and skip around in small circle, ending up on opposite side of partner so that the dance can begin again with new partners

Ah! si mon moine voulait danser

Traditional French Canadian folk song
English text by Edith Fowke

Ah! si mon moi - ne vou - lait dan - ser! Ah!
If you will come and — dance with me, If

si mon moi - ne vou - lait dan - ser! Un ca - pu - chon je lui
you will come and — dance with me. A fea - thered cap I will

don - ne - rais, Un ca - pu - chon je lui don - ne - rais.
give to thee, A fea - thered cap I will give to thee.

Refrain
Dan - se, mon moin', dan - se! Tu n'en - tends pas la
Come my lass, let's trip now! To - ge - ther let us

dan - se, Tu n'en - tends pas mon mou - lin, lon la, Tu
skip now, As light - ly on the mea - sures go, Our

n'en - tends pas mon mou - lin mar - cher.
feet move mer - ri - ly to and fro.

Circle dance: The children stand in a circle, holding hands. All the dance steps are done to the beat of the music.

mm. 1–2	("Ah! si mon moine voulait danser!): slide-gallop four steps clockwise
mm. 3–4:	slide-gallop four steps counter-clockwise
mm. 5–6:	four skips forward to centre of circle
mm. 7–8:	four skips back
mm. 9–10:	drop hands, turn to face partner, link arms and skip around in small circle
mm. 11–12:	change arms and skip around in the opposite direction
mm. 13–14:	reform large circle, join hands, and slide-gallop four steps clockwise
mm. 15–16:	slide-gallop four steps counter-clockwise

Bonavist' Harbour

Newfoundland folk song

Oh! There's, lots of fish in Bo - na - vist' har - bour,

Lots of fish right in a - round here, Boys and girls are

fish - ing to - geth - er, For - ty five from Car - bon - ear.

Oh! Catch - a - hold this one, catch - a - hold that one,

Swing a - round this one, dance a - round she.

Catch - a - hold this one, catch - a - hold that one,

Did - dle - dum this one, did - dle - dum dee!

Bonavist' Harbour (PEA 5, no. 3, CMC Archives) was collected by Kenneth Peacock,
and is used by courtesy of the Canadian Museum of Civilization.

Circle dance: The children stand in a circle next to their partners. All the dance steps are done to the beat.

mm. 1–2:   clap to the beat
mm. 3–4:   hold hands in big circle and side gallop four steps clockwise
mm. 5–6:   side gallop four steps counter-clockwise

mm. 7–8:	skip four steps into centre of circle
mm. 9–10:	skip four steps back
mm. 11–12:	drop hand and clap once loudly on "Oh"
mm. 13–14:	four-beat clapping pattern—slap hands on thighs, clap, snap snap
mm. 15–16:	turn to face partner, link arms, and skip around in small circle
mm. 17–21:	repeat actions from mm. 13–16, skipping around in opposite direction

Creating Dances

Teachers should also provide classroom opportunities for older elementary school children to create their own dances for additional songs, once they have become comfortable with a variety of the movements found in circle dances. Structure can be provided by asking children to work within the *form* of the song—for example the AB form in *Jack Was Every Inch a Sailor*. Children might create a dance for the A section and return to the security of a prescribed clapping sequence for the B section. Dance creation should be done in small groups. After initial experimentation and practice, invite each group to perform their dance for the rest of class. The performances should be videotaped and added to the children's portfolios. This activity should also include written reflection by the students on the dance-making process.

Jack Was Every Inch a Sailor

Traditional Maritime folk song

Now 'twas twen - ty-five or thir - ty years since Jack first saw the light, He

came in - to this world of woe one dark and storm - y night, He was

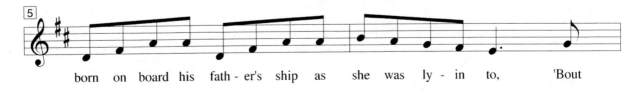

born on board his fath - er's ship as she was ly - in to, 'Bout

continued

G.S. Doyle (Ed.). (1966). From Old-Time Songs and Poetry of Newfoundland: Songs of the People from the Days of Our Forefathers (4th ed.). Reprinted with the permission of the Doyle family.

Prescribed or Creative Movement Used to Gain Kinesthetic Awareness of Musical Structure

Today's elementary music educators are indebted to Émile Jaques-Dalcroze for his pioneering work with music and movement.

The use of movement in the elementary classroom to kinesthetically reinforce children's growing understanding of the manipulation of musical structure can be historically linked to **eurhythmics**: *a series of movement-based activities that allow the child to express musical nuance by using the entire body as a musical instrument.* Eurythmics was advocated in the early years of the twentieth century by Swiss musician Émile Jaques-Dalcroze (1865–1950). Jaques-Dalcroze believed that such movement would help children to develop concentration, body coordination, memory, and a keen ear for musical changes—all of which, he suggested, would later be transferable to the playing of a musical instrument (Jaques-Dalcroze, 1928).

Today's elementary music educators who design their own movement activities to heighten children's sensitivities to the structural components of music are indebted to Jaques-Dalcroze's pioneering work. These teachers generally find that almost all musical concepts from any of the ten elements of music can be kinesthetically illustrated by children while listening to music. Such movement experiences play a significant role in helping children to achieve a higher musical understanding, as the more senses one brings into the learning process the more that is retained (Fauth, 1990).

Each of the following examples of movement activities for the elementary music classroom highlights at least one musical concept from the ten elements of music. Additional movement strategies of this kind may be found in Chapters 10–15.

Example 1: Beat (Grades 2–3)

The children walk around the room to a beat played by the teacher on a non-pitched percussion instrument, such as a drum. When the teacher periodically stops playing, the children continue walking at the same tempo, attempting to keep the beat going in their heads.

Example 2: Tempo (Grade 4)

The children sit in a circle while listening to a piece of recorded music that contains changing tempos The children are instructed to pass a beanbag on the beat; each time the tempo of the music changes, the beanbag changes direction. The music used for this activity should have a moderate tempo (approximately M.M. 80–106), so that the children will have little difficulty in passing the beanbag. One excellent choice for music is the *Slavonic Dance*, op. 46, no. 1 in C major by Antonín Dvořák (1841–1904).

Example 3: Metre (Grades 3–4)

The children stand in pairs facing their partners. While listening to music (either recorded or improvised by the teacher on the recorder) that is in **duple metre** (for example, 2/4 metre), the children first bounce and then pass/catch a ball back and forth with their partner in time to the music (1–bounce, 2–pass). When the music changes to **triple metre** (for example, 3/4 metre), the children illustrate the change by bouncing, then holding, and then passing or catching the ball (1–bounce, 2–hold, 3–pass). An excellent choice of recorded music for this activity is *Fall Fair* by Canadian composer Godfrey Ridout (1918–1984).

Example 4: Dynamics (Grades 1–2)

The children listen to a piece of recorded music in which the dynamics alternate between *forte* (loud) and *piano* (soft). Using their bodies, the children create one type of statue (for example, a giant) to illustrate the loud dynamics, and change to a different statue (for example, a mouse) to indicate the softer dynamics. The overture to *Die Entführung aus dem Serail* (*The Abduction from the Seraglio*) by Wolfgang Amadeus Mozart (1756–1791) works well for this activity.

Example 5: Rhythm (Grades 1–2)

The children are divided into groups of six to eight. After listening to the teacher tap a four-beat rhythm on a non-pitched percussion instrument such as a wood-block, children are asked to use their bodies to form the shape of the rhythm (for example two children might link arms to form a *ti-ti*).

Example 6: Pitch (Grades 1–2)

The children sit on the floor in their own space. While they sing a song they use their hands to "draw" the shape of the **melodic contour** on the floor. While singing the song a second time, they use their whole arm to "draw" the melodic contour in the air. An excellent song for this purpose is *Let Us Chase the Squirrel*.

Let Us Chase the Squirrel

Traditional children's song

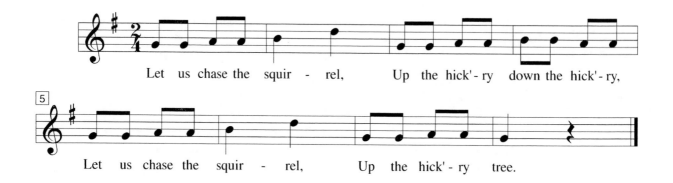

Let us chase the squir - rel, Up the hick'- ry down the hick'- ry,

Let us chase the squir - rel, Up the hick'- ry tree.

Example 7: Timbre (Grades 3–4)

The children listen to a piece of recorded music that features different instruments of the orchestra. While the music is playing, the children keep the steady beat on a part of their bodies. The children are instructed to move their beat motions to a different part of the body each time they hear an instrument change in the music. This activity may also be done by asking students to keep the beat with their feet while walking around the room and change direction each time they hear a change of instrument. One good choice of music for this activity is the "Polka" from the ballet *The Golden Age* by Dmitri Shostakovich (1906–1975).

The children are divided into small groups of five or six and invited to create movement to reflect the **phrase form**—*the arrangement of musical phrases into a structure of same, different, and/or similar phrases, and labelled with lowercase letters*—of a familiar class song. For example, with *On the Mountain*, the children's movement should illustrate aa[1] phrase form.

On the Mountain

Traditional children's song

Phrase 1: a

On the moun-tain stands a la - dy, Who she is I do not know.

Phrase 2: a'

All she wants is gold and sil - ver, All she wants is an ice cream cone!

Example 9: Texture (Grades 4–5)

The children are divided into groups of six to eight and asked to create movement to accompany the singing of a round or a canon in order to kinesthetically experience the texture of multiple parts, with one voice added at a time. Each group would be asked to perform their movement for the rest of the class while everyone sings the canon. One excellent canon for this activity is *Dona Nobis Pacem*.

Dona Nobis Pacem

Attributed to Giovanni Pierluigi da Palestrina (1525–1594)

Do - na, no - bis, pa - cem pa - cem,

Do - na no - bis pa —— cem.

continued

9 *2
Do - na, no - bis pa - cem,

13
Do - na, no - bis, pa —— cem.

17 *3
Do - na, no - bis —— pa - cem,

21
Do - na, no - bis, pa —— cem.

Example 10: Expressive Elements (Grade2)

The children stand in their own space, while the teacher plays a familiar tune (for example, *Twinkle, Twinkle, Little Star*) on the recorder. When the tune is played with **staccato** notes, the children hop in time to the music; when the tune is played with **legato** articulation, they sway back and forth.

Creative Movement That Accompanies Music in Order to Dramatize the Mood, Expression, or Story of the Music

Teachers and students should learn to value all "answers" during creative music-movement activities.

Music-movement activities of this type provide opportunity for children to express what they hear in music through personal creative movement. As in other creative experiences, it is important to remember there is no "right" answer, only individual responses that reflect the child's interpretation of the music. Children need to feel that their particular responses are valued by the teacher as well as by the other children in the classroom. Giving students opportunities to share their improvised movement creations with the rest of the class is an important part of this valuing process. Such responses can be permanently recorded on videotape for inclusion in the students' portfolios.

Sometimes composers write music for the purpose of telling a story or depicting an animal, scene, or event. Most children are familiar with the concept of **program music**, having heard such music especially written to accompany and illustrate the action in their favourite films or television programs. Here is a list of excellent classroom selections of program music:

Carnival of the Animals by Camille Saint-Saëns (1835–1921)

"Ballet of the Unhatched Chicks" from *Pictures at an Exhibition* by Modest Moussorgsky (1839–1881)

"The Little Train of Caipira" from *Bachianas Brasilieras* no. 2 by Heitor Villa-Lobos (1887–1959)

"The Flight of the Bumble Bee" from the *Tale of Tsar Saltra* suite by Nikolai Rimsky-Korsakov (1844–1908)

"The Moldau" from *Má Vlast* by Bedřich Smetana (1824–1884)

"Midnight" from *Cinderella Suite* by Sergei Prokofiev (1891–1953)

"Hoedown" from *Rodeo* by Aaron Copland (1900–1990)

"On the Painted Trail" from the *Grand Canyon Suite* by Ferde Grofé (1892–1972)

The Sorcerer's Apprentice by Paul Dukas (1835–1965)

The Music Box by Anatoly Lyadov (1855–1914)

Les patineurs (*Skater's Waltz*) by Émile Waldteufel (1837–1915)

"Dance of the Mosquito" from *Eight Russian Folk Songs, op. 58*, by Anatoly Lyadov (1855–1914)

Program music tells a story or depicts a scene.

In the elementary music classroom, children should be asked to discuss the kinds of actions appropriate to the title given by the composer to a piece of music of this kind. They should then be invited to express these actions through creative movement while listening to short segments of the music. *Do not be surprised if some children suggest the that the music doesn't sound much like the composer's intention.* In this case, invite students to improvise music on percussion instruments that they think *does* tell this story. Other children in the class can then be asked to move to the student's newly created version.

Personal reflection plays an important role in the creative music-movement process.

The majority of music is **non-programmatic**—*that is, it does not express a specific story or other non-musical idea.* Children should be encouraged to express non-programmatic music through creative movement as they hear it unfold. This can be done using either non-locomotor or locomotor motion. For example, Grade 2–3 students could be asked to make movements in their own space that express the mood of the music while listening to that music. Grade 3–4 children might be invited to "walk the way they hear the music," changing level and direction as appropriate to their interpretation. Grade 5–6 children, after hearing a short piece of music, could be asked to make a **tableau** (*a frozen picture*) in order to illustrate what they felt the music was about. Again, personal reflection plays an important role in the journey towards musical understanding and children should be encouraged to discuss the movement choices they make.

Questions for Discussion and Practice

1. Why is movement a natural accompaniment to music in the elementary school music classroom?

2. Define the two kinds of movement. Give an example of each by describing a music–movement activity that is not discussed in this textbook.

3. Discuss setting up an appropriate classroom atmosphere for using movement with music in the elementary music classroom. What parameters must the teacher take into consideration when planning for both structured and creative movement experiences?

4. Discuss the value of utilizing singing games in the elementary music classroom. Find examples for the early, middle, and late elementary grades using resources beyond those listed in this textbook.

5. What is eurhythmics? Do teachers still utilize this kind of activity in the contemporary elementary school music class? Why or why not?

References

Campbell, P. (1991). *Lessons from the World*. New York: Schirmer.

Jaques-Dalcroze, É. (1928). The child and the pianoforte: Thoughts for mothers. *Musical Quarterly, 14*, 203–15.

Fauth, B. (1990). Linking the visual arts with drama, movement, and dance for the young child. In Stinson, W. (Ed.), *Moving and Learning for the Young Child*. Reston, Virginia: American Alliance for Health, Physical Education, Recreation, and Dance

Rodgers, C., and Sawyers, J. (1988). *Play in the Lives of Children*. Washington D.C.: National Association for the Education of Young Children.

Stinson, W. (1990). Introduction. In Stinson, W. (Ed.), *Moving and Learning for the Young Child*. Reston, Virginia: American Alliance for Health, Physical Education, Recreation, and Dance.

CHAPTER 9

Reading and Writing Music

SYNOPSIS

Chapter 9 discusses the role of music literacy in the development of a comprehensive musical understanding. Music reading and writing readiness as well as guiding principles for developing music literacy within a learner-centred environment, are examined. Recommended teaching sequences for developing reading and writing skills with rhythm and pitch are also presented.

Introduction

Music literacy provides independent access to a variety of musical styles.

Music literacy—*the ability to read and write musical notation*—plays an important role in the development of children's musical understanding. As discussed in Chapter 2, children require competent skills in reading and writing music in order to richly experience two of the three authentic modes of musical encounter: performing and creating.

Without music literacy skills, students are wholly dependent on others to deliver music to them aurally. Although children may learn how to play music by ear, they can only learn music that is either performed for them live or has been recorded. This means that children without literacy skills have little independent access to musical styles, and therefore their chances at deriving personal meaning from any music, other than what is presented to them by someone else, are limited.

The ability to read notation opens the door for students to perform music independently or in ensemble with others. Music literacy also provides opportunities for children to sing or play music that is too long or complex to learn by rote. In addition, reading notation provides students with the opportunity to experience the history of music from the western hemisphere by performing music that was written down hundreds of years ago.

In regards to composing, music can be written without the use of standard notation, but the child composer may never be able to hear his or her music played unless the performers can be taught how to decipher the iconic symbols used to represent the musical sounds. In reality, as discussed in Chapter 6, the use of iconic notation for beginning activities in composing may indeed be pedagogically useful. However, children need to progress to composing music with standard notation in order to make sure that their music may be read and performed by generations to come.

Music Reading and Writing Readiness

Children's success at learning how to recognize, interpret, and translate notation into an appropriate musical response is directly related to the quality of their previous non-notational experiences with music: singing, clapping, moving, listening, and instrumental exploration. In learning music, as with learning language, children need to begin with aural, kinesthetic, and oral activities, and build on these experiences to the stage where they are able to make associations between aural sounds and the symbols that represent them.

As discussed in Chapter 2, this learning process, which is called **sound-before-symbol**, guides the instructional planning for teaching musical notation to children in the elementary grades. For students to be ready to learn how to read and write music, they first must have sung, played, and listened to a wide repertoire of music. Such music-making provides children with the oral and aural experience necessary to begin to hear the way music is put together. In addition, while experiencing this music, children need to have participated in a variety of non-notational classroom activities that provide them with opportunities to actively discriminate between:

1. same and different pitches
2. higher and lower pitches
3. melodic direction and contour
4. beat and rhythm
5. loud and soft dynamics
6. fast and slow tempos
7. repeated and contrasting phrases

Such classroom experiences provide the child with the necessary aural background in the sound-before-symbol process to set the stage for subsequently learning how to match notational symbols to these varying sounds. Chapters 10–15 provide a variety of classroom examples for helping children to experience these kinds of pre-notation music discrimination activities.

Music reading and writing readiness also implies that children have had contact with printed music. As research in **emergent language literacy** suggests (Prytuluk, 2000), physical familiarity with the printed word is an important part of the development process. For example, parents, caregivers, and early-childhood teachers often let pre-readers feel, touch, and notice the way printed language sits on the page before they actually ask children to begin to "read" the words themselves. This is frequently done during story time: while reading a story for the child, the adult holds the book for the child to look at.

Such interactions with books teach children how printed language is laid out: for example it usually starts on the left corner of a page, and the words are written from left to right. The same positive benefits resulting from these pre-reading contacts with printed language will occur with musical notation if elementary music teachers share musical scores with children periodically during the "sound" stage of the sound-before-symbol process (Montgomery, 1998). As when children examine books during emergent language literacy, elementary students in the music classroom are not asked to actually "read" the music. Instead, they should be directed to notice details such as the shapes of the musical symbols, how these symbols sit on and move up and down a five-line staff, and how the music is read left to right. Such early interactions with musical print should take place when the students listen to the teacher sing or play music, or after the children have sung a song themselves.

In the elementary grades, these activities usually take place in Kindergarten and early Grade 1. Students in Grade 1 will be ready to begin reading and writing very simple rhythms and melodies by the second half of the school year. You should remember however, that older elementary students who may be in a school situation where they received little or no previous experiences with music-making will also need to participate in such non-notational activities before attempting to learn to read and write music.

Contact with printed music is important for music reading and writing readiness.

Principles of Instruction

Activities in music literacy should use real music.

Teachers need to consider several variables surrounding the process of teaching children to read and write music. First, practice with reading and writing music always has more relevance to the child if the notation is embedded within real music rather than presented in an isolated exercise. If the notation to be read comes from a song the children want to learn to sing, they will see the significance of reading the music; moreover, the reading process itself will result in more artistic music-making. Teachers may use such reading activities as motivators to get into the music itself. For example, they may ask children to attempt to sight-read the rhythm of a song, and follow this by teaching the melody of the song by rote. A burning desire to write down the music one hears can be a tremendous motivator for children to become more familiar with the process of writing notation. The more the child can see the significance of classroom reading or writing activities for actual music-making, the easier it will be for the teacher to motivate the child to extend their growing music literacy.

Music used to practise reading notation will always be rhythmically and melodically simpler than music that is performed or listened to in the elementary music classroom. That means teachers should plan their yearly class repertoire such that they select both **note music** (*music that the children will be able to access through notation*) and **rote music** (*more difficult music that will be accessible only* *through learning by rote*). Obviously, the younger the children, the larger the proportion of classroom music that is taught by rote. Ideally, Grade 6 students should be able to interact with most of their classroom music through the process of reading notation.

Practice with music literacy should be as learner-centred as possible. This means expanding the supplies used for writing notation beyond the more traditional pencil and paper. Younger children are often quite motivated when writing music using concrete materials such as popsicle sticks for rhythms and round wooden disks, buttons, or bingo chips for note heads. Children in the middle elementary grades enjoy writing music on poster boards with markers, and students in the upper grades are keen to experiment with notation software on the computer.

Developing children's music literacy is a gradual process. Teachers will achieve greater success if such literacy activities are included in music lessons on a regular basis. This, of course, does not mean simply planning for five minutes of reading or writing music at the beginning of every lesson. Such practice usually results in elementary school children perceiving music literacy as an isolated incident, totally unrelated to actual music-making. Instead, find opportunities to interweave musical notation naturally into a variety of performing or creating activities that are already planned as part of a music lesson.

For example, in Grade 2, teachers might plan to have children review and play a familiar singing game. To add music notation into this activity, the teacher could notate the first phrase of the singing game on the board, ask the children to read the rhythm in their heads, and make a guess as to which song starts with this rhythm. After successfully answering, the children would move on to sing and play the game that goes with the song.

Another example, this time for Grade 4, might find the children learning a new song. Rather than teaching the whole song by rote, the teacher could dictate the rhythm of the song to the children, and invite them to "write" it down with popsicle sticks on the floor. After notating the rhythm, the children would then be asked to read it back (by clapping or by chanting rhythmic syllables). The lesson would then continue with the children learning the melody of the new song by rote and playing the *ostinato* accompaniment on non-pitched percussion instruments.

Other examples of classroom activities that naturally interweave musical notation into the elementary music lesson can be found throughout Chapters 10–15.

As with the teaching of any skill, teachers must break the learning process of reading and writing music down into smaller chunks that are then sequenced into an easy-to-complex teaching order. Teachers must be conscious of the difficulty level of the notational patterns they invite children to read or write in any lesson.

A recommended teaching sequence for introducing new rhythms to children for the purpose of learning to read notation is given below. Grade levels are included as a guide, but the easy-to-complex nature of the sequence is of most importance. This means, for example, that if Grade 4 students have had no experience with reading or writing music, they still should be introduced to rhythms beginning at the easiest levels of the sequence (for example, Grade 1), presumably, of course, using music that is appropriate to their social-emotional level

Contact with musical notation should be interwoven naturally throughout the elementary music lesson.

(rather than early-grades repertoire). Therefore, at whatever age, music literacy works best when introduced in small chunks of logically sequenced rhythms and/or pitches.

Sequence for introducing rhythms to children

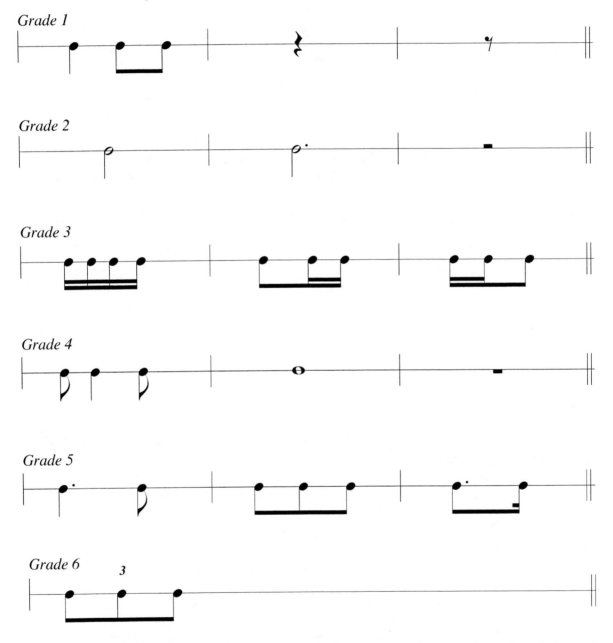

Developmental appropriateness also means using a variety of techniques for helping children learn to sight-read pitch and rhythm. During the twentieth century, elementary music educators found mnemonic devices such as **rhythmic syllables** to be very helpful for children when learning to read rhythm. These syllables were developed by Émile-Joseph Chevé (1804–1864) in France in the

1840s, and revitalized by Zoltán Kodály in the 1940s and 1950s. Today they are used by many Canadian elementary music educators to help children "hear" the way the rhythms should sound while clapping. For example, children speaking the following rhythm using traditional rhythmic names, would say "quarter-note, eighth-note, eighth-note, quarter-note, quarter-note."

However, these traditional names cannot be combined with clapping because the syllables of the names do not correlate with the actual rhythm. With rhythmic syllables, however, this problem is solved. When using rhythmic syllables, the child would chant "tah ti-ti tah tah"—here, there is a perfect match between what the child is clapping and what she or he is chanting. Thus, rhythmic syllables are used when reading new rhythms in the elementary music classroom because they allow the synchronization of the children's kinesthetic, oral, and visual learning modes.

Rhythmic syllable names

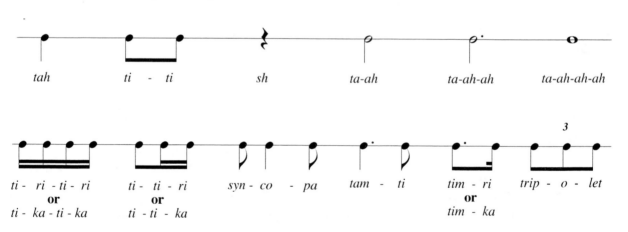

Successful techniques for helping children to learn to read pitch include **tonic sol-fa** or "moveable-*doh*"—a sight-singing system in which children utilize the syllables *doh, re, mi, fa, soh, lah,* and *ti* to sing the various pitches in a melody. This system, which originated with Guido d'Arrezo (ca 991–after 1033) and was popularized by the singing-school movement in England and by British teachers in Ontario during the last half of the nineteenth century, is used by Canadian elementary music educators today to help students learn intervallic relationships between pitches, since *doh* is always the first scale degree (hence the name *moveable-doh*). For example, *doh–mi* is always a major 3rd, *soh–doh* is always a perfect 4th, *ti–doh* is always a half-step, no matter what the key.

Tonic sol-fa syllables in F major

doh   re   mi   fa   soh   lah   ti   doh

Tonic sol-fa syllables in D major

doh   re   mi   fa   soh   lah   ti   doh

In minor keys, "lah" is the starting note of the scale, since a minor scale begins on the sixth scale degree (i.e., *lah*) of the major scale. Intervallic relationships, of course, stay the same for the tonic sol-fa syllables whether the song is in a major or a minor key.

Tonic sol-fa syllables in E harmonic minor

lah   ti   doh   re   mi   fa   si   lah

The tonic sol-fa system for learning to read musical notation is most often used in the elementary grades when helping children learn how to sight-read pitch in *vocal music*. This is important here because, unlike instrumental music, there are no holes to cover (as on a recorder) to produce the pitch changes. In order to sing at sight, children have to develop a basic working knowledge of the intervallic relationships between the notes that are written on the staff and what the voice must do to produce these pitches. Table 9.1 outlines a recommended teaching order for gradually introducing tonic sol-fa syllables to children in order to establish intervallic patterns for vocal sight-reading:

Table 9.1

Recommended sequence for introducing tonic sol-fa syllables in the elementary grades

Grade Level	Tonic Sol-fa Syllables
Grade 1	*soh-mi, lah*
Grade 2	*doh, re*
Grade 3	*soh-lah* below *doh*
Grade 4	high *doh*
Grade 5	*fa, ti*
Grade 6	*fi* (raised *fa*), *si* (raised *soh*)

Keep in mind that the goal of any sight-singing system is to bring children to the point where such a system is no longer necessary. Indeed, the ability to sight-read vocal music simply on the text is the goal of all choral musicians. Thus, when using notation, upper-elementary school children should be provided with some opportunities to attempt to sight-read simple songs using just the words of the song, rather than tonic sol-fa.

The use of **hand signs** to kinesthetically show individual pitches is another technique that may be useful to children when establishing a working knowledge of intervallic relationships in vocal music. Here, elementary school children physically make the shape of a particular hand-sign whenever they sing the corresponding pitches during sight-singing. These hand signs were developed by John Curwen and Sarah Glover in England during the 1870s and subsequently adapted and re-vitalized by Zoltán Kodály in Hungary in the mid-twentieth century. Today they are used to provide Canadian children with a vehicle through which they can visually "feel" the changes in pitch (see Table 9.2).

This type of kinesthetic reinforcement may be especially helpful for children in the younger grades where the kinesthetic mode of learning is very strong for most children. Older children will probably be able to eliminate the use of these hand signs once their pitch sense becomes more secure.

Learning to read pitch when playing classroom instruments is quite different. Here, students need to make an association between the location of the note on the staff and the correct hole to cover (on a soprano recorder) or the correct bar to strike (on a soprano glockenspiel). Traditional note names—A B C D E F G—for the staff are best here, with the child learning to translate this knowledge into playing the correct notes on the instrument. Most provincial curriculum guides across Canada advise introducing this kind of note reading in Grade 3, just before the children are introduced to playing the recorder in Grade 4. Such knowledge, of course, builds on the tonic sol-fa vocabulary previously established during vocal sight-singing in Grades 1–3. Reading with tonic sol-fa can also be carried forward if children are asked to sing as well as play their recorder pieces.

Children use techniques such as tonic sol-fa, rhythmic syllables, and hand signs to help them learn how to sight-read vocal music.

Table 9.2

Hand signs for kinesthetic reinforcement of pitches

Hand sign	Tonic sol-fa syllable
	doh
	ti
	lah
	soh
	fa
	mi
	re
	doh

The teaching sequence for traditional note reading relates to the physical parameters of playing the instrument itself. This means that the easy-to-complex teaching order for introducing notes will usually correspond to the degree of difficulty of the individual notes on a particular instrument. (For example, see the recommended sequence for teaching notes on the recorder on p. 99.) Ideally, by the end of Grade 6, children should feel comfortable about reading music notation while playing a variety of different classroom instruments.

Summary

The development of reading and writing music in the elementary grades may be said to journey through the following progression:

1. Music reading and writing readiness activities (Kindergarten–Grade 1)
2. Beginnings of reading and writing notation:
   - Step-by-step building of a rhythmic sight vocabulary for both vocal and instrumental music using rhythmic syllables (Grades 1–3)
   - Step-by-step building of an intervallic sight vocabulary for vocal music using tonic sol-fa and hand signs (Grades 1–3)
3. Further development of music literacy
   - Continued step-by-step building of a rhythmic sight vocabulary for vocal and instrumental music using rhythmic syllables (Grades 3–6)
   - Continued step-by-step building of an intervallic sight vocabulary for vocal music using tonic sol-fa (Grades 3–6)
   - Step-by-step building of note reading for instrumental music using traditional note names (Grades 3–6)
4. Advanced development of music literacy
   - Experience with sight-singing using words (i.e., no tonic sol-fa or rhythmic syllables)

The ability to read and write musical notation provides children with the tools of the trade necessary for access to deeper and richer experiences with music. When you facilitate children's acquisition of both, you will feel encouraged about having played a significant role in helping your students move closer towards the development of a comprehensive musical understanding.

Questions for Discussion and Practice

1. Why is the development of music literacy important for children's growth in musical understanding?
2. What is meant by music reading and writing readiness? At what grade level should this take place? Why?
3. Discuss a variety of ways a teacher can plan to make learning to read and write music a positive experience for elementary school children.
4. Describe some of the rhythmic and melodic systems used by teachers to help children learn how to sight-read musical notation? Which systems are used for vocal sight-reading and which are used for instrumental? Why?
5. Using the melodic sequence listed in this chapter, select one song for each grade level that meets the criterion for sight-singing at that grade level.

References

Montgomery, A.P. (1998). Music literacy: Connections to language literacy. Unpublished paper presented at the International Society for Music Education 23rd Biennial World Conference. Pretoria, South Africa.

Prytuluk, N. (2000). Sound-before-symbol teaching practices of early-childhood educators and elementary music teachers. Masters thesis: University of Alberta.

PART THREE

Classroom Activities

Part III discusses the *daily classroom activities* planned by the elementary music teacher to help children learn about the structure of music through the eight classroom experiences presented in Part II. As discussed in Chapter 2, such activities must be **learner-centred**, that is, *they must promote learning in ways that allow individuals to reach their potential through the most positive routes possible.* This means making daily activities as broad as possible in order to take into consideration the diversity of children's learning styles. In other words, in any given school year, students should be given the opportunity to become familiar with the musical concepts appropriate for study at that grade level through classroom activities using *a variety* of the eight musical experiences.

Daily classroom activities need to be **developmentally appropriate** in such a way that each *matches children's cognitive, psychomotor, and socio-emotional levels.* Children are most likely to gain a thorough understanding of a particular musical concept being highlighted if these classroom activities are a good match for their developmental levels. Thus, Chapters 10–15 place these daily activities in a logical simple-to-complex teaching order, based on children's *general* developmental levels. Teachers will need to make adjustments, of course, based on children's individual variability as to growth and development.

In addition, daily classroom activities are also arranged in each of the following six chapters in a **sound-before-symbol** progression. This means the activities involving non-notational aural, kinesthetic, and oral experiences are placed at the beginning of each chapter, and activities involving notation are placed at the end. This layout should help teachers plan daily lessons that will lead children towards the development of a comprehensive musical understanding.

CHAPTER 10

Beat, Tempo, and Metre

SYNOPSIS

Chapter 10 discusses daily classroom activities appropriate for the elementary music classroom that use experiences such as singing, playing instruments, or moving to highlight musical concepts from Beat, Tempo, and Metre. Activities for each structural element are presented in a sound-before-symbol progression within a developmentally appropriate simple-to-complex teaching order.

Beat: The Steady Pulse Underlying Music

Steady beat is an abstract concept that requires children to feel a silent, unwritten pulse.

Beat awareness—*the ability to feel a steady beat in music*—is one of the most basic concepts children develop in the elementary grades. In addition, **beat competency**—*the ability to keep a steady beat while singing or playing an instrument*—is an important musical skill that should also be developed during classroom activities that focus on beat. Beat awareness leads to a better cognitive understanding of the role that beat plays in making and creating music. Beat competency allows successful participation by the student in performing experiences that subsequently lead to a better psychomotor understanding of the importance of the structural element of beat.

Unlike rhythm, a steady beat is not always easily discernable by younger elementary school children. If you invite Kindergarten–Grade 1 students to clap along with music, they will often choose to clap the rhythm. Text is a very powerful element for young children and it often compels them to fixate first on *the way the words sound* or *the rhythm of the music*. Beat, on the other hand, is an abstract concept that involves feeling a silent, unwritten pulse.

Research suggests that even older students sometimes have difficulty keeping a steady beat with music. According to Rohwer (1998),

> Educators should not assume that all beginning instrumental students [junior high] have a sense of steady beat. The majority of the control group subjects [in her study] had difficulty synchronizing and performing to a steady beat. Attention clearly needs to be given to this basic skill [at an earlier age]. (p. 422)

Thus, elementary music teachers need to consider carefully the kinds of beat activities planned for children during both the non-notational and notational stages of the sound-before-symbol teaching process.

Movement in combination with singing, playing instruments, and listening is a useful classroom activity for helping elementary students overcome the abstract nature of beat. Success, of course, depends on the richness and age-appropriateness of these early **beat-movement activities** (*music activities that use movement to help children feel a steady beat*); each activity must be designed to complement both the socio-emotional and psychomotor developmental levels of the child.

Since research suggests beat awareness and beat competency may require long-term practice, movement activities involving beat should

Movement is an important pedagogical tool for helping elementary school students learn about steady beat in music.

1. motivate children towards participation,
2. hold their interest for numerous repetitions, and
3. allow for suitable practice in relation to a logical sequence of psychomotor development.

All three criteria are important for teachers to consider when planning for appropriate beat-movement activities in the elementary classroom.

In order to facilitate success with the first two criteria, teachers should plan beat-movement activities that are as **learner-centred** as possible. Since Kindergarten–Grade 1 students often focus on the text of a song or a rhyme, the teacher should select beat movements that relate to the story of the text rather than simply asking the children to routinely *patsch* the beat on their knees. For example, moving the arms back and forth in a see-saw motion while singing *See-Saw,* or moving the arms forwards and backwards to imitate train wheels while chanting *Engine, Engine* are wonderful examples of child-engaging beat-movement activities.

See-Saw

Traditional chant

See - saw, up and down, In the air and on the ground.

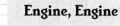

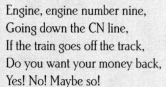

Engine, Engine   Traditional

Engine, engine number nine,
Going down the CN line,
If the train goes off the track,
Do you want your money back,
Yes! No! Maybe so!

*Consider
children's
psychomotor
development
when planning
beat-movement
activities to use in
the classroom.*

*Singing games
provide a learner-
centred way to
experience beat
practice.*

Success with the third criterion depends on the teacher's understanding of children's psychomotor development. Instructors need to consider which body movements might be easier for children, so that younger children will experience success when asked to find and keep the beat during music making or listening.

The following 17-step **Beat-Movement Teaching Sequence** has been created to offer teachers help in this direction. It is a simple-to-complex sequence for using movement with singing, playing instruments, and listening during the "sound" stage of beat development. Each level adds progressively more difficult beat motions for children to experience with music beginning with simple **non-locomotor motion** *(movement that is performed in a stationary position, i.e. movement in the child's own space)*, and gradually progressing to challenging **locomotor motion** *(movement that involves travelling from one space to another)*. Experiences at different levels of the beat-movement sequence require use of a variety of songs, rhymes, and recorded music in order to give children multiple opportunities for practising their beat skills.

Children may not need experiences at every stage of the teaching sequence in order to reach successful beat awareness and beat competency, but the logic of the pedagogical progression of simple-to-complex makes good sense for curricular planning. Children who are given these kinds of carefully selected beat-movement activities will usually begin to feel comfortable with beat by Grade 3. As with any psychomotor skill, however, ongoing practice is essential for maintaining excellent physical control. Thus, teachers should continue to use age-appropriate singing games throughout the elementary grades in order to carry forward joyful beat-movement practice. Examples of singing games that emphasize beat movements for children in the older grades include *Weevily Wheat* (p. 290), *Draw a Bucket of Water* (p. 224), *Great Big House*, (p. 163), *Circle 'round the Zero* (p. 164), *Built my Lady a Fine Brick House* (p. 165), and *Willoughbee* (p. 167).

The Beat–Movement Teaching Sequence for the Development of Beat Awareness and Beat Competency during the "Sound" Stage of the Sound–before–Symbol Process

Step 1: The child sings a song or chants a rhyme in his or her own space while moving his or her arms together in a repetitive beat motion with an end point for the beat.

This first step involves the elementary school child at the easiest level of motor development in the teaching sequence: non-locomotor movement in a child's own space with both arms moving together. This simple action is made even more accessible for the child because the movement provides a concrete **end point of the beat** (*a physical spot at which the beat is felt kinesthetically*).

Johnny Works with One Hammer is an excellent example for using movements from Step 1. Grade 1 students would be invited to gently tap their knee on the beat (as with a hammer) while singing the song. This movement is especially good for beginning beat competency as it involves a downward motion with the hand. In addition, the knee or other body parts serve as the end point for the hammer motion, making it much easier for the child to feel the beat in a concrete manner. Such text-related motions, applied to a variety of songs and rhymes, provide younger elementary school students with a learner-centred entry point for experiencing the pedagogical power of beat and movement.

Johnny Works with One Hammer

Traditional children's song

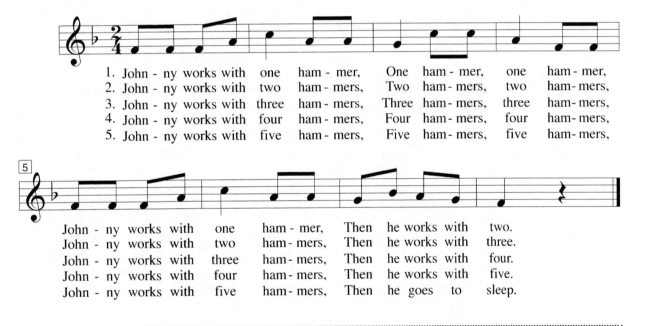

Step 2: The child sings a song or chants a rhyme in her or his own space while alternating her or his arms in a repetitive beat motion with an end point for the beat.

This level requires slightly more motor coordination than Step 1. Although still involving non-locomotor repetitive arm movements in the child's own space, the motions are slightly more difficult because of the alternating arm movements.

See-Saw (p. 191) provides an excellent classroom example for this kind of beat-movement activity. Here, Grade 1 children sit on the floor singing the song while stretching their arms out from the sides of their bodies. Each child should be invited to make a rocking see-saw motion from side to side, briefly touching the floor on the beat each time they rock to one side or the other. The floor serves as the end point in this example, which again helps the beginner to feel the beat in a concrete manner. Although this movement is still fairly simple, children should not be asked to attempt such alternating motions on the beat until they have achieved success with the easier arms-together movements described in Step 1.

Step 3: The child sings a song or chants a rhyme in his or her own space while moving his or her arms together or in alternation in a repetitive beat motion with no end point to the beat

This step utilizes repetitive arm beat motions that are similar to those in Steps 1–2, but this step requires the child to move to the beat without the benefit of a concrete end point. In this important step in the process of beat development, children must feel the beat in the air, much like they will later be required to feel the beat internally.

An excellent classroom example is to ask Grades 1–2 children to chant the rhyme *Engine, Engine* (p. 192) while swishing their arms forwards and backwards on the beat, like train wheels. With this movement, the children are required to stop and reverse direction at the appropriate moment on the beat, without the security of touching a concrete end point.

Step 4: The child sings a song or chants a rhyme in her or his own space while manipulating a concrete object on the beat.

When children have achieved success utilizing arm beat-movements described in Steps 1–3 with various rhymes and songs, they are ready to progress to moving an object to the beat. This is harder than simply moving the arms, because the children are required to manipulate an article on various parts of the body. The rhyme *Slowly, Slowly* is an excellent example for use with the early elementary grades. Here, children are instructed to walk a snail shell up their arm to the beat while chanting the rhyme. Although the arm serves as the end point for the beat, the end point changes location every time the child moves the snail farther up the arm. This may be challenging, but children delight in their growing skill at moving beat objects around their bodies.

Slowly, Slowly

Traditional

Slowly, slowly, very slowly,

Creeps the garden snail,

Slowly, slowly, very slowly,

Up the wooden rail.

The Guessing Game is a music example that is appropriate for older elementary school children (Grades 3-4) to practise this kind of beat movement.

Guessing Game

First Nations game
English text by A. Montgomery

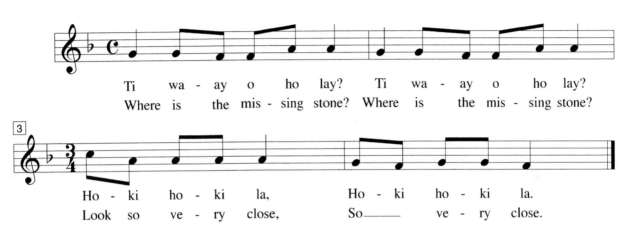

Ti wa - ay o ho lay? Ti wa - ay o ho lay?
Where is the mis - sing stone? Where is the mis - sing stone?

Ho - ki ho - ki la, Ho - ki ho - ki la.
Look so ve - ry close, So___ ve - ry close.

Game: The children are divided into two teams, standing in two lines facing each other. Two or three children on each team are given small stones to pass from one hand to another, while trying not to let the children on the other team see which hand holds the stone. At the end of the song, the children in each line try to guess exactly where the stones are in the other team. Points are awarded to each team for every correct guess. Then the game begins again with different children on each team manipulating the stones.

Step 5: The child sings a song or chants a rhyme in her or his own space while playing a percussion instrument on the beat.

Playing a percussion instrument on the beat is slightly more difficult than manipulating a concrete object. In this step, children are required to coordinate proper instrument technique at the same time as keeping the beat. It is helpful for children if the music and movement examples utilized with an instrument are the similar to those experienced during Steps 1–4.

For example, when Grade 1 children play a tonic **pedal tone** (F) on the beat on a bass xylophone while singing *Johnny Works with One Hammer* (p. 193) they use the same downward motion that they used to hammer the beat in Step 1. In this way, children may be able to transfer the successful feeling of beat movement in the arms with a particular song to a similar movement coordination on an instrument.

When children become more experienced with keeping the beat on instruments with songs from Steps 1–4, they should move to instrumental beat-keeping experiences with new songs. *Saturday Night* is an excellent example of a song to use with Grade 3 children to practise beat competency on a wood block or other non-pitched percussion instrument.

Saturday Night

African folk song
Arranged by A. Montgomery

Step 6: The child sings a song or chants a rhyme in his or her own space while moving his or her arms in a repetitive beat motion with a partner.

Step 6 allows children to explore arm beat-movement with a partner. The perennial favourite, *See-Saw* (p. 191), could be re-experienced here at a more complex motor skill level than in Step 2. Kindergarten–Grade 1 children sitting on the floor in their own spaces would be asked to face their partners while holding hands and rocking back and forth to the beat in a see-saw motion.

Re-visiting a song during several steps of the psychomotor teaching sequence has the added benefit of providing extended contact time to improve singing in tune. In addition, children's creative expression can rise to the surface as each pair may feel confident enough with the song to take turns suggesting novel ways to use their arms to show the see-saw beat.

Step 7: The child listens to recorded music in her or his own space while moving her or his arms together or in alternation in a repetitive beat motion with or without an end point for the beat

Step 7 gives children an opportunity to experience beat-movement with recorded music in a variety of styles and performing ensembles. Here, children might be asked to pat the beat on various parts of their bodies, changing to a different body part at the end of each musical phrase or section while listening to a piece of music. One excellent choice is the first movement of the *Brandenberg Concerto* no. 3 in G major, BWV 1048, by Johann Sebastian Bach (1685–1750). If music with a slower tempo—for example, "Jupiter" from *The Planets* by Gustav Holst (1874–1934)—is used, children might be encouraged to discover a swaying motion, as the longer motion will make beat awareness and beat competency with a slower tempo less difficult.

Although more abstract than the "music-making" beat-movement activities listed in Steps 1–6, keeping the beat with recorded music provides an opportunity for children to experience steady beat with music (for example, symphonies) that may be too difficult for them to perform at their particular age. Such activities help children to learn that steady beat is an important part of almost all music, not just the vocal music of childhood. See Chapter 7 for additional recommendations regarding recorded music appropriate for use in highlighting steady beat during the elementary grades.

Step 8: The child listens to recorded music in his or her own space while manipulating a concrete object on the beat.

This step is similar to Step 7, but here children are asked to add the skill of manipulating an object, either on the body or in the air, to the beat of the music. An example might include using scarves to pull the beat through the air to help illustrate the length of the beat while listening to music with slower tempos—for example, the "Dance of the Persian Slaves" from *Khovanshchina* by Modest Moussorgsky (1839–1881).

Step 9: The child sings a song, chants a rhyme, or listens to recorded music in her or his own space while passing an object to another person on the beat

By Step 9, children will have previously experienced manipulating an object to the beat both with singing and listening. Here, they are asked to perform the slightly more difficult movement of actually passing an object to another person while singing a song or listening to a recording. *Obwisana* is an excellent classroom example to use for Grades 3-4.

Obwisana

Traditional Ghanaian children's song
English text by A. Montgomery

Ob - wi - sa - na sa,   na, na,   ob - wi - sa - na sa,
Peace be with you now,   oh, oh,   peace be with you now,

Ob - wi - sa - na sa,   na, na,   ob - wi - sa - na sa.
Peace be with you now,   oh, oh,   peace be with you now.

Game: The children sit in a circle, each with a stone or a small object in their hand. On the first beat of m. 1, they tap their stone once on floor. On the second beat of m. 1, they move their stones to a point on the floor in front of the child to their right; on the first beat of m. 2, they pick up stone that has been placed in front (by the child to the left); and so on. This pick-up-and-pass routine continues through the rest of the song, and the children sing as many repetitions as needed for their stones to travel all the way around the circle.

Passing games such as this one abound in the children's music repertoire but frequently they are used too early in the beat-movement development process. Unless children can successfully manipulate an object with their own hands, they are unlikely to have much success in coordinating the passing of an object to another individual's hands.

Step 10: The child sings a song or chants a rhyme while his or her arms travel from space to space.

Step 10 provides children with a travelling beat experience before requiring them to actually use their feet to make the beat move from space to space. *Burnie Bee* is an excellent classroom example to use with Grade 2 students. Here, children stand in a circle with one of their outstretched palms holding a felt flower upright towards the sky. One child puts a bee puppet (Burnie) on his or her hand and flies the bee from flower to flower on the beat. Although the child's hand must travel from space to space, it is not necessary for his or her feet to move in a steady pattern as well. This is good preparation for the more difficult beat-movements required in Steps 11–12, when children will be asked to travel from space to space marking the beat with their feet.

Burnie Bee

Traditional

Burnie bee, Burnie bee,

Tell me when your wedding be,

If it be tomorrow day,

Take your wings and fly away.

Step 11: The child sings a song, chants a rhyme, or listens to recorded music in his or her own space while making stepping beat motions

This step requires children to begin transferring beat movements to their feet. Stepping beat motions are more difficult than feeling the beat with the arms, but they can be done while the child is either sitting or standing in one spot. Individual carpet squares placed on the floor for each child can be used to help define the space upon which the child can walk in place. It may also be useful for some children to revisit an easier arm beat motion in the part of the lesson that precedes the stepping beat experience.

For example, as Grade 1 children alternate arms in a train-wheel motion in the air while chanting *Engine, Engine* (p. 192), teachers would invite each child to move this beat motion from her or his hands to her or his feet. Another example utilizes the song *Ezekiel Saw the Wheel*. Here, Grade 4 children shift their beat motions from the circular "wheel" motions drawn in the air with their arms to a stepping motion in their feet. This kind of conscious transfer of beat movement from the upper to the lower body is an important psychomotor link for many children in the beat competency development process.

Ezekiel Saw the Wheel

Traditional African-American spiritual

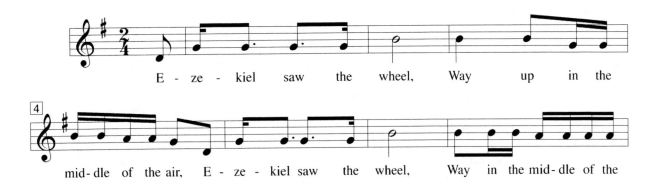

continued

air. Oh the big wheel run by faith, And the lit-tle wheel run by the

grace of God, A wheel in a wheel, Way in the mid-dle of the air.

Step 12: The child sings a song, chants a rhyme, or listens to recorded music while travelling from space to space with stepping beat motions.

Step 12 requires considerable beat-movement coordination by the child. Here, the child must walk from space to space on the beat while singing, chanting, or listening to recorded music. This is one of the most difficult beat skills in the development sequence, and children who can finally achieve success at this level are well on their way towards beat competency. Although there are many singing games suitable for practice of this kind, teachers might be wise to start with examples that provide aural or visual models for the children to follow.

For example, in the song *All around the Buttercup,* Grade 2 children have the opportunity to walk in and out of the circle to the beat while holding hands. This provides some beat security for children as they try and match their walking beat to their neighbour's pace.

All around the Buttercup

Traditional singing game

All a-round the but-ter cup, One two three,

If you want a spec-ial friend, Just choose me.

Game: The children stand in a circle with a space between each child. While everyone sings the song, one child walks to the beat, weaving in and out of the circle through the spaces. At the end of the song, the child invites another child from the circle to join hands with her or him. The song is sung again with the new child, followed by the original child both weaving in and out. This process continues, with a new child leading the line of "special friends" each time, until all the children have had a chance to become part of the weaving line.

A similar kind of beat-movement can be illustrated with the rhyme *Hicketty Picketty.*

Hicketty Picketty

Traditional

Hicketty picketty, my black hen,

She lays eggs in a great big pen.

Boys and girls come every day,

To see what my black hen did lay!

In this game, Grade 2 children sit in a circle chanting the rhyme while *patsching* the beat on their knees. A group of assorted percussion instruments are hidden in a covered basket in the middle of the circle (as if laid like eggs by a hen). One child walks around the outside of the circle trying to match her or his steps to the beat of the children's clapping. At the end of the game, the child outside the circle is allowed to go into the middle and choose an instrument to play as a mystery timbre for the other children. The child who identifies the correct name is allowed to play the instrument on the beat when the game begins again with a new child outside the circle.

This second example, too, provides a degree of beat security, as the child outside the circle attempts to match his or her stepping beat motion to the other children's clapping beat. *Hey Betty Martin,* on the other hand, is much more difficult in terms of the travelling beat movement (see next page). For this song, Grade 2 children are asked to use stepping beats as they individually tiptoe around the room. Because the children move independently from each other, they have little opportunity for matching their steps to with those of their classmates. This makes keeping the stepping beat movement more difficult than it would be either in *All around the Buttercup* or *Hicketty Picketty.* Teachers might provide some auxiliary help in this situation by standing on the sideline and tapping the beat on claves to help guide the children towards correct beat walking. Of course, as the children gain confidence in their stepping beats, such extra help should be eliminated so that the children can begin to hear the beat in the music on their own.

Hey Betty Martin

Traditional

Although *Hey Betty Martin* is categorized under Step 12, singing games such as this should only be attempted once the children have achieved success with easier travelling stepping beat motions, such as those described for *All around the Buttercup* or *Hicketty Picketty*. Many stepping beat games exist in children's repertoire and they are a joyful, learner-centred way to facilitate children's growth in successfully putting beat movements in their feet. Additional examples of singing games of this type may be found in Chapter 8.

Step 13: The child leads the class in keeping the beat in a repetitive arm beat motion or stepping beat motion while singing a song, chanting a rhyme, or listening to recorded music

At this level, children truly begin to take ownership of their beat competency. Roles are reversed, with children leading the class in beat-movements rather than the teacher. Re-visiting favourite music during this step is especially helpful, as children can use their psychomotor memory of their original experience to help guide their new beat experiences. Inviting children to lead the beat with both slower and faster tempos will provide practice in keeping the beat steady, and also reinforce their knowledge of tempo.

Step 14: The child sings a song, chants a rhyme, or listens to recorded music in her or his own space while keeping repetitive arm beat motions going, even when the music temporarily continues only in the child's inner hearing

Step 15: The child sings a song, chants a rhyme, or listens to recorded music in his or her own space while keeping stepping beat motions going, even when the music temporarily continues only in the child's inner hearing

Step 16: The child sings a song, chants a rhyme, or listens to recorded music while travelling from space to space with stepping beat motions, even when the music temporarily continues only in the child's inner hearing

Since later ensemble participation may require children to keep the beat going during rests while performing a piece of music, Steps 14–16 provide children with the opportunity to practise keeping the beat motions going even when the music is temporarily silenced, or when they are asked to temporarily sing the song inside their heads. Using a **cone puppet** (*a puppet that can pop its head in and out of a cone-shaped barrel*) as a visual cue to let the children know when to move their singing into their heads or back out into regular voice can be very motivating for children.

Step 17: The child in his or her own space is able to sing a song, chant a rhyme, or play an instrument with a steady beat by keeping the beat with a hidden motor movement in the toes

The musician's way of keeping the steady beat is to discreetly tap the toes inside her or his shoes.

Children who successfully reach this last stage in the beat-movement sequence are ready to give up the security of large motor movement to help to keep a steady beat while singing or playing an instrument. To help children become comfortable with the kinesthetic feel of the **musician's way of keeping the beat**—*discreetly tapping the toes inside one's shoes*—children might be encouraged to start the beat in their arms and slowly move it down to tapping their thighs, their knees, their feet, and finally to their toes. While singing each song, children should be encouraged to keep the beat hidden inside their shoes, moving only their toes rather than the whole foot. Indeed, this skill will require practice right through Grade 6 in order to bring it to fruition. When children are able to do this successfully, they will have reached true beat competency!

Elementary music classroom activities with the beat should, of course, not only lead children towards the development of beat awareness and beat competency, but should also provide a foundation for the development of beat literacy. As stated in Chapter 9, reading and writing music are important tools for children to develop because such music literacy opens the door to a whole world of musical understanding. Given the sound-before-symbol teaching process discussed in Chapter 2, teachers may be assured that any of the activities they use from the 17-step Beat-Movement Psychomotor Teaching Sequence will provide wonderful foundational experience for the symbol stage in the learning process for both beat and beat vs. rhythm (discussed in detail in Chapter 11). Thus, after children gain a variety of aural, kinesthetic, or oral experiences with the beat, they should move forward to beat experiences with symbolic interaction.

The Symbol Stage of Beat: Interacting with Iconic Representation

The heart shape (♥) is an excellent iconic representation for steady beat for grades 1–3.

Although beat is the one musical concept that in traditional notation has no symbol, the valentine heart shape (♥) has become recognized across Canada as an excellent iconic representation of beat during literacy activities with children in Grades 1–3. Another iconic shape frequently used with older elementary school students is a blank line (__).

Children in Grades 1–3 should have the opportunity to re-visit many familiar songs they have previously experienced only aurally, kinesthetically, or orally, now with the beat-movement tapped on an iconic symbol such as a piece of felt cut into a heart shape. For example, in a Grade 1–2 lesson, children could start by experiencing the beat with *Johnny Works with One Hammer* (see p. 193) as described in Step 1 of the Beat-Movement Psychomotor Teaching Sequence. Then, felt ♥s would be passed out to the children so that each could place one ♥ on her or his knee. While singing the song a second time, children would be asked to tap the beat on their felt ♥ while singing the song.

Ask early elementary students to read and write a song's ♥ patterns.

Another excellent idea is to sew eight felt ♥s in a row up the sleeve of a white shirt. While re-visiting the rhyme *Slowly, Slowly* (see p. 194), Grade 1–2 students could put on the special shirt and "walk" their snail up the arm tapping each of the felt ♥s on the beat. This kind of transfer of body beat-movement to beat tapping with the iconic symbol of beat (♥) is important for setting the stage for the reading and writing experiences with ♥ that should follow.

After these initial symbolic beat-keeping experiences, children should be presented with a variety of opportunities for individual decision making regarding music and the ♥. First, children might sing a song while counting the number of beats needed to "keep the song alive." *See-Saw* (see p. 191), for example, takes eight beats. Children could individually "write" these beats out on the floor with felt ♥s, and then should then be asked to sing the song again while pointing to the beats. This experience will help to strengthen the connection between the

Example of heart pattern for *See-Saw*

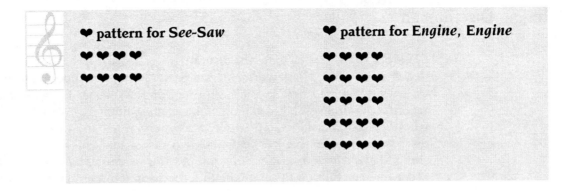

♥ pattern for *See-Saw*

♥ ♥ ♥ ♥

♥ ♥ ♥ ♥

♥ pattern for *Engine, Engine*

♥ ♥ ♥ ♥

♥ ♥ ♥ ♥

♥ ♥ ♥ ♥

♥ ♥ ♥ ♥

♥ ♥ ♥ ♥

previously learned kinesthetic response and the newly learned visual symbol♥. It will also reinforce the children's left-to-right music reading skills. Younger children often find this task difficult at the beginning, so a concrete object put beside the first ♥ may help them in the process of reading readiness (see photograph).

Reading and writing the ♥ patterns of a song can be followed by playing the Mystery Beat games. Here, the children see two complete ♥ patterns on the board—for example, one pattern for *Engine, Engine* (see p. 192) and one pattern for *See-Saw* (see p. 191). They are then asked to raise their hand if they recognize a ♥ pattern for a song they know.

These symbolic beat games go a long way towards helping children with reading and writing beat, and subsequently rhythm, in music. Chapter 11 describes classroom activities focusing on beat vs. rhythm that build upon the knowledge established first by these types of notational beat activities.

Tempo: How Fast or Slow the Beat Goes

A student's knowledge about tempo is built on previous experiences with steady beat.

It is important for students to develop tempo discrimination and tempo production.

Tempo is a structural characteristic frequently utilized by composers to make the music come alive for the listener. Elementary school students' sensitivity to tempo changes may be heightened through the use of a variety of classroom activities. Since tempo involves the speed of the steady beat, children should already have experienced initial activities from the 12-Step Beat-Movement Teaching Sequence before attempting to build upon this knowledge with ideas about tempo.

Beginning activities in tempo involve **tempo discrimination** *(the ability to hear the difference between faster and slower tempos)*. These are followed by activities involving **tempo production** *(the ability to use tempo effectively during performing or improvising)*, which lead to activities involving tempo with composing. Daily classroom activities involving tempo discrimination happen naturally in the "sound" stage of tempo development, and the activities involving tempo production can take place with or without the use of tempo markings (for example, *adagio* for a slow tempo). Composing with tempo obviously occurs in the symbol stage of the process only.

Tempo Discrimination

Classroom experiences in tempo discrimination involve the activities of listening and moving. First, Kindergarten–Grade 1 children are invited to listen to a variety of familiar and new music performed by the teacher (singing, playing the recorder or guitar, etc.) For example, the teacher might play *This Old Man* on the recorder, first at a slow tempo, then at a faster tempo, and invite the children to discuss the differences between the two performances. Initial performances should have distinctly contrasting tempos (for example, ***adagio*** and ***allegro***) in order for the children to gauge the differences in tempo more accurately.

This Old Man

Traditional children's song

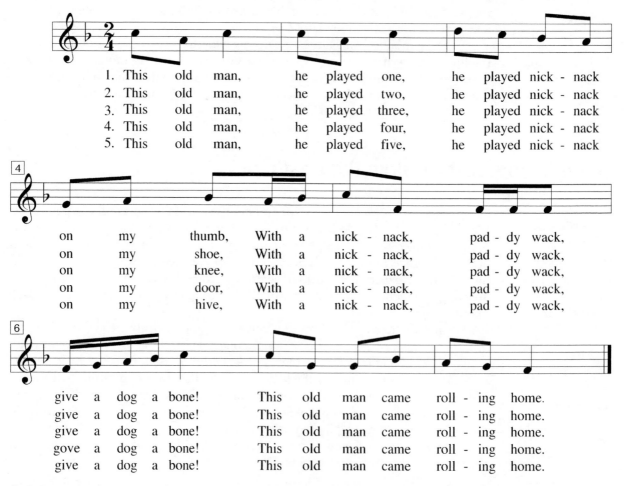

1. This old man, he played one, he played nick - nack
2. This old man, he played two, he played nick - nack
3. This old man, he played three, he played nick - nack
4. This old man, he played four, he played nick - nack
5. This old man, he played five, he played nick - nack

on my thumb, With a nick - nack, pad - dy wack,
on my shoe, With a nick - nack, pad - dy wack,
on my knee, With a nick - nack, pad - dy wack,
on my door, With a nick - nack, pad - dy wack,
on my hive, With a nick - nack, pad - dy wack,

give a dog a bone! This old man came roll - ing home.
give a dog a bone! This old man came roll - ing home.
give a dog a bone! This old man came roll - ing home.
gove a dog a bone! This old man came roll - ing home.
give a dog a bone! This old man came roll - ing home.

Subsequent listening experiences of this type should involve children listening to recorded music. Start with short pieces that have only one tempo. An excellent choice for *adagio* is the "Pie Jesu" from the *Requiem* by Gabriel Fauré (1845–1924), and a fine example for *allegro* is the "Bacchanale" from *Samson et Delila* by Camille Saint-Saëns (1835–1921). Then progress to music that has varying tempos: for example, *Slavonic Dance*, op. 46, no. 3 in A♭ major by Antonín Dvořák (1841–1904) Students might show their tempo discrimination with single tempo pieces through beat movement or through manipulating props such as scarves or hoops. Tempo discrimination for music with varying tempos could be expressed by having children participate in any number of the following activities.

1. The children sit at their desks and show a thumbs-up every time they hear a change in tempo of the music. (Grades 1–2)

2. The children walk around the room to the beat of the music, changing direction every time they hear a change of tempo in the music. (Grades 1–2)

3. The children create two or three different movement patterns to keep the beat while listening to music; they perform one with the first tempo and the others when the tempo changes. (Grades 3–4)

4. The children sit in a circle and pass a ball on the beat; the ball changes direction every time they hear a change of tempo in the music. (Grades 3–4)

Tempo Production

Tempo discrimination in the sound stage of the learning process is followed by tempo production. Here Kindergarten–Grade 1 children begin to learn how to use tempo to vary their performance of familiar songs. This is not as easy as it sounds, because it is always less difficult to sing a song such as *Johnny Works with One Hammer* (see p. 193) with a steady beat at a moderate **andante** tempo than at either a very fast *allegro* or a very slow *adagio*.

Call-and-response songs, such as *Down by the Bay*, provide greater success at the beginning of this process as younger children have the benefit of hearing the teacher establish the tempo first in the call portion of the song.

Down by the Bay

Traditional folk song

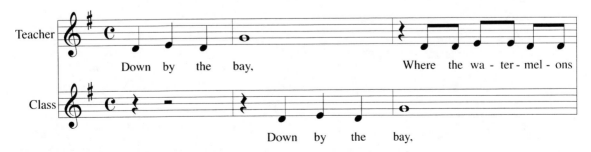

continued

Another example—a game version of *Mary Had a Little Lamb*—uses tempo changes to help illustrate the story of the text, sometimes making it easier for children to practise the production of tempo variations.

Mary Had a Little Lamb

Traditional nursery song

Game (as taught to the author by Dianne Edwards, Toronto, Ontario): The children stand in a circle with about a metre of space between each child. The child chosen to play the part of Mary walks in and out of the circle, stepping on the beat, while the children sing mm. 1–8 at an *adagio* tempo. At m. 9, another child takes the part of the lamb and chases Mary in and out of the circle, stepping on the beat, while the song continues at an *allegro* tempo. At the end of the song, the game can begin again with new children playing the parts of Mary and the lamb.

Children should be given time for careful reflection as they learn how tempo is used in music. For example, the teacher might invite Grade 1 children to sing the lullaby *Bye Baby Bunting* at several different tempos, and then pose questions such as "Which tempo do you think is best for helping the baby to fall asleep?"

Bye Baby Bunting

Traditional lullaby

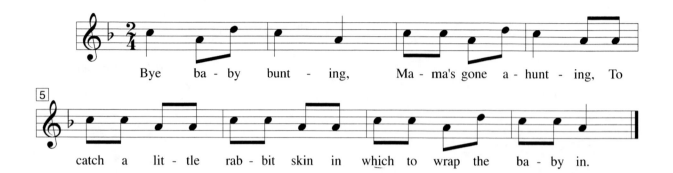

Bye ba - by bunt - ing, Ma - ma's gone a - hunt - ing, To

catch a lit - tle rab - bit skin in which to wrap the ba - by in.

Another example, for Grade 4 students, uses the song *Mango Walk* (p. 148). The teacher asks the children to experiment with different tempos and find the tempo they think works well for accompanying the song with a mango walk movement. This kind of aesthetic judgment-making is an important step in the journey towards students having success with tempo both in performing and in composing.

The symbols used to give tempo directions in music involve both the metronome marking and the tempo word descriptor placed at the beginning of a piece of music and wherever else a tempo change occurs in the music.

Moderato ♩= 96

D'ou viens - tu ber - gè - re, D'ou viens - tu?

Children can easily incorporate these markings into their music production and composition activities by having such directions included on the music they are asked to read or write. From the beginning of the labelling process, children feel very comfortable using terms such as *adagio* or *allegro* rather than the more generic terms of fast and slow. Children may be given the opportunity to experiment with a **metronome** (*a mechanical or electronic device used to show and/or sound a steady beat at a given tempo*) in order to better understand how the metronome markings in the music are used. When given the opportunity to choose a tempo for performing a familiar song during a lesson, Grade 2–6 students may try several different metronome settings in order to find the one that best suits their concept of the perfect performance tempo. Practice with this kind of decision-making again leads the child to a more comprehensive understanding of the importance of tempo in music.

Metre: The Periodic Accenting of Specific Beats over Others

Metre involves the pattern of strong and weak steady beats in music.

In music, the term **metre** refers to *the periodic accenting of specific beats over others*. Generally thought of as an abstract concept, elementary school children initially come to understand metre through a variety of classroom activities such as listening, singing, and playing instruments with each activity including movement as a key pedagogical partner.

As when learning about steady beat, children need the help of kinesthetic experiences—this time by responding to stronger and weaker beats—in order to be able to feel the flow of the music. Initial experiences, generally beginning at the end of Grade 1 or early in Grade 2, involve a variety of body motions used to show the strong and weak beats. These experiences can be followed by the use of conducting to help older children continue to feel the different kinds of beats in metre.

Kinesthetic response helps children to feel metre in music.

Elementary teachers may need to provide a good deal of leadership in the beginning of the learning process in order for children to have a visual model to reinforce their aural experiences. Activities appropriate for the sound stage of the metre development process start by helping children compare the accented beat patterns in 2/4 and 3/4 metres, later leading to experiences with 4/4 metre. Here are several examples of appropriate aural, kinesthetic, or oral activities.

1. Invite Grade 2–3 students to explore a variety of body-percussion patterns that help to illustrate a strong-weak pattern (as in 2/4) and a strong-weak-weak pattern (as in 3/4). Examples for 2/4 might be "*patsch*-snap" or "stamp-clap"; examples for 3/4 might include "*patsch*-snap-snap" or "stamp-slide-slide." Next, play a variety of recorded music in 2/4 metre—for example, the "Russian Sailors Dance" from *The Red Poppy* by Reinhold Glière (1875–1956)—and 3/4 metre—for example, the third movement from the Symphony no. 39 in E♭ major by Wolfgang Amadeus Mozart (1756–1791). Ask the children to perform the appropriate body percussion pattern on the beat while they listen to the music.

2. Review a 2/4 song, such as *Bounce High, Bounce Low*, with Grade 2 children. Then give each child a large rubber ball, instructing them to manipulate the ball in a two-beat bounce-catch pattern. The "bounce" will help the children feel the strength of the first beat in the 2/4 metre with the "catch" simulating the weaker beat.

Bounce High, Bounce Low

Traditional song

Bounce high, bounce low, bounce the ball to Shi - loh.

3. Review a song with alternating 3/4 and 2/4 time signatures, such as *Ton moulin*, with Grade 2–3 children. Instruct the students to use the ball in a "bounce-catch-hold" pattern during the 3/4 section, and change to a "bounce-catch" pattern during the 2/4 section. Then have them sing the song again, this time performing the game described below, which also emphasizes the changing metre in the song.

Ton moulin

Traditional French folk song

Game: The children stand and join hands with their partners. Five pairs form a wheel, with each pair making one of the spokes. During the first 3/4 section, the children walk the wheel around in a circle on the beat, indicating the strong and weak beats with movement as they go (for example, "bend-sway-sway"). During the 2/4 section, the partners link arms and twirl around in a small circle on the beat. During the **da capo** repeat of the 3/4 section, the children reform the wheel and repeat their motions to indicate the beat.

4. Choose familiar songs in 2/4 or 3/4 time and ask children to use movement (as in activity 1) to feel the strong and weak beats while singing. Then, sing the song a second time, asking children to sing "1" on the strong beats and count how far they get before they have to sing "1" again (for example, **1**-2, **1**-2 in 2/4, or **1**-2-3, **1**-2-3 in 3/4).

Multiple experiences of this kind during the sound stage of metre development prepare Grade 2 children for the introduction of the symbols of metre; **time signatures** and **bar lines**. Here, teachers should ask children to re-visit a familiar song such as *Bounce High, Bounce Low* using movement to reinforce the strong-weak metre pattern. Teachers and children should write the rhythm of the song on the board, and place accent marks (>) above the strong beats. Teachers could then explain that bar lines may be placed in front of the notes with accent marks to show the beat pattern groupings, thereby allowing elimination of the accents. The **2/4** time signature may then be introduced and placed at the front of the first measure. This is also an appropriate time to explain to children the tradition of using **double bar lines** at the end of a piece of music.

Children should re-experience this four-step process with many of their familiar songs:

1. Sing a familiar song showing the strong and weak beat pattern through movement.

2. Write the rhythm of the song, and place accent marks (>) above the appropriate notes.

3. Replace the accent marks with bar lines and add the appropriate time signature (2/4 or 3/4) at the beginning of the first measure.

4. Place a double bar line at the end of the rhythm.

Children can now learn conducting patterns to help them to reinforce their kinesthetic response to metre. Grade 3–6 students should be given the opportunity to use appropriate conducting patterns both while listening to recorded music and while singing. Older children should have the opportunity to take turns being the conductor during group singing or while playing instruments. Such leadership helps elementary school students come to a deeper understanding of the importance of metre in music (James, 1998).

Students are ready for introduction to 4/4 metre when they begin to become comfortable with feeling 2/4 and 3/4, generally in Grades 3–4. This corresponds nicely with the introduction of the recorder in Grade 4, which will provide multiple examples of music in 4/4 time. Much of the children's classroom vocal music is in 2/4 metre rather than 4/4, so instrumental music provides an excellent opportunity to experience a four-beat metre during the elementary grades.

Most provincial curricula across Canada recommend introduction of **compound metres** (such as 6/8 or 9/8) and the more complex irregular metres (such as 5/4 or 7/4) in Grades 4–6. Although there is a great deal of suitable vocal music for teaching the strong-weak patterns in 6/8 time (including *I'se the B'y*, p. 90; *Bonavist' Harbour*, p. 128; *En roulant ma boule*, p. 246–7), teachers generally turn to recorded instrumental music to help children learn about other compound meters (such as 9/8) and irregular metres in which the beat groupings are not all the same length. One example of 9/8 can be found in the first movement (just after the introduction, which is in 3/4) of the Symphony no. 4 in F minor by Pyotr Il'yich Tchaikowsky (1840–1893). The second movement of the Tschaikovsky's Symphony no. 6 in B minor provides an excellent example of 5/4. Examples of several irregular metres can be found in the music of jazz artist Dave Brubeck (born 1920), including *Take Five* (in 5/4), *Unsquare Dance* (in 7/4) and *Blue Rondo à la Turk* (in 9/8, where the eighths are grouped into four beats: 2-2-2-3). Experiences of this kind help children in the upper grades expand their knowledge of how metre works in music.

Metre should become part of the symbols manipulated during composing activities as soon as the appropriate symbols have been introduced to the children. Even younger children writing short rhythmic compositions can include time signatures. Older students might try writing short melodies and experimenting with which metre they feel is best for performing their melody. Chapter 6 provides additional ideas on how to use metre within the activity of composing.

Questions for Discussion and Practice

1. Why do movement activities help to make learning about beat less abstract for children?

2. Briefly discuss the criteria teachers need to consider when planning for beat-movement activities in the elementary music classroom.

3. Describe the kinds of movement activities that are appropriate at the beginning, middle, and end of the 12-Step Beat-Movement Teaching Sequence.

4. What is the difference between tempo discrimination and tempo production? Give an example of an appropriate classroom activity for each.

5. Why do children need to develop an understanding of steady beat before learning about metre? What other structural characteristic of music should children be familiar with before they learn about the symbols of metre. Why?

References

James, L. (1998). Action research: Conducting activities for third graders. *Teaching Music, 5(5)*, 42–3.

Rohwer, D. (1998). Effect of movement on steady beat perception, synchronization, and performance. *Journal of Research in Music Education, 46(3)*, 414–24.

CHAPTER 11

Rhythm

SYNOPSIS

Chapter 11 discusses daily classroom activities appropriate for the elementary music classroom that use experiences such as singing, playing instruments, and moving to highlight the four musical concepts from Rhythm. Activities are presented in a sound-before-symbol progression within a developmentally appropriate simple-to-complex teaching order.

Introduction

Young children often think of rhythm as the way the words sound.

Rhythm—*the varied durations of notes or silences over a steady beat*—is a structural property of music that is easily accessible to many children (Veenker, 1999; Demorest and Serlin, 1997; and Moore et al., 1997). This is due in part to young children's immediate focus on the text whenever they hear music. In fact, children in Kindergarten–Grade 1 often think of **rhythm** as *the way the words sound*.

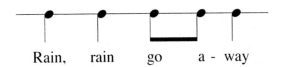

Rain,   rain   go   a - way

This kind of phonemic reinforcement is, of course, positive, as children's focus on text leads to the recognition of rhythmic patterning. Indeed research indicates that Kindergarten children who have strong **phonemic awareness skills** (*sensitivity to aspects of the phonological structure of language such as rhyming, alliteration, and phonemes*) are also successful at perceiving and identifying easy rhythmic patterns in music (Montgomery, 1998a; Montgomery, 1998b).

Pedagogically, elementary music teachers build on children's fascination with language by using movement activities such as clapping "the way the words sound" in songs and rhymes in order to begin developing rhythmic concepts. Early classroom experiences highlight the rhythm of individual words in songs or rhymes—for example, the "B-I-N-G-O" in *Bingo* (p. 160)—later leading to clapping the rhythm for entire songs or rhymes, such as *Old Mother Witch*.

Old Mother Witch

Traditional

Old mother witch,

Fell in a ditch,

Picked up a penny,

And thought she was rich!

These initial aural-kinesthetic experiences with the concrete feeling of rhythm, combined with the beat-movement experiences discussed in Chapter 10, set the stage for the eventual labelling and symbolic association of rhythmic notation during the "symbol" stage of the learning process.

Principles of Instruction

Rhythm, rhythm vs. beat, individual rhythmic values, and rhythmic patterns are all important concepts of the structural property of rhythm.

Learning about the structure of rhythm can be divided into four main concepts:

1. *rhythm*—the way the words go
2. *rhythm vs. beat*—the difference between rhythm and beat
3. *individual rhythmic values*—specific note or rest durations such as *ta, ti-ti,* and *ti-ka-ti-ka*
4. *rhythmic patterns*—combinations of individual rhythmic values

The first two concepts are experienced through aural, kinesthetic, and oral activities in the classroom. The third and fourth concepts are experienced through activities using rhythmic notation. Generally, the first two concepts are experienced by children in Kindergarten–Grade 1, and the second two are taught in Grades 1 through 6. *However, if teachers find themselves working with older elementary school students who have had little aural or kinesthetic experience with rhythm, they should initiate the learning process with activities involving the first two concepts.*

Classroom Activities for Highlighting Rhythm

The following classroom activities can be used in the elementary grades to highlight the concept of *rhythm*.

Activity 1: The children sing songs or chant rhymes while clapping the rhythm of particular words or phrases from the music. (Kindergarten–Grade 2)

Children are asked to clap or tap "the way the words sound" or the "rhythm" of words of particular interest to the children while singing a song or chanting a rhyme. This activity provides children with the initial experience of feeling rhythm, without having to concentrate on hearing the complete rhythm of a song or rhyme. Excellent examples include, for Kindergarten, clapping the words "teddy bear" in *Teddy Bear* (p. 49), and for Grade 1, clapping the words "eidel dum" in *Hop Old Squirrel*.

Hop Old Squirrel

Traditional

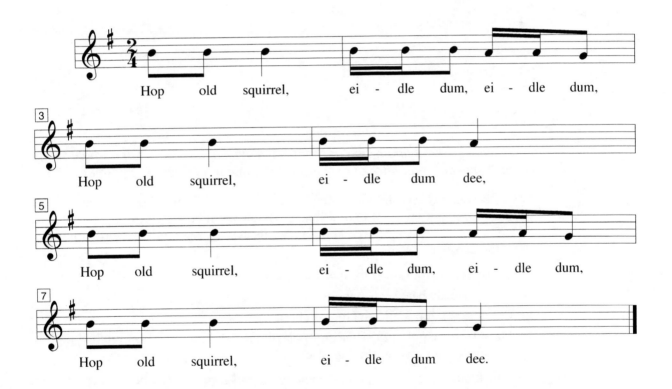

....

Activity 2: The children sing songs or chant rhymes while playing the rhythm of particular words or phrases from the music on non-pitched percussion instruments. (Kindergarten–Grade 2)

This is similar to Activity 1, but here the children are asked to move their kinesthetic awareness of the rhythm of highlighted words from clapping to playing on a non-pitched percussion instrument. One excellent example is the call-and-response song, *One, Two, Tie My Shoe* (p. 41). For this Grade 1–2 activity, the teacher sings the "call" parts of the song ("One, two," etc.), and the children answer by singing and playing the rhythm on wood blocks during the "response parts" ("tie my shoe," etc.).

Activity 3: The children sing or chant while clapping the rhythm of a whole song or rhyme (Kindergarten–Grade 6)

Here children experience "the way the words sound" for complete rhymes or songs. Children should learn how to sing these short songs or chant the rhymes before attempting to clap the rhythm at the same time as they sing or chant the music. An excellent example for Grade 1 is the rhyme *Criss Cross*.

Criss Cross   Traditional

Criss cross, apple sauce,

Spiders crawling up your back,

Cool breeze, tight squeeze,

Now you've got the shivereeze!

Activity 4: The children sing or chant while playing the rhythm of a whole song or rhyme on a non-pitched percussion instrument. (Kindergarten–Grade 6)

This activity is similar to Activity 2, but the children are now asked to move their feeling of the rhythm of a song or rhyme from hand clapping to performing on an instrument. Children should try this activity by completing the following steps in order:

1. Learn to sing the song or chant the rhyme.
2. Keep a steady beat while singing or chanting.
3. Clap the rhythm while singing or chanting.
4. Move from clapping the rhythm to playing the rhythm on a non-pitched percussion instrument while singing or chanting.

This kind of sequential process is helpful *at all grade levels* when doing any kind of classroom rhythmic activities involving instruments.

Activity 5: The children echo-clap or echo-play a rhythm. (Kindergarten–Grade 6)

Students are asked to listen to a rhythm tapped by the teacher or another student on a pair of claves, and then echo-clap it back or echo-play it back on a non-pitched percussion instrument. This makes a wonderful warm-up activity for a lesson that involves teaching a new song: use some of the rhythms from the song in the echo-clapping activity.

The children listen to the teacher tap the rhythm of a "mystery" song or rhyme on the claves, and then try to identify the name of the song, selecting from any of their familiar class repertoire. Children can check their answers by singing the song while the teacher taps the rhythm a second time, to see if the two are a match. If not, another song can be tried, and so on.

Rhythmic activities in music should always include keeping a steady beat.

Activities for Highlighting Beat vs. Rhythm

Classroom experiences that highlight *beat vs. rhythm* are important for children, once they are comfortable with the concepts of both *beat* and *rhythm*. Contrasting the differences between the two in music is significant because children will learn the third rhythmic concept—**individual rhythmic values**—by listening for *the number of rhythmic sounds heard over a steady beat.* For example, when clapping this rhythm,

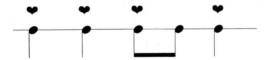

children will eventually be asked "On which beats do you hear one tap, and on which beats do you hear two?" They will subsequently learn that:

- one tap per beat is a *"tah"* (a quarter note),
- two even taps per beat is a *"ti-ti"* (two eighth notes),
- four even taps per beat is a *"ti-ri-ti-ri"* (four sixteenth notes),
- one tap that lasts over two beats is a *"ta-ah"* (a half note).

Thus, multiple classroom experiences that help children contrast *beat vs. rhythm* are a critical part of the rhythmic development process, because they lay the groundwork for learning rhythmic notation. Here are four examples of classroom activities that will help in this regard.

Activity 1: Half of the class sings a song or chants a rhyme while keeping the beat on non-pitched percussion instruments (for example, skins); at the same time, the other half of the class sings or chants the song or rhyme while playing the rhythm on non-pitched percussion instruments of a contrasting timbre (for example, wood). (Kindergarten–Grade 3)

In this activity, timbre is used to help the children hear the difference between the way the *beat* feels (in this case, "sounds") and the way the *rhythm* sounds. Songs with active rhythms (rhythms that contain shorter note values such as eighth notes or sixteenth notes) are helpful for this activity because the faster rhythm prevents confusion between the beat and the rhythm. For example, the rhythm of a song such as *Bounce High, Bounce Low* (p. 211) has so many quarter notes that children might not hear the difference between the quarter-note rhythm and the 2/4 quarter-note beat. A song such as *Lucy Locket* (p. 154), on the other hand, has enough eighth notes for the rhythm to sound distinctly different from the steady beat.

Activity 2: Children sing songs or chant rhymes while tapping the steady beat on a felt ❤, and then sing or chant the same song or rhyme while playing the rhythm on rhythm sticks. (Kindergarten–Grade 2)

In this activity, children experience the contrast between beat and rhythm in the same song or rhyme in close proximity to each other. As discussed in Chapter 5, rhythm sticks are most successful when they are played by striking one stick against the middle of the other with the bottom stick held firmly in place. This technique will help the children to play the rhythm more accurately. Children in the early elementary grades should have experience playing both the rhythm and the beat in this way with a variety of songs from their regular classroom repertoire.

Activity 3: Children write the beat pattern for a song on the floor using felt ❤s (see Chapter 10). Then they sing a short familiar song or chant a familiar rhyme while clapping the rhythm, moving their hands along the ❤ pattern to mark the beats. (Grades 1–2)

Here, children experience the relationship between the flow of the rhythm claps and the actual "steady beats needed to keep the song alive." This activity should be done with a variety of classroom songs in order to prepare for the symbolic association between rhythm sounds and beats that will follow. It is helpful at this point in the process to include some songs containing only *tah*s and *ti-ti*s since these are the individual rhythmic values children will be introduced to first through notation. Excellent examples to use for this include *See-Saw* (p. 191), *Criss Cross* (p. 218), *Engine, Engine* (p. 192), and *Lucy Locket* (p. 154).

*Activity 4: Children sing songs or chant rhymes while alternating between keeping the beat by patting their knees and clapping the rhythm with their hands; during the activity, the teacher guides them with a **beat-rhythm sign** (a reversible sign with one side showing a large iconic beat ❤ symbol and the other side showing a pair of rhythm sticks). (Grades 1–3)*

In this activity, which is slightly more difficult than Activity 3, the children alternate between feeling the beat to making the sound of the rhythm as directed by the teacher, who holds the sign and turns it at selected moments. This will take considerable practice and should be tried with a variety of classroom songs and rhymes. Since this is the last step in the beat vs. rhythm activity sequence, teachers should also make sure children practice this activity with songs containing only *tah*s and *ti-ti*s to prepare for the symbolic stage in the learning process.

Classroom Activities for
Introducing Individual Rhythmic Values

Quarter notes and eighth notes are the first rhythmic values to be introduced to children in the elementary grades.

Elementary school children reaching this stage in the rhythmic learning process are ready to begin associating their aural and kinesthetic knowledge of beat vs. rhythm with the notation of specific **rhythmic values**. As discussed in Chapter 9, many provincial curriculum guides recommend that this symbolic association begin in Grade 1 with quarter notes (*tah*) and eighth notes (*ti-ti*) and continue in a logical introduction order through to Grade 6 (see page 183).

The classroom activities used to introduce children to the label and symbol of any *new rhythmic value* need to be carefully thought out. It is recommended that teachers consider using the following steps to organize instruction for any such "introduction" lessons for Grades 1–6:

- Step 1: Ask the children to sing a familiar song.
- Step 2: Ask the children to sing the song again while keeping the steady beat.
- Step 3: Instruct the children to sing the song again, this time, clapping or playing the rhythm on a non-pitched percussion instrument.
- Step 4: Invite the children to play a beat vs. rhythm game with the song (see pp. 219–220).
- Step 5: Invite the children to notate either part or all of the rhythm of the song, using popsicle sticks or other concrete manipulatables. Instruct them to try to determine how the new rhythmic value (for example, a half note) differs from the other more familiar rhythmic values in the song (for example quarter notes and eighth notes). Questions such as, "How many taps does our new rhythm sound over one beat?" or "How many beats does our new rhythm take?" may help to lead the children towards determining the parameters of the new rhythmic value.
- Step 6: Tell the children the labels for the new rhythmic value—both the rhythmic syllable name and the traditional note name (for example, *tah*, quarter note)—and show them the appropriate notational symbol.
- Step 7: Ask the children to practise reading the rhythmic notation of the whole song, including the new rhythm, using the appropriate rhythmic syllable names
- Step 8: End this experience by singing the complete song with the students one last time.

Music selected for introducing new rhythms to elementary school children is critical to the success of the learning process.

Music selected for use during these introductory lessons can be critical to the student's ability to come to a personal understanding of how the symbol is manipulated in music. Carefully selected songs will promote *student discovery* of the new rhythm, thus making a more teacher-directed approach during the lesson unnecessary. As a result, the children will take greater ownership in the learning process.

Teachers should consider the following criteria carefully when selecting songs to introduce the label and symbol of a new rhythmic value to children.

1. *The song should be a* **review song** (*a song that has been taught to the children in a previous lesson*). This will help the children build their new symbolic knowledge upon previous aural and kinesthetic experience with the rhythm of that song.

2. The song should not contain any rhythmic notation the children have not yet experienced symbolically except for the one new symbol to be highlighted. For example, the song used to introduce the half note in Grade 2 should contain one or more half notes, plus any previously-taught rhythmic values (such as quarter notes, eighth notes, or quarter rests), but there should not be any symbolically unknown rhythmic values (such as sixteenth notes or whole notes). This kind of careful pedagogical planning ensures that students focus on determining the parameters of only one new rhythmic value at a time, thereby promoting the building of a thorough knowledge base.

3. The new rhythmic value to be highlighted should occur only a few times in the song, and it should always be in the same context (i.e. with a similar text and/or a similar rhythm). The ideal placement of a new rhythmic value in the music provides opportunity for children to draw clearer comparisons with their previously learned symbolic knowledge of other rhythmic values when determining how the new rhythm differs from the other rhythms in a song.

Excellent examples of children's songs which meet these criteria include:

See-Saw—*tah* and *ti-ti* (Grade 1, see p. 191)

Pease Porridge Hot—quarter rests (Grade 1)

Jolly Old St. Nicholas—*ta-ah* (Grade 2)

Who's That?—*ti-ri-ti-ri* or *ti-ka ti-ka* (Grade 3, see p. 48)

À Saint-Malo, beau port de mer—*ti ti-ri* or *ti ti-ka* (Grade 3)

Draw a Bucket of Water—*ti-ri ti* or *ti-ka ti* (Grade 3)

Weevily Wheat—*syn-co-pa* (Grade 4, see pp. 290–91)

In the Bleak Midwinter—*tam-ti* (Grades 4–5)

Vive la canadienne!—*tim-ri* or *tim-ka* (Grades 4–5)

I'se the B'y—6/8: *tam; ti-ti-ti; ta-ti* combinations (Grade 5, see pp. 90–91)

Rise Up Shepherd and Follow—*trip-o-let* (Grade 6)

Pease Porridge Hot

Traditional chant

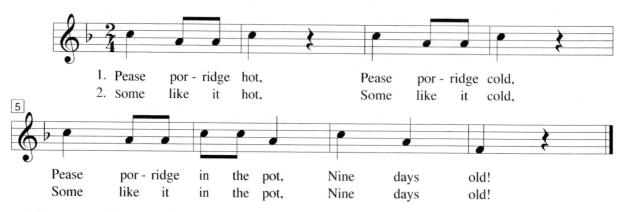

Jolly Old St. Nicholas

Traditional Christmas song

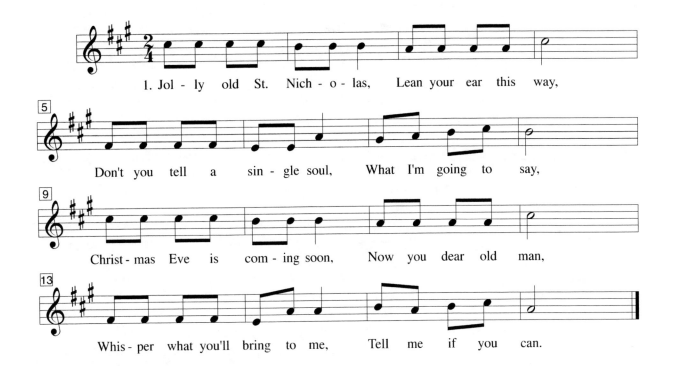

1. Jol-ly old St. Nich-o-las, Lean your ear this way,
Don't you tell a sin-gle soul, What I'm going to say,
Christ-mas Eve is com-ing soon, Now you dear old man,
Whis-per what you'll bring to me, Tell me if you can.

2. When the clock is striking twelve,
   When I'm fast asleep,
   Down the narrow chimney flue,
   With your pack you'll creep,
   Soon you'll find the stockings there,
   Hanging in a row,
   Mine will be the shortest one,
   Mended at the toe.

3. Johnny wants a choo-choo train,
   Susie wants a sled,
   Nelly wants a box of paints,
   Yellow, blue, and red,
   Now I think I'll leave to you,
   What to give the rest,
   Choose for me dear Santa Claus,
   You will know the best!

À Saint-Malo, beau port de mer

Traditional French Canadian folk song
English text by Edith Fowke

À Saint Ma - lo beau port de mer, À Saint Ma - lo beau
At Saint Ma - lo be - side the sea, At Saint Ma - lo be -

port de mer, Trois gros na - vir's sont ar - ri - vés, Nous i -
side the sea, Float - ed at an - chor ves - sels three, We are

rons sur l'eau nous y prom - pro - me - ner, Nous i -
sail - ing out on the great sal - ty sea, We are

rons jou - er _____ dans l'î - le
sail - ing sail - ing far a - way.

Draw a Bucket of Water

Traditional North American singing game

1. Draw a buck-et of wa - ter, For my la - dy's daugh - ter,
2. Draw a buck-et of wa - ter, For my la - dy's daugh - ter,
3. Draw a buck-et of wa - ter, For my la - dy's daugh - ter,
4. Draw a buck-et of wa - ter, For my la - dy's daugh - ter,
5. Draw a buck-et of wa - ter, For my la - dy's daugh - ter,

One   in   the bush   and   two   in   the bush,   And   num - ber   one   pops   un - der.
One   in   the bush   and   two   in   the bush,   And   num - ber   two   pops   un - der.
One   in   the bush   and   two   in   the bush,   And   num - ber   three   pops   un - der.
One   in   the bush   and   two   in   the bush,   And   num - ber   four   pops   un - der.
One   in   the bush   and   two   in   the bush,   And   all   of   us   pop   out! _____

Game: The children stand in circles of four, and number off around the circle (1–2–3–4). In each circle, "1" and "3" join hands together. "2" and "4" do the same, holding their hands over "1" and "3." During the first verse, the pairs pull each other back and forth across the circle to the beat, and at the end of the verse, "1" pops under the arms of "2" and "4." The same action continues through the next three verses with the "2," "3," and "4" popping under. During the last verse, the circles of four step around in a circle to the beat, with their arms still wrapped around each other. On the last line, they all pop out to form a regular circle.

In the Bleak Midwinter

Gustav Holst (1874–1934)
Text by Christina Rossetti (1830–1894)

In   the bleak mid - win   -   ter,   fros - ty wind made moan,

Earth   stood hard   as   i   -   ron,   wa - ter   like   a   stone.

Snow   had fal - len,   snow on snow,   snow —   on —   snow,

In   the bleak mid - win   -   ter,   long —————— a - go.

Vive la Canadienne

Traditional French Canadian folk song

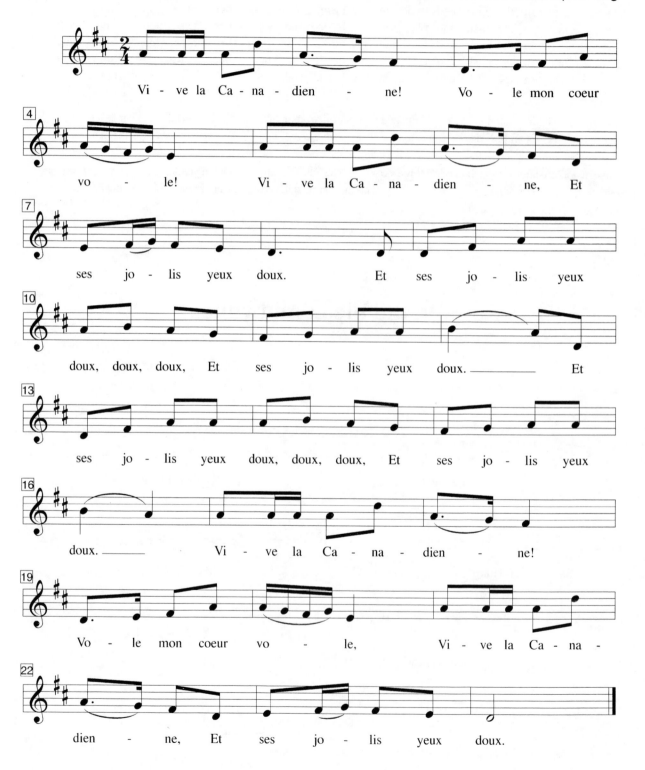

Rise Up Shepherd and Follow

Traditional spiritual

There's a star in the east on Christ-mas morn,
Rise up shep-herd and fol-low, It'-ll lead to the place where the
Sav-ior's born, Rise up shep-herd and fol-low.
Leave your sheep and leave your lambs, Rise up shep-herd and
fol-low, Leave your ewes and leave your rams,
Rise up shep-herd and fol-low. Fol - low,
Fol - low, Rise up shep-herd and fol-low,
Fol-low the star of Beth-le-hem, Rise up shep-herd and fol-low.

Classroom Activities For Highlighting Rhythmic Patterns

After the initial introduction of rhythmic notation, children need to experience the use of rhythm in music from a variety of perspectives in order to gain practice in and to reinforce their growing knowledge of how individual note values are combined to make rhythmic patterns in music. Here are a number of classroom activities suitable for this purpose.

Activity 1: The children use movement to "write" a rhythmic phrase from a familiar song or rhyme. (Grades 1–3).

The students are divided into groups of five or six, and each group is invited to use their bodies to form the rhythm of a phrase from a familiar song or rhyme. For example, one student might stand by herself to represent a *"tah,"* two children might link their arms together to form a *"ti-ti,"* and one student might pretend to be asleep to represent a rest.

Activity 2: The children use movement to illustrate changes in rhythmic values. (Grades 2–3)

For this activity, the teacher might improvise a melody on the recorder or piano, alternating between groups of quarter notes and groups of eighth notes. Children are instructed to walk around the room to the beat when they hear quarter notes being played, and to stop and clap on the beat when they hear eighth notes.

Activity 3: The children play the Mystery Rhythm game: "Which song starts like this?" (Grades 1–6)

This time, students are presented with the rhythmic notation of the first phrase of a familiar song and asked to identify which one of their class songs begins with this rhythm. Experience indicates that children remember the first phrase of a song most readily, so this is an excellent place to begin notational practice with rhythm.

Activity 4: The children change the rhythm of the first phrase from one familiar song to turn it into the first phrase of a different familiar song. (Grades 1–6).

Students take a rhythmic phrase from Activity 3 and change it so as to make the starting phrase of a different familiar song.

Activity 5: The children write part or all of the rhythm of a familiar rhyme or song using concrete materials. (Grades 1–6).

In this activity students are asked to write the rhythm of a familiar song using age-appropriate materials (popsicle sticks, markers and poster board, pencil and

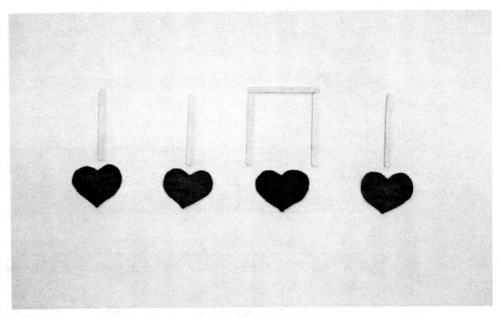

paper, music notation software, etc.). Younger children using popsicle sticks should also be given felt ❤s above which to write their rhythms so that there is a continual association between the beat and the different rhythmic values.

Activity 6: The children read rhythms from flash cards either by chanting rhythmic syllables or by playing the rhythms on a non-pitched percussion instrument. (Grades 1–6)

Here students are asked to read rhythms that are written on large flash cards. Teachers should ask the children to keep a steady beat either on their knees or on another body part while they read the phrases, in order to keep the rhythms as even as possible. The flash cards should be read consecutively without missing a beat between cards. In order for this activity to be as musical as possible, the rhythms on the flash cards should be chosen from one of the children's favourite songs, although the cards should not be presented in any particular order. At the end of the reading activity, the children can be invited to place the flash cards in the correct rhythmic order for the song.

Activity 7: Writing part or all of the rhythm of a familiar song or rhyme using mini flash cards. (Grades 1–6)

In this variant of Activity 6, students are invited to "write" the rhythm of a song or rhyme using individual mini flash cards. Each child is given a package containing small flash cards with different rhythmic patterns written on them. The children sort through their cards to find the ones that can be put together to make the rhythm for a familiar song or rhyme. Since a number of songs will use several of the same rhythmic patterns, children can put together a variety of songs from any one group of mini-cards. The photograph below shows the rhyme *Criss Cross* (p. 218) being written with **mini flash cards**:

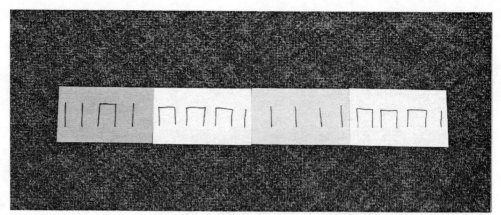

Assembling flash cards to notate the rhythm of a rhyme

Activity 8: The children chant rhythmic syllables while echo-clapping or echo-playing. (Grades 1–6)

The children chant the appropriate rhythmic syllables while clapping back or playing back on a non-pitched percussion instrument a rhythmic pattern that has been tapped to them by the teacher. Again, rhythmic patterns from familiar songs can be used in this activity to help reinforce children's visual recognition of this notation.

Activity 9: The children check the teacher's reading of a rhythm notated on the board to determine where he or she has made a mistake. (Grades 1–6)

The children read the rhythm of a familiar song or rhyme written on the board silently while the teacher reads the rhythm out loud, deliberately making a few mistakes. Then, the children are asked to identify where the teacher made mistakes in the rhythm.

Activity 10: The children play a more advanced version of Mystery Rhythm: "Which song is this?" (Grades 1–6)

In this variant of Activity 3, the children are invited to read the complete rhythmic notation of a familiar song or rhyme written on the board and then asked to name the song. When an answer is given, all the children should be asked to sing the song while the teacher claps the rhythm on the board to see if the suggested song matches the actual rhythm on the board. If the children discover there is no match, a different song should be tried, and so on.

Activity 11: The children listen to recorded music and identify familiar rhythmic patterns used in the music. (Grades 2–6)

The children are asked to listen for a particular rhythmic pattern used by the composer either in the melody or in an *ostinato* bass line. Examples of appropriate music for this kind of experience can be found in Chapter 7.

Activity 12: The children play the Rhythm Erase game. (Grades 2–6)

The teacher writes the rhythm of a familiar song or a new rhythm on the board, one phrase per line. The children read this rhythm out loud, and then are asked to memorize the rhythm as the teacher or a student erases one line at a time after each subsequent reading. When the entire rhythm has been erased, individual children are asked to come to the board and write one phrase of the rhythm back on to the board until the rhythm has been completely re-written. This is a great game for helping children improve their musical memory.

Activity 13: The children sight-read the rhythm of a new song using rhythmic syllables. (Grades 2–6)

In this activity, children build on their previous notational experiences with familiar songs and apply their knowledge to reading the rhythm of a brand new song. Success in this exciting moment for children leads to the beginnings of real music literacy with rhythm.

Activity 14: The children sight-read the rhythm of a new song using non-pitched percussion instruments. (Grades 2–6)

In this variant of Activity 10, children gain notational practice with rhythm while benefiting from the motivational aspect of playing a classroom instrument. Additional activities in which children use improvisation and composition to practise their knowledge of rhythmic patterning can be found in Chapter 6.

Questions for Discussion and Practice

1. Why do young children think of rhythm as "the way the words sound"?
2. What are the four important concepts of the structural property of rhythm? How does knowledge of one concept lead to building knowledge of the next?
3. Identify age-appropriate songs that could be used with the beat vs. rhythm activities listed in this chapter during Kindergarten–Grade 1.
4. Discuss the content and teaching process of the "introductory lesson" for teaching new rhythmic values to elementary school children. Find two additional "introductory" songs for each of the individual rhythmic values listed in this chapter using music found in other parts of this textbook.
5. Make a list of five selections of recorded music that are appropriate for children in Grades 3–6 to listen to and to identify rhythmic patterns embedded within the music.

References

Demorest, S., and Serlin, R. (1997). The integration of pitch and rhythm in musical judgement: Testing age-related trends in novice listeners. *Journal for Research in Music Education, 45(1)*, 67–79.

Montgomery, A.P. (1998a). Music literacy: Links for advocacy. In B. Roberts (Ed.), *Communication in the Arts*. Sydney, NS: University of Cape Breton Press.

Montgomery, A.P. (1998b). Music for a literate society. Unpublished paper presented at the 23rd World Conference of the International Society for Music Education. Pretoria, South Africa.

Moore, R., Brotons, M., Fyk, J., and Castillo, A. (1997). Effects of culture, age, gender, and repeated trials on rote song learning skills of children 6–9 years old from England, Panama, Poland, and the United States. *Bulletin of the British Council of Research in Music Education, 133*, 83–8.

Veenker, R. (1999). *Children's short term memory processing of melody, rhythm, and text reproduction of song*. Unpublished doctoral dissertation, University of Minnesota.

CHAPTER 12

Pitch

SYNOPSIS

Chapter 12 discusses daily classroom activities appropriate for the elementary music classroom that use experiences such as singing, playing instruments, and moving to highlight the musical concepts from Pitch. Activities are presented in a sound-before-symbol progression within a developmentally appropriate simple-to-complex teaching order.

Introduction

Melody is made up of an organized sequence of high and low pitches.

The term **pitch** refers to *the highness or lowness of a note*; pitch is determined by the frequency of the sound (that is, the number of vibrations per second). High and low pitches strung together in an organized sequence make a **melody**—what children sometimes refer to as *the way the tune goes*.

According to Sloboda (1985), "Melody is the aspect of music which is nearest the surface and that which, for most listeners, most immediately characterizes the music" (p. 52). This makes sense, as children's love of melody starts early, with their initial attempts to string together pitches as they babble and make up little melodies to entertain themselves at their play.

Although pitch and pitch patterns are at the centre of what children think of as music, becoming sensitive to the way the concept of pitch is utilized in music is not an easy process. Students in the elementary grades need a variety of classroom activities—such as singing, moving, and listening—to help them come to a deeper understanding of the significance of pitch in music.

Beginning activities with pitch involve **pitch discrimination**: *the ability to hear whether two notes are the same pitch or whether one is higher or lower than* the other (Kindergarten–Grade 1). Subsequent activities involve recognition of **melodic contour**: *the upward and downward linear shape that high and low pitches make when strung together in a melody* (Kindergarten–Grade 1). **Pitch production**—*the ability to make higher and lower pitches with the voice*—is also important during this initial stage of pitch development, and is discussed in detail in Chapter 4.

Following numerous aural, kinesthetic, and oral classroom experiences with the first two concepts, children are taught to associate the tonic sol-fa names (*doh, re, mi, fa, soh, lah, ti*—see p. 184) of *individual pitches* with the sounds of the high and low notes they have been singing and listening to in melodies (Grades 1–5). Soon after, children learn where these individual pitches sit on a **staff** (*the lines and spaces upon which musical notation is written*). Such knowledge sets the stage for the important process of learning how to read simple melodies with the voice (Grades 1–3).

High vs. low, melodic contour, pitch names and locations on the treble staff, scales, accidentals, and key signatures are all important concepts of pitch.

Students in Grades 4–6 continue their practice with reading melodic notation using tonic sol-fa, adding experience with the **treble clef** (*a symbol placed at the beginning of the staff to identify the second line of the staff as G*) and **absolute pitch names** (*the musical alphabet, A–B–C–D–E–F–G, that is used to label the lines and spaces on the staff*) that they use to read music when playing recorders or pitched percussion instruments. Older elementary school students learn about more complex aspects of pitch, such as **scales** (*a group of pitches arranged in ascending and/or descending order*) as well as some of the signs that tell musicians which pitches to play, including **accidentals** (*sharps, flats or naturals placed in front of a note to alter its pitch by a half step: a sharp raises a note, a flat lowers a note, and a natural cancels a flat or a sharp*) and **key signatures** (*a group of sharps or flats following the clef at the beginning of the staff to indicate which notes are to be altered throughout the music*). Knowledge of such concepts of pitch lay the groundwork for eventually learning about **harmony** (*the simultaneous sounding of two or more pitches*), which is discussed in detail in Chapter 15.

Developing sensitivity to pitch begins with rote-singing of age-appropriate children's songs.

As with the development of beat and rhythm, classroom activities with pitch follow a sound-before-symbol teaching progression with initial experiences in Kindergarten–Grade 1 being at the aural, kinesthetic, and oral stage of the learning process. Beginning activities involve the rote singing of age-appropriate children's songs (see Chapter 4) that provide the aural vocabulary necessary to begin building the children's knowledge about the first concepts of pitch. Concepts are taught in an easy-to-complex sequence leading from initial "sound" experiences to the subsequent labeling and symbolic association of these pitches with the appropriate melodic notation.

The Pitch Concept of High vs. Low

Understanding the *high vs. low* concept of pitch means being able to hear the pitch difference between two notes—that is, whether one note is higher or lower than another. This means that melodies containing more than *two* different pitches (for example, *Twinkle Twinkle Little Star*, which has six pitches) are inappropriate for use in teaching this concept. Since very little children's music falls into the two-note category, teachers in the elementary grades turn to stories, rhymes, and instruments to help illustrate the concept of high and low for students.

Initial experiences begin with the comparison of high and low pitches that are more than an **octave** apart, and gradually introduce pitches that are closer and closer together, thus progressively improving the child's pitch discrimination abilities.

Intervals for comparing high vs. low pitches

Intervals larger than an octave for initial high-low experiences

Moderate size intervals for second stage of high-low experiences

Small intervals (minor 3rd) for final high-low development

An **interval** is *the distance between two notes*; intervals can be measured in terms of **whole** and **half steps**. When students are able to successfully hear the difference between two pitches that are separated by the interval of a **minor 3rd** (*the interval distance between two notes that have one letter name between them and that are a step and a half apart*—for example, A to C, or E to G, but not A to B sharp or F flat to G) they are ready to move on to learning the tonic sol-fa names of individual pitches.

Classroom activities appropriate for helping children develop their ability to discriminate between high and low are included below:

Activity 1: The teacher reads a story that involves the use of a high and low speaking voice. (Kindergarten–Grade 1)

A story such as *Goldilocks and the Three Bears* is excellent for this activity. When reading the story for the children, the teacher uses a very high speaking voice for Baby Bear's lines and a very low speaking voice for Papa Bear's lines. Children enjoy joining in with this familiar story when it comes time to use the contrasting voices.

Activity 2: The children chant familiar rhymes using Baby Bear's high speaking voice or Papa Bear's low speaking voice. (Kindergarten–Grade 1)

Invite children to use their *high* Baby Bear speaking voices or their *low* Papa Bear speaking voices when chanting a favourite rhyme (for example, *Hicketty Picketty*, p. 72) during a music lesson. Baby Bear and Papa Bear puppets could be used to motivate children to move their voices very high or very low. This activity should be done with a variety of selections from the children's rhyme repertoire in the music classroom.

Activity 3: The children use different movements to show the difference between high notes and low notes played by the teacher on an instrument. (Kindergarten–Grade 1)

Here, the children move their skills from distinguishing between and producing high and low speaking voices to distinguishing between single high and low pitches played on instruments. The teacher can use a variety of instruments for this activity, including different sizes of handbells, different sizes of bars on a xylophone, or high and low notes on the recorder. Start with two notes that are a great distance apart and, in repetitions of this activity, move the children's discrimination to pitches that are closer and closer together. Instruct the children to use different movements to illustrate the high and low pitches. For example, students might pretend to be at the ocean, standing on tiptoe to reach towards the stars in the sky when they hear a high note, and stooping down to reach towards a starfish in the sand when they hear a low note. Encourage the children to make the distance between the two movements smaller as the two pitches played by the teacher grow closer together.

Activity 4: The children place "higher" or "lower" signs on barred instruments such as xylophones to identify where the higher notes are located on an instrument. (Kindergarten–Grade 1)

Here the children learn the visual concept that bigger or longer on an instrument usually means lower pitches, and shorter or smaller usually means higher pitches. This activity may be done in conjunction with Activity 3 using either barred instruments or different sizes of hand drums, triangles, or handbells.

Activity 5: The children echo-sing or echo-play high and low pitches that are a small interval (for example, a minor 3rd) apart. (Grades 1–2)

In this activity, the teacher sings high and low pitches using a neutral syllable such as "loo" and the children echo these pitches back. The children can respond by singing "loo," by singing the words "high" or "low," or by playing the appropriate high and low notes on a prepared soprano xylophone (with all the bars removed except for two notes a minor 3rd apart).

Activity 6: The children notate high and low pitches that are a small interval (for example, a minor 3rd) apart using iconic symbols. (Grades 1–2)

The children sit on the floor and use concrete manipulatables—for example, felt cut-outs of stars (★) to designate the high and low pitches, and a black shoelace about 40 cm long as the line dividing high from low. The children notate the high and low pitches as they hear them played on the recorder. Encourage students to place the stars just above or just below the shoelace line since the notes are only a minor 3rd apart. This activity will prepare children for eventually writing pitches close together on a musical staff.

Activity 7: The children read high and low pitches that are written on the board using iconic ★ notation. (Grades 1–2)

Here, the children read melodic patterns of high and low notes that are written on the board, again using iconic ★s and a black line. Children sight-sing the pitches, using two pitches a minor 3rd apart that have been given to them by the teacher (either with his or her voice or played on a recorder). When the children see a star representing a high pitch, they sing "high" on the high note; when they see a low star, they sing "low" on the low note. This activity is a wonderful preparation for reading staff notation as the children experience the concept of left to right reading with each symbol representing a pitch.

Activity 8: The children write the high and low pitch patterns of songs that contain only two pitches that are a minor 3rd apart using iconic notation. (Grades 1–2)

In this activity, the children learn by rote to sing a variety of two-pitch minor 3rd songs, such as *Star Light Star Bright*.

Star Light, Star Bright

Traditional chant

After they sing the song, the children attempt to write down the patterns of high and low pitches in each phrase of the song using felt ★s for the notes and a black shoelace for the line dividing high from low.

Activity 9: The children compose high-low two-note (minor 3rd) songs using iconic symbols. (Grades 1–2)

Here, children compose their own four- to eight-beat high-low melodies using iconic felt ★s to represent the high and low pitches and a black shoelace for the line dividing high from low. The children can also add text to turn the melodies into "real" songs, and they will delight in performing their compositions for the rest of the class. The songs can be transferred to paper, using crayons, and placed in the students' music portfolios for later assessment purposes.

The Pitch Concept of Melodic Contour

Once children understand that high and low pitches may be combined into a sequence to create melodies or short songs as described in the earlier activities, they are ready to discover that melodies can be made up of a variety of high and low pitches that move upwards, downwards, or are repeated. Melodic contour is the linear shape that could be "drawn" by tracing the movement of these high and low notes with a pencil on paper.

For example, imagine drawing a line to connect the notes in the song *All around the Buttercup,* as in a dot-to-dot game. The line you draw represents a visual picture of the *melodic contour* of the song.

All around the Buttercup

Traditional singing game

All a-round the but-ter cup, One two three,

If you want a spec-ial friend, Just choose me.

Melodic Contour of All around the Buttercup

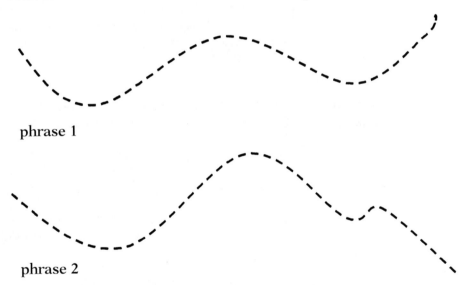

phrase 1

phrase 2

Children in the early grades experience melodic contour through a variety of listening, performing, and movement activities. Here are some examples.

···

Activity 1: The children "draw" the melodic contour of a melody using movement. (Grades 1–2)

While the children sing a short familiar song (for example, *Johnny Works with One Hammer*, p. 193) or listen to a short recorder piece played by teacher, they use their hands to "draw" the melodic contour in the air.

Activity 2: The children "draw" the melodic contour of a melody using a flash-light on the wall. (Grades 1–2)

As in Activity 1, the students sing a short familiar song or listen to a short melody played on the recorder by the teacher and use flashlights to "draw" the melodic contour of the melody on the wall.

Activity 3: The children use movement to show a change of direction in the melodic contour. (Grades 1–2)

While the teacher sings a song or plays a melody on the recorder or the xylophone, the children walk around the room to the beat. When the melody moves upward, they walk forward; when it moves downward, they walk backward; when it stays on a repeated note, they walk in place.

Activity 4: The children "draw" the melodic contour of the melody using movement and a rope (Grades 1–2)

Divide the children into groups of eight to ten, and give each group a rope about four metres long. The children sing a short familiar song or listen to a short melody played on the recorder by the teacher. During the music, the groups arrange themselves into a line, bending or standing tall in order to hold the rope in the shape of the melodic contour of the melody.

Activity 5: The children listen to two short melodies and determine whether the melodic contours are the same or different. (Grades 1–2)

Here, the children can use thumbs-up or thumbs-down to show whether they think the melodic contours of two melodies played by the teacher on a recorder are the same or different.

Activity 6: The children draw the melodic contour of a melody on paper. (Grades 1–2)

As in the previous activities, the children draw the melodic contour of a melody they either sing or listen to. Here they use poster paper and markers, crayons, paint, or any other art medium. Because the drawn contours are more "permanent", the children should have the opportunity to reflect on the nature of the contours (for example, Are they jagged or smooth? Mostly up or mostly down?).

Activity 7: The children trace the melodic contour of a notated melody. (Grades 1–2)

This activity gives the children an opportunity to examine the melodic contour of familiar melodies they have sung in relation to the printed notation. Using any favourite class song—for example *Les petites marionettes*—instruct the children to place tracing paper on top of the notation, and trace the melodic contour of the melody by connecting the note heads in a dot-to-dot fashion. This is an excellent reading-readiness activity to prepare children for reading the upward and downward motion of the melody of songs using standard notation.

Les petites marionettes

Traditional French children's song
English text by A. Montgomery

Ain - si font, font, font! Les pe - ti - tes ma - rio -
Watch them turn, turn, turn! All the lit - tle mar - ion -

net - tes, Ain - si font, font, font! Trois p'tits tours et puis s'en vont.
ettes, — Watch them turn, turn, turn! Three small turns and off they go.

....

Activity 8: The children compose a melodic contour. (Grades 1–3)

In this activity, the children work in pairs. One child draws a melodic contour on poster paper using markers. The second child uses the soprano xylophone to perform her or his version of the first child's composition. The roles are reversed as the activity continues. A video camera could be used to record the results of this activity, thereby providing another assessment sample for the students' music portfolios.

Classroom Activities for Introducing the Labels and Symbols for Individual High and Low Pitches

Children's practice with individual pitches grows out of their initial experiences with high and low pitches and melodic contour in music.

Children in Grades 1–2 who reach this stage in the pitch learning process are ready to begin associating their aural, kinesthetic, and oral knowledge of *high-low pitches* and *melodic contour* with the *labels and symbolic notation for specific pitches*. As discussed in Chapter 9, many provincial curriculum guides recommend that this symbolic association begin with *tonic sol-fa names* in Grade 1, in order to promote the intervalic sight-vocabulary needed for vocal sight-reading. *Absolute pitch names* are added in late Grade 3 or early Grade 4 to coincide with the beginnings of instrumental note reading with the recorder (see pp. 186–87).

The two initial pitches introduced to Grade 1 children using tonic sol-fa are *soh* and *mi*. The aural sound and visual placement of this minor 3rd interval will have been previously established with the children during the high-low pitch activities discussed earlier in this chapter. Thus, the introduction of the labels and visual placement of *soh–mi* pitches on the staff can progress quite quickly for children if the proper preparatory activities have been experienced in the classroom. When moving on to writing melodies using *soh–mi* patterns, round wooden note heads (•), in combination with a black shoelace line, may now be substituted for the iconic felt ★s. Such activities will make the transition to writing pitches on the staff a comfortable process.

The introduction of the traditional five-line staff should come shortly after the children have been introduced to the *soh–mi* labels. Some teachers like to use a two- or three-line staff as a transition activity, but most children find the five-line staff quite simple to understand. Teachers should use a body part—such as the hand turned with the palm facing the child's chest—as a comfortable analogy for talking about the five lines and four spaces on the staff. Children find it quite enjoyable to play little pointing games to learn that the bottom line of the staff is line 1 (the pinky finger), the top line is line 5 (the thumb), the bottom space is space 1 (the space between the pinky and ring fingers), and so forth.

line 5 ⸻
line 1 ⸻

Students should learn that every line or space may have a note or a rest on it and that the higher a note is on the staff, the higher it sounds. Children need to experience such activities on an actual staff as well, and may be given tools such as **individual staff boards** (*poster boards with large staffs laminated on top*) on which to practise moving their wooden note heads from line to line.

When ready, children may transfer their visual knowledge learned by manipulating wooden note heads with a shoelace line to manipulating wooden note heads on the lines and spaces of the staff. Teachers need to show children that "when *soh* is on a space, *mi* is on the space below" and "when *soh* is on a line, *mi* is on the line below."

Soh-mi space-to-space   *Soh-mi* line-to-line

soh   mi   soh   mi

Students will need to practise writing *soh–mi* songs such as *Star Light, Star Bright* (see p. 238) starting on different lines or spaces so that they learn that songs may be written anywhere on the staff. *Songs should be sung as close as possible to the actual pitch of the written starting note on the staff* in order for children to gain oral and aural experience with the basic highness and lowness of the various lines and spaces.

Elementary school children use tonic-solfa to help them initially write melodies of familiar songs on the musical staff.

If possible, children should indicate the rhythmic value of the *soh–mi* pitches when writing melodies on the staff. Children will need practice at putting the **stem** of the note (for example, the popsicle stick) in the correct place of the staff: *to the right of the note pointing up if the note is below the third line; to the left of the note pointing down if the note is on the third line or above.* This implies that it is desirable for Grade 1 students to have concrete practice with rhythmic syllables such as *tah* and *ti-ti* before they are introduced to *soh–mi* pitches. As a rule of thumb for any grade level, most students find rhythmic symbols much easier to learn than melodic symbols. Thus, new rhythmic concepts should be taught earlier in the school year so as to allow more time for the aural, kinesthetic, and oral stage of the melodic development process.

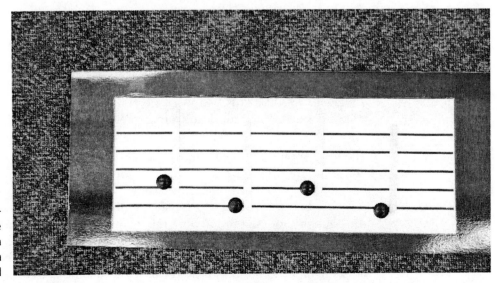

Using wooden note-heads and popsicle sticks to create a melody on a staff-board

Activities used to introduce children to the labels and symbols of pitches beyond *soh* and *mi* (*lah* in Grade 1; *doh* and *re* in Grade 2; *soh* and *lah* below *doh* in Grade 3; high *doh* in Grade 4; *fa* and *ti* in Grade 5; and *fi* and *si* in Grade 6) should also be carefully thought out. Teachers should consider organizing instruction through the following recommended steps during any such "introduction" lessons for Grades 1 to 6.

- Step 1: Ask the children to sing a familiar song.

- Step 2: Ask the children to sing the song again while keeping the steady beat and clapping the rhythm.

- Step 3: Invite the children to "draw" the melodic contour of the song in the air while singing.

- Step 4: Invite the children to notate either part or all of the melody of the song using wooden note heads, popsicle sticks, and staff boards or other concrete manipulatables. Instruct them to try to determine how the new pitch differs from the other more familiar pitches in the song. A question such has, "Is the new note higher or lower than ____?" may help to lead the children towards determining the parameters of the new pitch in relation to the other notes in the melody.

- Step 5: Tell the children the tonic sol-fa label for the new pitch, show the hand sign that is used to kinesthetically feel the pitch (see Chapter 9), and indicate where the note goes on the staff in relation to the rest of the song.

- Step 6: Ask the children to attempt to read the melodic notation of the whole song, including the new note, using appropriate tonic sol-fa names and/or hand signs.

- Step 7: End this experience by singing the complete song with the students again, this time using text.

Music selected for these "introductory" lessons can be critical to the student's ability to come to a personal understanding of how a particular pitch is presented in notation. Carefully selected songs will promote *student discovery* of the new pitch, thus making a more teacher-directed approach during the lesson unnecessary. Also, by making their own discovery, the children will take greater ownership in the learning process.

As a result, teachers should consider the following criteria carefully when selecting songs to introduce the label and symbol of a new pitch when introducing new pitches to children:

1. *The song should be a* **review song** (*a song that has been taught to the children in a previous lesson*). This will help the children build their new symbolic knowledge upon previous aural and kinesthetic experience with the melody of that song.

2. The song should not contain any pitches the child has not yet experienced symbolically other than the pitch being highlighted. For example, the song used to introduce the notation of *doh* in Grade 2 should logically contain the pitch *doh* plus any combination of previously taught pitches (such as *soh*, *mi*, or *lah*). The song should not contain other symbolically unknown pitches (such as *re* or *fa*). This kind of careful pedagogical planning allows students to focus on determining the parameters of only one new pitch at a time, and thereby promotes the building of a thorough knowledge base of melodic patterning.

3. The new pitch to be introduced should occur only a few times in the music, and should be approached from another pitch in a manner that makes it easier to hear the new note. Ideal placement of the new pitch in the music provides opportunity for children to draw clearer comparisons with their previously learned symbolic knowledge of other pitches when determining whether the new pitch is higher or lower than the other pitches in the song. The following table provides advice in this direction:

Table 12.1

Ideal Pitches for Introducing New Notes to Students

New Note	Ideal Pitch to Approach the Note
lah	*soh:* one step below, in a *soh-lah-soh* pattern
doh	*soh-mi:* a perfect 5th and a major 3rd above, in a *soh-mi-doh* pattern
re	*mi:* one step above, in a *mi-re-doh* pattern
low *soh*	*doh:* a perfect 4th above, in a *doh-soh-doh* pattern
low *lah*	*soh:* one step below, in a *soh-lah-soh* pattern
high *doh*	*soh:* a perfect 4th below, in a *soh-doh* pattern
fa	*soh:* a step above, or *mi:* a half step below, in a *soh-fa-mi-re-doh* or a *mi-fa-so* pattern
ti	*lah:* a step below, in a *lah-ti-doh* pattern

Excellent examples of songs that meet these criteria for introducing new pitches include:

Star Light, Star Bright—*soh–mi* (Grade 1), see p. 238

Brown Bear, Brown Bear—*lah* (Grade 1)

Pease Porridge Hot—*doh* (Grade 2), see p. 222

Bow Wow Wow—*re* (Grade 2), see p. 157

En roulant ma boule—*soh* and *lah* below *doh* (Grade 3)

Jingle at the Windows—high *doh* (Grade 4), see p. 73

J' entend le Moulin—*fa* (Grade 5)

D' où viens-tu, bergère—*ti* (Grade 5), see p. 249

Brown Bear, Brown Bear

Traditional fill-in-the-blank song

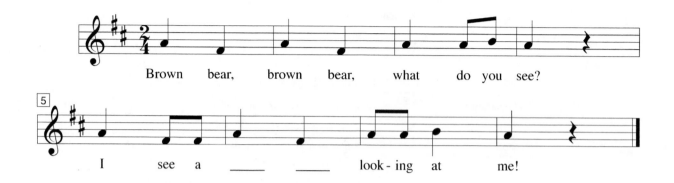

En roulant ma boule

Traditional French Canadian folk song

J'entends le moulin

Traditional French Canadian folk song
English text by Edith Fowke

D'où viens-tu, bergère

Traditional French Canadian carol
English text by Edith Fowke

D'où viens-tu, ber-gè-re, d'où viens-tu?
Whence O shep-herd maid-en, whence come you?

D'où viens-tu, ber-gè-re, d'où viens tu?
Whence O shep-herd maid-en, whence come you?

Je viens de l'é-ta-ble, de m'y pro-me-ner,
I come from the sta-ble, where this ver-y night,

J'ai vu un mi-ra-cle, ce soir ar-ri-vé.
My eyes have been daz-zled, by a won'-drous sight.

After initial introduction of tonic sol-fa names, children need to experience the use of pitch in music from a variety of perspectives in order to gain practice and to reinforce their growing knowledge of how individual pitches are combined together to make melodic patterns in music. Here are a number of activities that are suitable for this purpose.

Activity 1: The children echo-sing using tonic sol-fa names and hand signs. (Grades 1–5)

The teacher sings a short melodic pattern using tonic sol-fa names and hand signs, and the children echo it back the same way. This is a wonderful warm-up activity for a lesson that involves teaching a new song. Use some of the melodic patterns from the song in the echo-singing warm up.

Activity 2: The children echo-play melodic patterns on xylophones that have been sung to the children by the teacher using tonic sol-fa names. (Grades 2–5)

Here the teacher sings a short melodic pattern using tonic solf-fa names, and the children are asked to play it back on soprano xylophones. This is more difficult than Activity 1, since children have to translate a *soh–mi–re–doh* pattern, for example, to the correct bars to be played on the xylophone.

Activity 3: The children echo-sing (using tonic sol-fa names and hand signs) short melodic patterns that the teacher has either sung (using a neutral syllable such as "loo") or played on a recorder. (Grades 2–5)

This activity is similar to Activity 1, but here the teacher does not use tonic sol-fa syllables. The children have to listen to a short melodic pattern the teacher either sings on a neutral syllable (such as "loo") or plays on a recorder. The children listen to these sounds and attempt to translate them into the appropriate tonic sol-fa names to use in echo-singing the pattern back to the teacher. This process is similar to a later activity involving melodies of songs sung on text.

Activity 4: The children play the Mystery Melody game: "Which song starts like this?" (Grades 1–6)

Elementary students are presented with the melodic notation of the first phrase of a familiar song and asked to identify which one of their class songs begins with this melodic sequence. Experience indicates that children remember the first phrase of a song most readily, so this game is an excellent way to begin notation practice with pitch.

Activity 5: The children change the pitches of the opening phrase of one familiar song to turn it into the opening phrase of a different familiar song. (Grades 1–6).

In this activity, students take a melodic phrase from Activity 4 and change the pitches so as to write the opening phrase of a different familiar song.

Activity 6: The children use movement to "write" a melodic phrase from a familiar song or rhyme. (Grades 1–3).

Divide the students into groups of five or six, and invite each group to use their bodies to form the pitches of a melodic phrase from a familiar song by standing on the appropriate lines or spaces of a large staff on the floor. (For this activity, teachers could use huge sheets of poster paper or a large bed sheet or tarp with lines painted on.)

Activity 7: The children write part or all of the melody of a familiar song using concrete materials. (Grades 1–6)

Students are asked to write the melody of a familiar song using age-appropriate materials: wooden note heads, popsicle sticks, and staff boards; markers and poster board; pencils and paper, or music notation software.

Activity 8: The children play the Mystery Melody game: "Which song is this?" (Grades 1–6)

In this variant of Activity 4, the children are invited to read the complete melodic notation of a familiar song off the board and determine the name of the song. When an answer is given, all the children should be asked to quietly sing the song while the teacher sings the melody written on the board, using a neutral syllable such as "loo," to see if the the two melodies match. If the children "discover" there is no match, they can try a different song, and so on.

Activity 9: The children echo-sing melodic patterns (using tonic sol-fa) that the teacher has "sung silently," to the students using only hand signs.

This activity is a more difficult variant of Activities 1 and 2. Here the children have to hear the melodic pattern in tonic sol-fa in their heads as the teacher gives the pattern to them using only silent hand signs.

Activity 10: The children read melodic patterns from flash cards either by singing tonic sol-fa syllables (Grades 1–5), or by playing the notes on a pitched percussion instrument such as a xylophone (Grades 1–6) or on a recorder (Grades 4–6).

In this activity, students are asked to read melodic patterns that are written on large flash cards. The children should tap a steady beat on their knees or other body parts in order to keep the melodies as rhythmically accurate as possible. The flash cards should be read consecutively without missing a beat between cards. In order for this activity to be as musical as possible, the melodic patterns on the flash cards should be taken from one of the children's favourite songs, although the cards should not be presented in any particular order. At the end of the reading activity, the children may be invited to place the flash cards in the correct order to "write" the melody of the song.

Activity 11: The children write part or all of the melody of a familiar song using mini flash cards. (Grades 1–6).

In this variation of Activity 9, students are invited to "write" the melody of a song using individual **mini flash cards**. Each child is given a package of mini flash cards containing a variety of melodic patterns The children sort through their cards to find the ones that can be put together to make the melody for a familiar song. Since a number of songs will use some of the same melodic patterns, children can put together a variety of songs from any one group of flash cards.

Activity 12: The children check the teacher's reading of melodic notation off the board to determine where he or she has made a mistake. (Grades 1–6)

The children are asked to read along silently while the teacher sings the melody of a familiar song that is written on the board, using tonic sol-fa syllables and making a few deliberate mistakes. Then the children are asked to identify where the mistakes were made by the teacher in the music.

Activity 13: The children identify familiar melodic patterns used in a selection of recorded music. (Grades 2–6)

In this activity, children are asked to listen for a familiar melodic pattern that has been used by the composer, either in the melody or in an *ostinato* bass line. Examples of appropriate music for this kind of experience can be found in Chapter 7.

Activity 14: The children play the Melody Erase game. (Grades 2–6)

Here the teacher writes a melody on the board, one phrase per line. The children read this melody out loud and then are asked to memorize the melody as the teacher or a student erases one phrase at a time after each subsequent reading. When the entire melody has been erased, individual children are asked to come to the board and re-write one phrase from the melody until the whole song has been completely re-written. This is a great game for helping children improve their musical memory.

Activity 15: The children sight-read the melody of a new song using tonic sol-fa syllables. (Grades 2–6).

Here, the children build on their previous notational experiences with familiar songs and apply this knowledge to reading the melody of a brand new song. Success in this exciting moment for children leads to the beginnings of real vocal music literacy.

Additional activities in which children use improvisation and composition to practise their knowledge regarding melodic patterning can be found in Chapter 6.

The Pitch Concepts of Absolute Pitch and the Treble Clef

Absolute pitch names (the musical alphabet: A–B–C–D–E–F–G) in combination with the significance of the *treble clef* are appropriate for children to begin learning at the end of Grade 3 or early Grade 4, just prior to the introduction of the recorder in Grade 4 (see p. 99). By this time, the children will already have some experience with manipulating tonic sol-fa notes around on the staff, and they will find the opportunity to add the traditional labels for the lines and spaces quite exciting.

Since elementary school children's voices and classroom instruments sound—and are written—in the treble clef, instruction with absolute pitch names begins here. *Note names for the various lines and spaces should be introduced gradually as needed, rather than all at once.* It makes sense to start by labelling the second line as G. This line serves as a handy reference point for the children since the treble clef curls its tail around this line. Notes above and below G may be added slowly over several lessons, as appropriate.

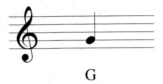

G

Children might begin by reading three-note songs from the staff while playing instruments such as the recorder or the soprano glockenspiel. Three-note songs include *Grandma Grunts* (p. 100), *Closet Key* (p. 266), *Merrily We Roll Along* (p. 100), and *Hot Cross Buns* (p. 100). Students can then expand to reading four-note songs (for example, *Les cloches*, p. 102), five-note songs (for example, *The May Song*, p. 103), and six- or seven-note songs (for example, *Alleluia Canon*, p. 109). This progression can be easily coordinated with teaching new notes on the recorder (see p. 99), thereby increasing the personal significance of learning notation for the students. Any of the simple three- to seven-note songs listed above can be read off the staff, starting on different notes as appropriate to the instrument, thereby giving children experience with all the lines and spaces.

Teachers should provide opportunities for children to practise their sight-reading of absolute pitches with a variety of simple music. As discussed in Chapter 9, music used to practise reading notation will always be easier than other music performed or listened to in the classroom. This is fine as long as the teacher maintains a healthy balance between music taught by *rote* (i.e., taught orally) and music taught by *note* (i.e., taught through notation) in each grade level. In reality, many teachers use some combination of the two, sometimes asking children to practise reading selected parts of a song and teaching the rest of the song by rote. This habit generally results in a positive classroom experience for children, taking care of the continual need to expand children's repertoire while at the same time, nurturing children's development in music literacy.

The Pitch Concepts of Major and Minor Scales

Many elementary music teachers introduce major and minor scales in Grades 4 or 5, once the children have gained symbolic experience with the tonic sol-fa syllables *fa* and *ti*. The process of using familiar class songs to help children come to a better understanding of the importance of musical concepts is helpful here as well. Rather than explaining that scales are made up of eight consecutive pitches, and that major and minor scales have different patterns of whole and half steps (a **major scale** *has half steps between notes 3 and 4 and notes 7 and 8;* a **natural minor scale** *has half steps between notes 2 and 3 and notes 5 and 6),* teachers can use familiar songs that will help students to discover this information for themselves through experiences with real music.

One suggestion for beginning this process of "discovery" is to have students compare a song built on a major scale—such as *Tickle Cove Pond*—with a song built around a minor scale—such as *Jesous Ahatonhia* (*The Huron Carol*). Ask students to write down all the notes used in each song on the staff in ascending order, like a scale, and compare the different whole- and half-step patterns of the two scales.

Tickle Cove Pond

Newfoundland folk song

In cut - tin' and haul - in' in frost and in
snow, We're up a - gainst trou - bles that few peo - ple
know, And ____ on - ly by pa - tience with
cour - age and grit, And eat - in' plain food can we
keep our - selves fit. The hard and the ais - ey we
take as it comes, And when ponds freeze o - ver we
shor - ten our runs, To ____ hur - ry my

haul - ing   the   spring   com - ing   on,   Near   lost   me   my

Chorus

mare ____ on   Tick - le   Cove   Pond.   Oh   lay

hold   Wil - liam   Old - ford,   lay   hold   Wil - liam   White,   Lay

hold   of   the   cord - age   and   pull   with   your   might,

Lay _____ hold   of   the   bow - line   and   pull   all   you

can,   And   give   me   a   lift   for   poor   Kit   on   the   pond!

G.S. Doyle (Ed.). (1966). From Old-Time Songs and Poetry of Newfoundland: Songs of the People from the Days of Our Forefathers (4th ed.). Reprinted with the permission of the Doyle family.

Jesous Ahatonhia
(The Huron Carol)

16th-century French melody
Huron text attributed to Jean de Brébeuf (1593–1649)

Es - ten - nia - lon de tson - ou - e Je - sous a - ha - ton -

hia, On - naou - a - te - ou - a d'o - ki n'on - ouan - da - skoua - en -

tak, En - non - chien skou - a - tri - ho - tat, n'on - ou - an - di - lon -

ra - cha - tha, ____ Je - sous a - ha - ton - hia,

Je - sous, A - ha - ton - hi - a

Further comparisons made within the same song—for example *Sweetly Sings the Donkey* sung first in F major and then in F minor—will help students to come to a clearer understanding of the aural impact of the difference between music that is written in major keys and music that is written in minor keys.

Sweetly Sings the Donkey
(in F major)

Traditional round

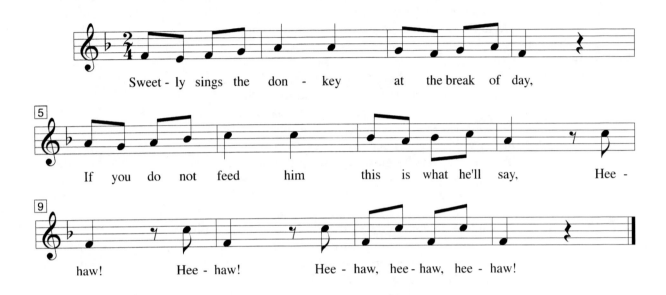

Sweet - ly sings the don - key at the break of day,

If you do not feed him this is what he'll say, Hee -

haw! Hee - haw! Hee - haw, hee - haw, hee - haw!

Sweetly Sings the Donkey
(in F minor)

Traditional round

Sweet - ly sings the don - key at the break of day,

If you do not feed him this is what he'll say, Hee -

haw! Hee - haw! Hee - haw, hee - haw, hee - haw!

Recorded music helps children to better understand the significance of major and minor tonalities.

Students need opportunities to reflect on the expressive properties of music.

Children should also have opportunities to listen to a variety of recorded music in major keys—for example, the Canon in D major by Johann Pachelbel (1653–1706)—and minor keys—for example, "The Old Castle" from *Pictures at an Exhibition* by Modest Mussorgsky (1839–1881)—as well as music that combines both major and minor tonalities within a single composition—for example, the minuet of the Suite in F major, HWV 348, from *Water Music* by George Frideric Handel (1685–1759). Listening examples such as the third movement of Gustav Mahler's Symphony no. 1 (where the composer shifts the traditionally major melody of *Frère Jacques* into a minor key) may also be helpful. Music based on scales that contain a raised seventh degree (*si*) or raised sixth and seventh degrees (*fi, si*) will help Grade 5–6 students come to an understanding of the differences between the **harmonic** and **melodic** forms of the minor scale.

Teachers should be careful not to place judgment value on the differences in the sounds created by major and minor tonalities (for example, suggesting that music written in a major key sounds "happy" or that music written in a minor key sounds "sad"). As with learning about other the expressive properties of music (rhythm, harmony and texture, dynamics, etc.), children should be given time to reflect on their own reactions as to how such manipulations in music make them feel.

Older students in the elementary grades should also be given experience with performing scales, both with their voices and on instruments such as the recorder or the soprano xylophone. A study of **key signatures** (*groups of sharps and flats placed directly to the right of the clef to indicate which notes are to be played sharp or flat throughout an entire piece of music*) and their relationship to scales makes sense here, as it will lead the students towards the ability to make independent decisions regarding appropriate *harmony* to use to accompany their singing (for example, with *borduns* and I–IV–V chords—see Chapters 5 and 15).

Other scales that Grade 6 students may find interesting to study include the **chromatic scale** (*a scale made up of twelve notes, each a half step apart*), **blues scales** (*scales based on blues tunes and songs: these scales resemble a major scale but some degrees of the scale—often the third and the seventh—are lowered*), or the **whole tone scale** (*a scale made up of six notes, each a whole step apart*). Each new scale should be studied in reference to specific music the that the children perform, create, or listen to, rather presented as isolated theoretical knowledge.

Questions for Discussion and Practice

1. What are the main concepts of the structural property of pitch? How does knowledge of one concept lead to building knowledge of the next?

2. What is the difference between "high and low" and "melodic contour"? Briefly describe age-appropriate activities for practicing each of these musical concepts during the early grades.

3. Discuss the content and teaching process of the "introductory lesson" for teaching new tonic sol-fa pitches to elementary school children. Find two appropriate introductory songs for each of the individual pitches listed in Table 2.1 using music found in this textbook.

4. Locate at least five three- to five-note songs appropriate for playing on the recorder that could be used to initially practise note reading on the musical staff with students in Grades 4–5.

5. Make a list of five selections of recorded music appropriate for children in Grades 4–6 to listen to and identify major and minor tonalities in the music.

Reference

Sloboda, J. (1985). *The Musical Mind.* Oxford: Clarendon Press.

CHAPTER 13

Dynamics, Timbre, and Expressive Elements

SYNOPSIS

Chapter 13 discusses daily classroom activities appropriate for the elementary music classroom that use experiences such as singing, playing instruments, and moving to highlight musical concepts from Dynamics, Timbre, and Expressive elements. Activities are presented in a sound-before-symbol progression within a developmentally appropriate simple-to-complex teaching order.

Dynamics

Dynamics—*the loudness or softness of music*—is a structural characteristic frequently used by composers to make music more expressive. Children are receptive to dynamic contrasts and enjoy the mood changes they create in music (Montgomery, 1996).

Beginning elementary school classroom experiences with dynamics should involve **dynamics discrimination**—*the ability to hear the difference between music performed loudly and music performed softly.* This can be followed by activities involving **dynamics production**—*the ability to use dynamics effectively while performing or improvising*—which in turn, lead to composing with dynamics—activities including the use of dynamic markings in the writing of music. Daily classroom activities involving *dynamics discrimination* and/or *dynamics production* take place either at the "sound" stage of the learning process or at the "symbol" stage, with the inclusion of musical symbols such as:

Initial experiences
with dynamics in
the elementary
music classroom
involve dynamic
discrimination.

pp—pianissimo (very soft),

p—piano (soft),

mp—mezzo piano (medium soft),

mf—mezzo forte (medium loud),

f—forte (loud),

ff—fortissimo (very loud).

Composing with dynamics occurs at the symbol stage of the learning process only.

Dynamics Discrimination

Classroom experiences with *dynamics discrimination* involve the activities of listening and moving. First, Kindergarten–Grade 1 children are invited to listen to a variety of familiar and new music pieces either sung or played by the teacher on an instrument such as the recorder or the guitar. For example, the teacher might play *Hey Betty Martin* on the recorder using soft dynamics (for example, *pianissimo* or *piano*), and repeat the performance using loud dynamics (for example, *forte* or *fortissimo*), inviting children to discuss the differences between the two performances. Next, the teacher might sing the song using the dynamic contrasts indicated in the score below, giving the children time to reflect on how the contrasting dynamics support the story of the text. In initial performances, the teacher should vary the dynamics quite distinctly—as between *pianissimo* (*pp*) and *fortissimo* (*ff*)—in order for the children to gauge the differences they hear in the dynamics as accurately as possible.

Hey Betty Martin

Traditional

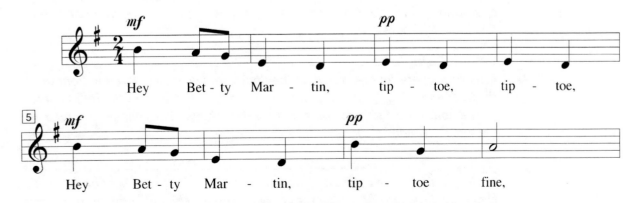

continued

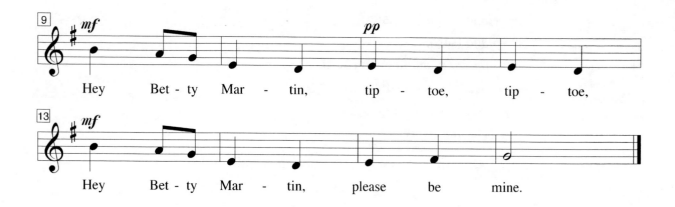

Hey Bet-ty Mar-tin, tip-toe, tip-toe,

Hey Bet-ty Mar-tin, please be mine.

Subsequent listening experiences of this type should involve the children responding to dynamics in recorded music. Start with short selections that have a single dynamic level—for example, *forte* in "Promenade no. 1" from *Pictures at an Exhibition* by Modest Mussorgsky (1839–1881)—and progress to music that contains contrasting dynamics—for example, the *Sonata pian' e forte* by Giovanni Gabrielli (ca 1554–1612). Students might show their discrimination skills with single-dynamic pieces using movement. For example, invite the students to move to the music in their own space as an imaginary "loud" animal (such as an elephant) when they hear music that is *forte* (*f*), and an imaginary "soft" animal (such as a mouse) when they hear music that is *piano* (*p*).

Children could express dynamics discrimination with recorded music that has contrasting dynamics by participating in any number of the following activities.

Activity 1: Invite the children to sit on the floor, holding their hands close together out in front of their bodies when they hear soft dynamics, and spreading their hands wide apart when they hear loud dynamics. Make certain that the children perform this movement horizontally rather than vertically, to ensure that there is no confusion with the pitch concept of high vs. low. (Grades 1–2).

Activity 2: In this variation of Activity 1, children place a large piece of elastic sewn together in a loop around their wrists, and stretch it or slacken it as appropriate to the dynamic changes in the music, using an in-and-out horizontal motion. (Grades 1–2).

Activity 3: Invite children to sit on the floor with two signs placed in front of them: one reading "f" and the other reading "p." Instruct the children to hold up the appropriate sign to correspond with each dynamic change they hear in the music. (Grades 1–2)

Activity 4: Direct the children to walk around the room to the beat of the music, changing direction every time they hear a dynamic change in the music. (Grades 1–2)

Movement is an important tool used by children to express their discrimination of dynamics.

Activity 5: *Ask the children to create two or three different movement patterns to keep the beat while listening to the music; instruct them to perform one with the first dynamic level they hear and the others when the dynamics change. (Grades 2–3)*

Activity 6: *Instruct the children to sit in a circle and pass a ball from one child to the next, changing direction every time they hear a dynamic change in the music. (Grades 2–3)*

Dynamics Production

Elementary school children sometimes confuse the musical concepts of loud and soft with fast and slow.

Dynamics discrimination at the sound stage of the learning process is followed by *dynamics production*. Here, children in Grades 1–6 begin to learn how to use dynamics to vary their performance of familiar music. This is not as easy as it sounds, because children tend to confuse dynamics with tempo, often speeding up the beat when asked to sing *forte* or slowing down when asked to sing *piano*. Teachers can help children learn how to avoid this pitfall by taking time to practise familiar songs with a variety of tempo and dynamic combinations (for example, an *adagio* tempo with *forte* dynamics, or an *allegro* tempo with *piano* dynamics).

Dynamics production may be experienced by children in Grades 1–6 with classroom rhymes, stories, and songs. For example, Grade 1 students might chant a rhyme such as *Who's That Coming Down the Street?* using a variety of dynamic levels to express the text.

Who's That Coming Down the Street?   Traditional

Who's that coming down the street?

Sounds like someone's great big feet.

Who's that coming down the hall?

It's the softest one of all.

Who's that coming through the town?

Sounds like the man with the big trombone!

Grade 4 students could do the same while singing *Les raftsmen*.

Les raftsmen

Traditional French Canadian voyageur song

Là ous-qu'y sont tous les rafts-men? Là ous-qu'y
Here come the rafts - men, tra - la - la, Here come the

sont tous les rafts - men? Dans les chan - quiers i'
rafts - men, tra - la - la, In - side their boats they

sont mon - tés, Bing sur le ring! Bang sur le rang!
pad - dle through, Bing on the bell! Bang on the bell!

Lais - sez pas - ser les rafts - men, Bing sur le ring! Bing, bang!
Hear the rafts - men come right now, Bing on the bell, Bing, bang!

Grade 6 students could use the *Nova Scotia Song*.

Nova Scotia Song
(Farewell to Nova Scotia)

Traditional Maritime folk song

The sun was — set - ting — in the — west, The —

2. I grieve to leave my native land,
   I grieve to leave my comrades all,
   And my aged parents whom I always held so dear,
   And the bonny, bonny lass that I do adore.
   Chorus

3. The drums they do beat and the wars do alarm,
   The captain calls, we must obey,
   So farewell, farewell, to Nova Scotia's charms,
   For it's early in the morning I am far, far away.
   Chorus

This version of the Nova Scotia Song was collected by Helen Creighton.
It is used here with the permission of Nova Scotia Archives and Records Management, Halifax, Nova Scotia.

Students should be given time for careful reflection as they experiment with how to use dynamics effectively in music. Discussion about the power of dynamics for helping express text, establish mood, or create excitement may be included as a direct result of such exploration.

Following experience with producing the various dynamic levels in music, students in Grades 2–3 might be introduced to other dynamic concepts such as:

crescendo: *a gradual increase in dynamics from soft to loud*

decrescendo (or diminuendo): *a gradual decrease in dynamics from loud to soft*

sforzando (sfz), *a sudden strong forte on a note, as directed by the marking "sfz"*

Grade 2 students experimenting with the *crescendo* might play the singing game *Closet Key,* which requires the children to sing *crescendos* and *decrescendos* to help their classmates find a hidden key.

Closet Key

Traditional singing game

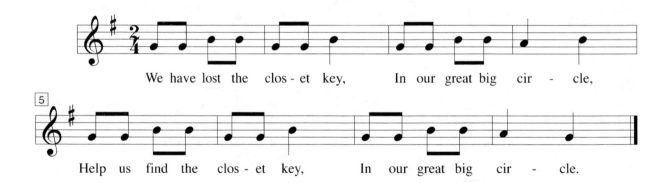

Game: The children sit in a circle, approximately one metre apart, with their hands in their laps. Each child pretends to hold a key in his or her hands. One child temporarily leaves the room, and in his or her absence, the teacher gives a child in the circle a real key to hold. Then the child who was outside is invited back in to walk around the inside of the circle to try to find the hidden key. The children help by repeatedly singing the song, using *crescendos* as the child gets closer to the key and *decrescendos* as the child walks away. Once they key is found, the game begins again with another child leaving the room.

Older children should have opportunities to experiment with adding *crescendos* into a variety of music from their classroom repertoire—for example *The Lumber Camp Song*:

The Lumber Camp Song

Traditional New Brunswick folk song

Come all you jol - ly fel - lows and

lis - ten to my song, It's all a - bout the

shan - ty boys and how they get a - long, We're the

jo - liest bunch of fel - lows that ev - er you could

find, The way we spend our win - ter months is

hurl - ing down the pine.

Recorded music—for example, the "Hungarian March" from *The Damnation of Faust* by Hector Berlioz (1803–1869)—can also be incorporated, giving students in Grades 2–6 access to the excitement created by the use of *crescendos* and *decrescendos* in orchestral music music that is beyond their psychomotor developmental levels. Again, reflection time is important so that the students have ample opportunity to discuss the impact they think *crescendos* and *decrescendos* have on making such music more expressive.

Sforzandos and sudden *fortissimos* can be experienced in a similar manner, first through experimentation with various pieces of music, including songs such as *Kelligrew's Soirée*.

Kelligrew's Soirée

Newfoundland folk song

G.S. Doyle (Ed.). (1966). From Old-Time Songs and Poetry of Newfoundland: Songs of the People from the Days of Our Forefathers *(4th ed.). Reprinted with the permission of the Doyle family.*

Students should also have the opportunity to listen to recorded music that highlights these effects—for example, the sudden *fortissimo* chord in the second movement from the Symphony no. 94 in G major ("Surprise") by Franz Joseph Haydn (1732–1809). All of these experiences provide elementary school students with the understanding of dynamics that is needed in order to make meaningful choices about how to use dynamics when composing their own music.

Timbre

Students learn about timbre through singing, moving, playing instruments, listening, and creating experiences in the classroom.

The term **timbre** refers to *the tone colour* of an instrument or voice: for example, the tuba has a deep, dark timbre while the piccolo has a tinkling, bright sound. Composers use timbre to provide variety and contrast in music, as a melody played on one instrument may sound completely different when played by another instrument.

As with dynamics, elementary school students need *discrimination, production*, and *composing* experiences in order to come to a thorough understanding of different instrumental timbres including:

1. *the four voices*: whispering, shouting, talking, and singing;
2. *body percussion*: using the body as an instrument to make different sounds, such as snapping, clapping, stamping;
3. *non-pitched percussion*: percussion instruments that sound on only one pitch;
4. *pitched percussion* : percussion instruments that sound on multiple pitches;
5. *recorder*: the flute-like wind instruments played by students starting in Grade 4.

Teachers generally use singing, moving, and listening to help children learn to *discriminate* between these timbres; playing instruments is the main experience used during *timbre production* activities.

Other instrumental timbres experienced in elementary school music classes—such as **orchestral instruments** (*instruments from the string, percussion, wind, and brass families that are used to play orchestral music*)—are usually encountered only through *timbre discrimination* activities, as *timbre production* is reserved for band and orchestra performance classes. In some Canadian schools, these instrumental classes are included as early as Grades 5–6, while in the majority of schools they begin in Grades 7–9.

Kindergarten and Grade 1 students begin their timbre exploration with the *four different voices*. Including rhymes, poetry, and stories alongside children's songs during music lessons in these early grades helps children gain hands-on timbre discrimination and production experience with both the singing and the talking voice. This is important as children work steadily towards the goal of singing in tune. Specific activities in this regard can be found in Chapter 4 (pp. 39–41).

The four voices and body percussion are the initial timbres experienced by children in the early elementary grades.

Body percussion also plays an important role in providing early timbre experiences for children in Kindergarten–Grade 2. As discussed in Chapter 5 (p. 67), exploration with body percussion begins with *simultaneous imitation* (the children imitate the teacher's body percussion movements) and continues to a point where the students in Grades 1–3 are able to make choices regarding particular body percussion timbres to provide "colour" when highlighting the text of rhymes, poetry, stories, and songs. *Wee Willie Winkie* can be used with Grade 1 students to highlight the text of a rhyme with body percussion.

Timbre discrimination and production experiences with *non-pitched percussion instruments* follow naturally from body percussion activities, as these instruments may also be used to provide "colour" to help highlight the text of rhymes, poetry, stories, and songs. Prior to such decision making, however, young elementary school students need opportunities to become familiar with the variety of timbres available to them through the use of such instruments. The following series of discrimination and production activities are appropriate for this purpose.

Wee Willie Winkie

Wee Willie Winkie <u>runs</u> through the town,

<u>Upstairs</u> and <u>downstairs,</u> in his nightgown,

<u>Rapping</u> at the window, <u>crying</u> through the lock,

Are the children now in bed because it's <u>eight-o-clock</u>?

Activity: Invite the students to use body percussion to help express the underlined words in the rhyme.

Activity 1: "Where is the sound coming from?" (Kindergarten–Grade 2)

Invite the children to close their eyes and listen for where the sounds of two non-pitched percussion instruments (for example, a triangle and a wood block) are coming from in the classroom. As the teacher walks around the room playing one of the instruments, the children use their hands to point to the place where they hear the sound. When the teacher changes instruments, the children stand up to indicate the change in timbre and continue with their pointing. The game continues with the children alternating between standing and sitting as appropriate to the timbre changes they hear played by the teacher.

Activity 2: Same and different sounds (Kindergarten–Grade 2)

This activity is a variation of Activity 1. Here, the children use movement to show their discrimination of non-pitched percussion timbres. The children close their eyes and switch back and forth between hopping and marching in their own space whenever they hear the teacher switch from playing one instrument (for example, finger cymbals) to another (for example, a hand drum).

Activity 3: Keeping the beat (Grades 1–3)

Elementary school children need the opportunity to become familiar with a wide variety of non-pitched percussion timbres.

In this activity, the children keep the beat on a non-pitched percussion instrument while chanting or singing familiar classroom rhymes or songs. At the beginning, only one beat instrument should be used in any single lesson, in order to give the children adequate opportunity to become familiar with the instrument's name, its proper playing technique, and its unique timbre. Throughout Kindergarten–Grade 2, however, children should have opportunities to keep the beat with a variety of non-pitched instruments from each of the three categories (wood, skins, and metals).

Activity 4: Identify the hidden sound (Grades 1–3)

Here, the students have the opportunity to test their aural knowledge of the timbres of the non-pitched percussion instruments they have experienced during Activities 1–3. Using a rhyme such as *Hicketty Picketty* (p. 72) makes this kind of timbre identification experience as learner-centred as possible for the children.

Activity 5: Classifying sounds (Grades 1–3)

Divide the students into groups of three or four, and give each group a variety of non-pitched percussion instruments. Instruct the children to first play each instrument and then to organize the instruments into groups according to *tone colour* or *timbre*: for example, *ringing timbres, tapping timbres, booming timbres*. Encourage the children to experiment with a variety of ways to play each instrument, since some instruments might be classified in more than one category. (For example, a hand drum played on the skin makes a *booming* sound, but played on the rim it makes a *tapping* sound.)

These five activities provide elementary school students with the necessary timbral foundation to be able to make aesthetic decisions regarding which non-pitched instruments to select when providing "colour" to highlight the text of rhymes, poetry, stories, and songs. Such activities also instill the necessary timbral understanding for students to use when deciding whether rhythmic *ostinati* used to accompany singing (see Chapters 5 and 15) should be played by an instrument that has a *ringing* sound or one that has a *tapping* sound.

In *This Little Light of Mine*, for example, finger cymbals might be selected to highlight the word "shine," and guiro and hand drum chosen as the timbres for the *ostinato* accompaniment.

This Little Light of Mine

Traditional spiritual
Arranged by A. Montgomery

continued

Pitched percussion and recorder timbres are experienced through performance activities.

After initial classroom experiences with non-pitched percussion timbres, Grade 2–6 students experience the timbres of *pitched percussion instruments* by playing harmonic accompaniments such as *borduns*, melodic *ostinati*, and descants on glockenspiels, xylophones, and metallaphones. Information for using these instruments with elementary school students can be found in Chapter 5, and a discussion of their function in supporting harmonic understanding is found in Chapter 15. In addition, students in Grades 4–6 experience recorder timbre by playing melodies, descants, and melodic *ostinati*. Recommendations for teachers in this regard are also located in Chapter 5.

Instruments of the Orchestra

Experiences with the instruments of the orchestra during elementary school music are grouped under two topics. Grade 3–4 students learn about the *four instrument families*—**strings**, **brass**, **woodwinds**, and **percussion**—and why

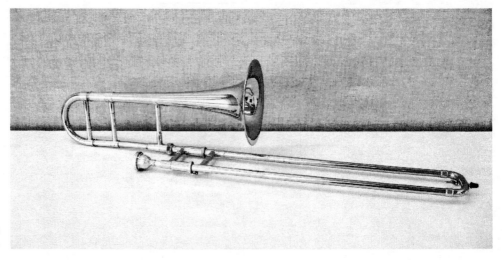

Trombone
(from the brass family)

Clarinet
(from the woodwind family)

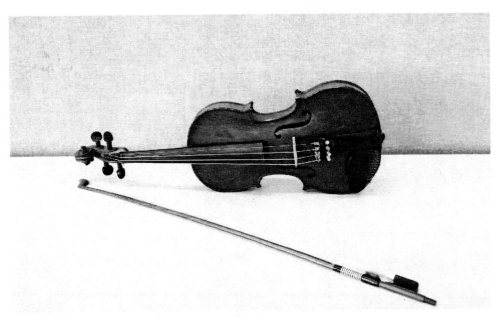

Violin
(from the string family)

Conga drums (from the percussion family)

Live
performances are
the most powerful
way to experience
the timbre of
orchestral
instruments.

individual instruments are grouped together into one of these four families. Grade 5–6 students take this process one step further by focusing their timbre discrimination on individual instruments within each family—for example comparing the timbres of the **trumpet** and the **tuba** within the brass family.

Live performances are usually the most powerful medium through which children can gain an understanding of how orchestral instruments sound. Yearly visits to the elementary music classroom from the local junior-high band director and some of her or his students is an excellent source for these kinds of live performances. Teachers working in communities where universities are located will most likely find undergraduate music education students who are more than happy to pay a visit to an elementary classroom for the purpose of giving live demonstrations of wind, brass, and string instruments. Further, some Canadian orchestras offer an *Adopt-a-Player* program, whereby a musician from the orchestra will pay a number of visits to a school. In addition, student concerts, which are often presented by local orchestras once or twice a year, provide a wonderful listening field trip for elementary school students.

In light of the infrequent nature of these live listening experiences, however, most teachers must turn to a variety of other resources, including recorded music, videos, computer software, instrument sites on the Internet, and books, in order to facilitate children's understanding of the timbres of orchestral instruments. The following types of recorded music will prove useful.

1. Music that highlights individual instruments from all four families—for example, *The Young Person's Guide to the Orchestra* by Benjamin Britten (1913–1976)

2. Music that highlights one particular instrument family—for example, the *Serenade for Strings* by Pyotr Il'yich Tchaikowsky (1840–1893)

3. Music that features individual instruments from several different families—for example, *Peter and the Wolf* by Sergei Prokofiev (1891–1953)

4. Music that highlights an individual instrument from one family—for example, the snare drum and the percussion section in the overture to *The Thieving Magpie* by Gioachino Rossini (1792–1868)

Table 13.1

Orchestral instrument family	How the sound is made	How the pitch is changed	What gives individual instruments their unique timbres
Percussion *pitched instruments:* tympani, chimes, xylophone, etc. *non-pitched instruments:* bass drum, snare drum, small percussion, etc.	The player strikes or shakes the instrument, causing part or all of it to vibrate and resonate	*pitched instruments:* The player changes the tension of the drum head (tympani), strikes a different size or length of bar or tube (xylophone, chimes), or chooses a different size of instrument (triangle, gong)	the size, shape, and/or material of each instrument, combined with the type of mallet (yarn, metal, wood, rubber, etc.) used by the player
Strings violin (highest) viola cello double bass (lowest)	The player bows or plucks the strings, making the string vibrate, which causes the body of the instrument to resonate	The player changes the length of a vibrating string by placing a finger on the string part way along	the size and/or the material of the instrument, combined with unique bowing techniques
Brass trumpet (highest) French horn trombone, baritone tuba (lowest)	The player's breath vibrates the lips, causing the instrument tube to resonate	The player changes the length of the resonating tube by pressing a valve (or for the trombone, moving the slide)	the size and/or the shape of the instrument; the placement of a mute in the bell
Woodwinds flute (highest)	The player blows across or down into the mouthpiece, causing the air column inside the instrument to resonate	The player changes the length of the vibrating air column in the instrument by covering holes with keys or with the fingers	the size and shape of the instrument, and/or the material of which it is made
oboe bassoon (lowest)	The player's breath vibrates a double reed, causing the air column inside the instrument to resonate	(same)	(same)
clarinet saxophone (rarely)	The player's breath vibrates a single reed against the mouthpiece, causing the air column inside the instrument to resonate	(same)	(same)

Such recordings are excellent when supplemented by videos, including Rubin (1990) and Gamble (1992a, 1992b). Films from the National Film Board of Canada (**www.nfb.ca**) such as *McGill, Mahler, and Montreal* (1998), *La symphonie fantastique (La marche au supplice)* (1986), *Concerto grosso modo* (1985), *Viola* (1980), *Music for Wilderness Lake* (1980), *Canada Vignettes: The Violin Maker* (1978), and *The Violin* (1977) are also recommended. Excellent storybooks that encourage individual students to learn about orchestral and band instruments through reading include Van Kampen and Eugen (1989), Meyrick (1991), Stuchner (1998), Wellbrun (1998), Trottier and MacAulay-MacKinnon (1997), Kalman (1997), Lohans (1996), Gillmor and Gay (1996), Martchenko (1993), Jeunnese and Delafosse (1994), Hayes (1991), Young and Hartmann (1990), Lillegard (1987a, 1987b, 1987c), Kuskin (1982), Kushner (1980), and Koscielniak (2000). Multiple experiences of these kinds provide a strong foundation for the child's development in understanding the instrumental timbres of orchestral instruments.

Composers sometimes insert environmental sounds into orchestral music to provide special timbral effects. Recorded selections such as *And God Created Great Whales* by Alan Hovhaness (1922–2000), which includes taped sounds of humpback whales, or *Parade* by Erik Satie (1866–1925), which includes the sound of a typewriter, are excellent examples for introducing this concept to children.

Listening to other instruments that are not traditionally part of a symphony orchestra—such as electric guitar, electric bass, banjo, bagpipe, drum set, synthesizer, and electrified violin, as well as ethnic instruments from around the world (for example, the *didjeridu*), should also be included in the elementary music curriculum. Many of these instruments contribute important timbres in musical styles such as:

1. *pop* and *rock*: synthesizer, electric guitar, electric bass, drum set, electrified violin
2. *country and western*: banjo, guitar
3. *jazz*: electric guitar, drum set, electric bass,
4. *music of First Nations peoples*: particular types of drums and wind instruments
5. *folk music*: fiddles and bagpipes (for Celtic music of Cape Breton), zither and hurdy-gurdy (for music of Eastern Europe)

Timbres of non-orchestral instruments should be studied in the context of the music in which those instruments are frequently used.

Students in Grades 5–6 should learn about these instruments when such music is included in the classroom. Visits by parents or cultural groups in the community can be a wonderful way to demonstrate different and unusual instruments to children. National Film Board of Canada videos such as *Spirits of Havana* (2000), *The Montreal Jazz Package* (1999), *Opre Roma: Gypsies in Canada* (1999), *Singing Our Stories* (1998), *The Fiddlers of James Bay* (1980), *World Drum* (1987), and *Celtic Spirits* (1978) are also excellent resources.

Expressive Elements

Concepts from this structural property of music refer to performance directions added to the music that help the performer to give the rhythm and melody of a piece of music a distinctive character. For example, articulation directions such as **staccato** (*short, separated, detached*) or **legato** (*smooth, flowing, connected*) tell the musician to play the notes in a certain way, resulting in a specific musical sound. Students might be asked to sing a song such as *Sakura* (p. 126) to experience the concept of a *legato* performance, or *Lukey's Boat* to get a feel for the inclusion of *staccato* notes in music.

Lukey's Boat

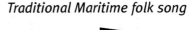
Traditional Maritime folk song

2. Oh Lukey's boat has cotton sails,
   A-ha, me by's,
   Oh Lukey's boat has cotton sails,
   And planks put down with galvanized nails,
   A-ha, me riddle-di-day!

3. Oh Lukey's rolling out his grub,
   A-ha, me by's,
   Oh Lukey's rolling out his grub,
   A barrel a bag a ten pound tub,
   A-ha, me riddle-di-day!

4. Oh Lukey's sailing down the shore,
   A-ha, me by-s,
   Oh Lukey's sailing down the shore,
   To catch some fish in Labrador,
   A-ha, me riddle-di-day!

Children should also experience *legato* and *staccato* by playing instrumental music (for example, on the recorder), since the production of these articulations differs depending on the instrument. In addition, listening to selections of recorded music that emphasize one particular articulation—such as *staccato* in the "Pizzicato Polka" from *Ballet Suite no. 1* by Dmitri Shostakovich (1906–1975)—or selections that contain contrasting articulations—such as *staccato* and *legato* in *Danse Macabre* by Camille Saint-Saëns (1835–1921)—plays an important role in the learning process.

Other directions sometimes found in music, such as a **fermata** (*a sign that directs the player to hold a note longer than its normal duration*) could be introduced with a song such as *The Ryans and The Pittmans (We'll Rant and We'll Roar)*. Again performance experiences for elementary school students in regards to this concept should include both vocal and instrumental music.

The Ryans and the Pitmans
(We'll Rant and We'll Roar)

Words and music by Henry W. LeMesurier (ca 1875)

2. I'm a son of a sea-cook and a cook in a trader,
   I can dance, I can sing, I can reef the mainboom,
   I can handle a jigger, and cuts a big figure,
   Whenever I gets in a boat's standing room.

3. If the voyage is good, then this fall I will do it,
   I wants two pound ten for a ring and the priest,
   A couple of dollers for clane shirt and collars,
   And a handful of coppers to make up the feast.

4. Then here is a health to the girls of Fox Harbour,
   Of Oderin, and Presque, Crabbes Hole, and Bruley,
   Now let ye be jolly, don't be melancholy,
   I can't marry all or in chokey I'd be!

G.S. Doyle (Ed.). (1966). From Old-Time Songs and Poetry of Newfoundland: Songs of the People from the Days of Our Forefathers *(4th ed.). Reprinted with the permission of the Doyle family.*

Composing activities in the later grades should include decision making by the students regarding articulation, *fermatas*, tempo, dynamics, and timbre. All of these elements may contribute greatly to how the rhythm and melody sounds, and students should be conscious of the potential of these structural properties for helping to create a distinct musical composition and subsequently, a meaningful musical performance.

Questions for Discussion and Practice

1. What is the difference between dynamics discrimination and dynamics production? Briefly describe five classroom activities that help children develop either or both of these skills.

2. Find three pieces of recorded music (other than those listed in this book) that will help to illustrate the concept of *crescendo* for children.

3. Briefly describe a variety of classroom activities that will help children in the early grades to become familiar with the timbres of non-pitched percussion instruments. Use examples both from this chapter and from Chapter 5.

4. Search out five selections of recorded music that highlight the timbres of individual instruments from the brass family. Now, find five selections that highlight instruments from the woodwind family.

5. On the Internet, find at least three different Web sites that are useful for helping children learn about various instrument timbres.

References

Gamble, J. (1992a). *Peter and the Wolf* [video]. Los Angeles: Bogner Entertainment.

Gamble, J. (1992b). *Carnival of the Animals* [video]. Los Angeles: Bogner Entertainment.

Gilmor, D., and Gay, M.-L. (1996). *The Fabulous Song*. Toronto: Stoddart

Hayes, A. (1991). *Meet the Orchestra*. New York: Voyager Books.

Jeunesse, G. and Delafosse, C. (1994). *Musical Instruments*. New York: Scholastic (originally published 1992 in French: *La Musique*. Paris: Gallimard)

Kalman, B. (1997). *Musical Instruments from A to Z*. Niagara-on-the-Lake, ON: Crabtree Press.

Koscielniak, B. (2000). *The Story of the Incredible Orchestra*. Boston: Houghton Mifflin

Kuskin, K. (1982). *The Philharmonic Gets Dressed*. New York: HarperCollins.

Kushner, D. (1980). *The Violin Maker's Gift*. Toronto: MacMillan.

Lillegard, D. (1987a). *Woodwinds*. Chicago: Children's Press.

Lillegard, D. (1987b). *Percussion*. Chicago: Children's Press.

Lillegard, D. (1987c). *Brass*. Chicago: Children's Press.

Lohans, A. (1996). *Nathaniel's Violin*. Victoria, BC: Orca Books.

Martchenko, M. (1993). *Jeremy's Decision*. Don Mills, ON: Oxford University Press.

Meyrick, K. (1991). *Lost Music*. New York: Child Play

Montgomery, A.P. (1996). The effect of tempo on the musical preferences of elementary and middle school children. *Journal of Research in Music Education, 42(3)*, 119–128.

Rubin, M. (1990). *The Orchestra* [video]. Waterbury, VT: Mark Rubin Productions.

Rubin, M., and Daniel, A. (1984). *The Orchestra*. Toronto: Groundwood.

Stuchner, J. (1998). *The Kugel Valley Klezmer Band*. Richmond Hill, ON: North Winds Press.

Trottier, M. and MacAulay-MacKinnon, P. (1997). *Heartsong—Ce ol cridhe*. Sydney, NS: University of Cape Breton Press.

Van Kampen, V., and Eugen, I. (1989). *Orchestranimals*. Richmond Hill, ON: North Winds Press ; New York: Scholastic.

Wellburn, E. (1998). *Echos from the Square*. Oakville, ON: Rubin Publishers.

Young, D., and Hartmann, P. (1990). *The Abaleda Voluntary Firehouse Band*. Edmonton: Tree Frog Press.

CHAPTER 14

Form

SYNOPSIS

Chapter 14 discusses the daily classroom activities appropriate for the elementary music classroom that use experiences such as singing, playing instruments, and moving to highlight musical concepts from Form. Activities are presented in a sound-before-symbol progression within a developmentally appropriate simple-to-complex teaching order.

Introduction

Composers use form to help create unity and variety in music for the listener.

Form—*the way in which music is structured into an organized journey*—is a property of music that involves the composer's arrangement of the melodic and rhythmic sections into an ordering of same, different, or similar parts. According to Aiello, (1994), "In listening to music, the listener seeks an equilibrium: there must be a proportion of novelty within a background of predictability" (p. 57). Thus, the repetition created by the return of *same parts* (parts that are identical in both pitch and rhythm) in a composition provides unity for the listener, while the use of *different* parts (parts that are different in both pitch and rhythm) creates contrast. *Similar* parts (parts that are the same in pitch but different in rhythm, or vice versa) provide the listener with unity interwoven with some variety.

Three kinds of musical phrases: same, similar, and different

Initial experiences with form in the elementary grades focus on determining phrase form.

Elementary school children learn about two kinds of musical form, both of which involve **phrases** (*complete musical sentences that are delineated by a pause or a breath*).

Phrase form *is the arrangement of individual phrases into a structure of same, different, or similar phrases;* the individual phrases are usually labelled with lowercase letters (a, b, c, etc.).

Sectional form *is the arrangement of larger sections of music made up of several phrases into a structure of same, different, or similar sections;* the individual sections are usually labelled with capital letters (A, B, C, etc.).

In addition, the children learn about two auxiliary sections of music that are sometimes used to supplement a larger structural organization:

introduction, *a short section of music placed at a beginning of a piece of music, usually to serve as a prologue*

coda, *a short section of music placed at the end of a piece of music, usually to serve as an epilogue*

Phrase form is used to label the structure of shorter songs consisting of only a few phrases, while *sectional form* is used to label longer pieces consisting of many phrases. Since children in the early elementary grades sing shorter songs (about two to four phrases), phrase form is traditionally introduced in Grade 1. Sectional form follows naturally in Grade 3 as classroom songs become longer and instrumental music (played, for example, on the recorder) is included.

Phrase Form

The introduction of phrase form in Grade 1 begins with learning about *musical phrases*. Many teachers find movement a useful, learner-centred activity with which to illustrate this concept for children in the sound-before-symbol sequence.

For example, while singing the song *Diddle Diddle Dumpling*, Grade 1 students could be invited to walk around in a circle keeping the beat with their feet. The teacher would then invite the children to follow her or his lead, changing direction in the circle every time a new phrase is begun. On the second try, students would be asked to listen to the music and try to anticipate where the teacher might be planning to change direction. (Note that no mention of phrases is made at this point.)

Diddle Diddle Dumpling

Traditional rhyme

After returning to their chairs, students would be asked to listen to the teacher sing *Diddle Diddle Dumpling* again, this time placing both of their hands on top of their heads and lifting them off temporarily every time they hear the teacher take a breath during the singing of the song.

On completion of this sequence, the teacher should explain that **musical phrases** are *complete musical sentences separated from each other in music by a breath,* perhaps using the analogy of sentences in language. Children should then be instructed to imitate the teacher in counting the number of musical phrases found in *Diddle Diddle Dumpling,* moving their arms in a "rainbow" or arch-like motion from left to right in order to show each of the four phrases in the song.

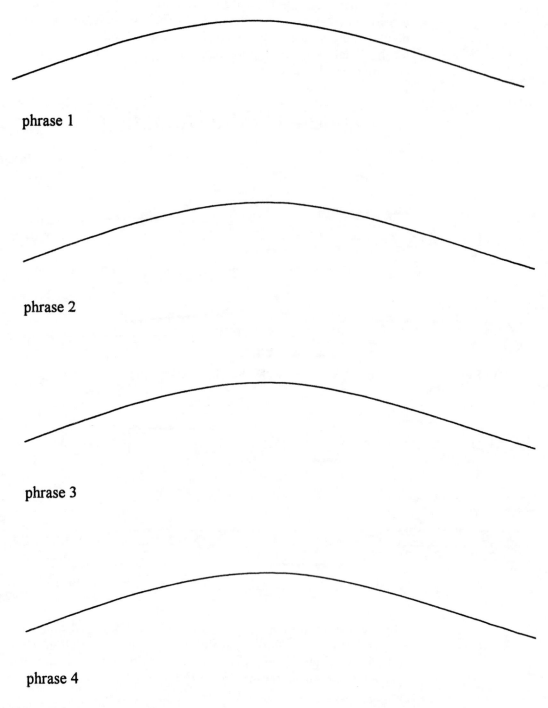

phrase 1

phrase 2

phrase 3

phrase 4

Grade 1 students should be given considerable practice at illustrating the correct number of phrases in other familiar class songs, using the rainbow arch movement, before attempting to classify these musical phrases according to the particulars of phrase form.

When ready to introduce *phrase form* in the later part of Grade 1, teachers should use songs that contain only *same* and *different* phrases, leaving music containing *similar* phrases until later in Grade 2. With a song such as *Hot Cross Buns*, the children should first attempt to determine the number of phrases in the song, using the arch-like rainbow motion. Then the teacher should sing each individual phrase for the children, without text, on a neutral syllable such as "loo." This is important, as children may confuse a repetition of the text with a "same" phrase when the rhythms or pitches of the two phrases may be quite different.

As each phrase is sung and compared with the previous one, children can begin to label the phrases *a, b, c* as appropriate. As indicated below, *Hot Cross Buns* has a phrase form of *aaba*. For beginning experiences with labelling musical phrases, some teachers prefer to use iconic labels (for example, pictures of fruit: apples for phrase *a*; bananas for phrase *b*, etc.), and move to labelling with letters later in Grade 2.

Hot Cross Buns

Traditional rhyme

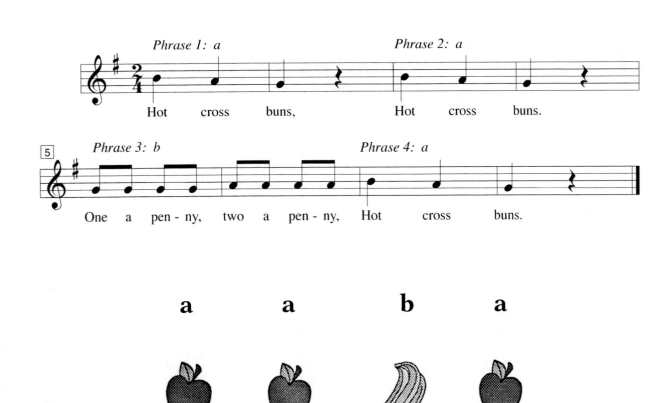

Rocky Mountain is an example of a Grade 2 song that contains same, different, and similar phrases. For this song, the phrase form would be labeled *abcc¹*. Phrase forms involving "similar" phrases occur frequently in the repertoire of elementary school children's songs.

Rocky Mountain

Traditional folk song

Phrase 1: a

1. Rock - y moun - tain, rock - y moun - tain, rock - y moun - tain high,

Phrase 2: b

When you're on that rock - y moun - tain, hang your head and cry.

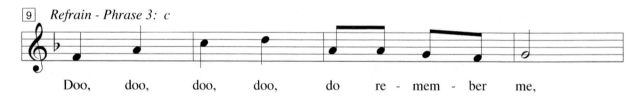

Refrain - Phrase 3: c

Doo, doo, doo, doo, do re - mem - ber me,

Phrase 4: c¹

Doo, doo, doo, doo, do re - mem - ber me.

2. Sunny valley, sunny valley, sunny valley low,
   When you're in that sunny valley, sing it soft and slow.
   Refrain

3. Stormy ocean, stormy ocean, stormy ocean wide,
   When you're in that stormy ocean, hang your head and hide.
   Refrain

Sectional Form

When composers write longer pieces—that is, music written in a number of phrases—they use bigger structural forms, called *sectional forms*, to provide unity and variety in their music. Although each section is divided into several shorter phrases, when these phrases are put together, they sound as if they belong together in a larger complete unit.

The Bridge at Avignon is an excellent example of sectional form. Although the song has ten individual phrases (abab¹cc¹abab¹), when sung as a complete song, it is easy to hear the larger ABA sectional organization. Indeed, these sections sound like complete units that could stand on their own.

The Bridge at Avignon / Sur le pont d'Avignon

Traditional French folk song

The introduction of *sectional form* in elementary school music follows a logical sequence of easy-to-complex:

1. *Binary (AB) form*—music that is organized into two contrasting sections
2. *Ternary (ABA) form*—music that is organized into two contrasting sections with a return of the first (A) section at the end
3. *Rondo (ABACA) form*—music that is organized into three contrasting sections, with the first (A) section repeated after each contrasting (B or C) section
4. *Theme and variations (A A^1 A^{2}2 A^3 A^4 A^5 A^6, etc.) form*—music that consists of a theme section and a number of subsequent sections that present the theme with one (or more) alterations (for example, tempo changes, dynamic changes, rhythmic changes)
5. *Fugue form*—polyphonic music that consists of a theme (melody)—called a "subject"—that is presented by one part and taken up imitatively in turn by the other parts; sometimes the subject is accompanied by a contrasting theme, which is called a "counter subject."

Music that is organized in binary (AB) and ternary (AB) forms (organizational structures that are commonly found in vocal music) can be introduced using familiar songs from the Grade 3–4 children's repertoire. *Weevily Wheat* is an example of a song in AB sectional form, and *Vive la Canadienne* (p. 226) is an example of a song in ABA sectional form.

AB and ABA are the two most common sectional forms in children's vocal music.

Weevily Wheat

Traditional singing game

twen - ty five, / for - ty five,   Five times six is thir - ty, / Five times ten is fif - ty,

Five times sev - en is thir - ty five, / Five times e - leven is fif - ty five,   Five times eight is for - ty. / Five times twelve is six - ty

Game: The children divide into groups of four, stand in small circles, and number off (1–2–3–4) around the circle. During the A section (mm. 1–8), the children hold hands and skip around in a circle to the beat, changing direction at the beginning of the new phrase (m. 5). During the B section (mm. 9–16), each child (starting with number 1) in turn puts one hand into the centre of the circle, on the quarter note beat. By the end of the B section (16 beats), each child will have put both hands into the centre twice—the hands end up stacked on top of each other, like a stack of pancakes!

Composers use forms such as rondo, theme and variations, and fugue to organize instrumental music.

Composers generally use *rondo* (ABACA), *theme and variations* (A A¹ A² A³ A⁴, etc.), and *fugue* forms when writing instrumental music. Elementary school teachers might use a variety of recorded music to help illustrate these forms for students in Grades 4–6. Examples include *Scherzo for Stephen* by Canadian composer Saul Honigman (b. 1926) for rondo form; the final movement (air and variations, "The Harmonious Blacksmith") from the Suite no. 5 in E major, HWV 430 by George Frideric Handel (1685–1759) for theme and variations form; and the Little Fugue in G minor, BWV 578, by Johann Sebastian Bach (1685–1750) for fugue form.

In addition, children will gain a greater understanding of the inner workings of such musical forms by being involved in their initial creation. For example, a rondo form might be created with any of the following strategies:

1. Combine three songs to create an ABACA form: for example, *Lukey's Boat* (p. 279) as the A section, *I'se the By* (pp. 90–91) as the B section, *Bonavist' Harbour* (pp. 128–29) as the C section.

2. Combine two songs and a recorder piece to create an ABACA form: for example, *Iroquois Lullaby* (p. 32) played on the recorder as the A section, *My Bark Canoe* (p. 75) as the B section, and *Ojibwa Song* (p. 294) as the C section.

3. Combine three songs played on instruments to create an ABACA form: for example, *Ah! si mon moine voulait danser* (p. 169) played on the recorder as the A section, *The Lumber Camp Song* (p. 267) played as a rhythm on non-pitched percussion as the B section, and *En roulant ma boule* (p. 246) played as a melody on glockenspiel as the C section.

Creating sectional forms helps elementary students to understand the inner workings of form.

Theme and variations form can be created using a familiar melody such as *Twinkle, Twinkle Little Star* (see activity in Chapter 6, pp. 133–34). This creative experience could be followed by having the students view the National Film

Board of Canada video, *Variations on Ah! vous dirai-je, maman*, which features a theme and variations by Wolfgang Amadeus Mozart (1756–1791) on the melody of *Twinkle, Twinkle Little Star*. Here, Grade 4–5 students have the opportunity to experiment with compositional practices that are used by orchestral composers, thereby setting the stage for the potential use of this structural organization for their own music written in Grade 6.

Introduction and Coda

These two auxiliary sections of music may be introduced to elementary school children as early as Grades 2–3, using short rhythmic compositions written by the children. Here, students play brief rhythmic patterns (four to eight beats) of their own creation as introductions and *codas* to familiar songs and rhymes. Played by the children on non-pitched percussion instruments, these rhythmic introductory and finishing sections of music add greatly to the performance of simple songs the children are already singing in the classroom. The following arrangement of *An Inuit Lullaby* is an example.

An Inuit Lullaby

Cape Dorset lullaby
Arranged by A. Montgomery

Sleep	through	the	night	my	dar	-	ling.
Thanks	be	to	God	who	sent		her.
She	is	so	sweet	I'm	sing	-	ing.

Coda

Older elementary school students could be invited to write short melodic introductions and/or rhythmic *codas* such as those included with this arrangement of *Ojibwa Song:*

Ojibwa Song

Traditional Ojibwa song
Arranged by A. Montgomery

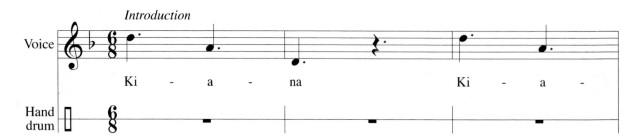

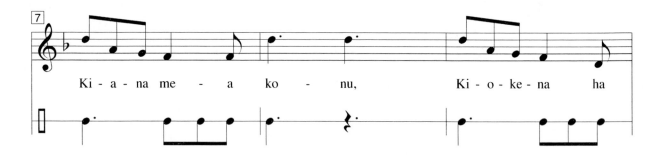

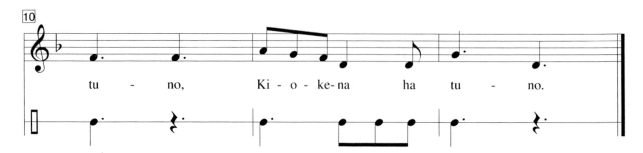

Questions for Discussion and Practice

1. How does form in music help create unity and contrast?

2. Find three songs in this book (other than *Rocky Mountain*) with phrase forms that include at least one phrase from each of the three phrase types (same, different, similar).

3. Find two songs in other chapters in this book that have an AB sectional form. Now find two examples of songs with an ABA sectional form.

4. Find three listening selections appropriate for the elementary grades that could be used to help illustrate music in either rondo form and/or fugue.

5. Using a simple melody such as *Mary Had a Little Lamb*, write a series of variations on this melody, using alterations involving dynamics, tempo, rhythmic changes, etc.

Reference

Aiello, R. (1994). Music and language. In Aiello, R. and Sloboda, J. (Eds.), *Musical Perceptions*. Oxford: Oxford University Press.

CHAPTER 15

Harmony and Texture

SYNOPSIS

Chapter 15 discusses daily classroom activities appropriate for the elementary music classroom that use experiences such as singing, playing instruments, and moving to highlight the musical concepts from Harmony and Texture. Activities are presented in a sound-before-symbol progression within a developmentally appropriate simple-to-complex teaching order.

Introduction

Harmony is a structural property of music that refers to *the simultaneous sounding of two or more notes.* For example, two-part harmony might be a melody and a rhythmic *ostinato* accompaniment.

Example of two-part harmony: voice and rhythmic ostinato

Traditional rhyme

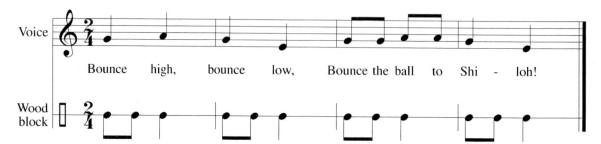

An example of three-part harmony might be a melody accompanied by both a rhythmic *ostinato* and a *bordun*.

excerpt from a traditional First Nations song

Voice: Ho, ho— wa - ta - nay, Ho, ho— wa - ta - nay,
Sleep, sleep— ba - by now, Sleep, sleep— ba - by now,

Hand drum

BX

Children are generally excited by the sounds of harmony, especially when they are provided with tools (for example, playing classroom instruments) that allow them to be responsible for performing both the "tune" and the "accompaniment" of the music.

The term **texture,** refers to *the nature of the multiple sounds created by harmony in music.* For example, music with multiple parts might be described as having a **polyphonic** texture: that is, it has *two or more parts that move independently from each other,* as in the round *Laugh Ha! Ha!*

Laugh Ha! Ha!

Traditional English round

Voice 1: Laugh ha, ha! Here's a mer - ry jest,

Voice 2: Laugh ha, ha!

continued

Or, music in two or three parts might be described as having a **homophonic** texture: that is, it has *two or more parts that move together rhythmically but have different pitches,* as in this three-part choral arrangement:

Harmony and texture are taught together.

Children in the elementary grades usually study harmony and texture in conjunction with each other, since texture is actually the *aural result* of adding harmony to music.

Harmony is introduced to elementary school children in a logical easy-to-complex sequence based on both the children's developmental readiness for singing in more than one part (see Chapter 4), and the children's psychomotor ability at playing non-pitched instruments, barred instruments, or recorder (see Chapter 5). Thus, initial textural experiences in music for kindergarten children are **monophonic**—meaning that the children sing songs that have only one part, with no harmony. When harmony is first introduced in Grade 1, with simple *rhythmic ostinati* and *pedal tone* accompaniments, texture experiences move from being *monophonic* in nature to being *polyphonic* and this format is maintained throughout most of the elementary grades.

Harmony and texture may be introduced to elementary school students using the teaching sequence shown in Table 15.1. Each of these types of harmony may be introduced to the children through **harmonic discrimination**—*the ability to hear and identify when two musical parts are sounding simultaneously.* The children may then derive the definition for the particular harmonic concept under consideration from their experiences of hearing and reflecting on the character of the harmonic accompaniment.

For example, when introducing the harmonic concept of *rhythmic ostinato*, the teacher might ask Grade 1 children to sing a familiar song such as *Johnny Works with One Hammer.* The teacher would then ask the children to sing the song again while he or she claps either the beat or the rhythm with the song,

Table 15.1

Recommended Teaching Sequence for Introducing Harmony and Texture

Harmony	Texture
1. Singing without accompaniment (Kindergarten)	Monophonic
2. Singing with simple rhythmic *ostinato* (Grade 1)	Polyphonic
3. Singing with simple pedal tone accompaniments (Grade 1)	
4. Singing with chordal and/or broken *bordun* accompaniments (Grades 2–3)	
5. Singing or playing simple two-part music (Grades 2–3) • Easy partner songs • Easy rounds • Easy two-part music incorporating melodic *ostinati* • Easy two-part music incorporating descants	
6. Singing with accompaniments using more complex rhythmic and melodic *ostinato* and *bordun* patterns (Grades 4–6)	
7. Singing or playing intermediate two-part music (Grades 4–6) • More complex rounds and canons • Polyphonic two-part songs or instrumental pieces	
8. Singing or playing simple polyphonic three-part songs or instrumental pieces (Grades 5–6)	
9. Singing and/or playing I–IV–V chordal accompaniments (Grades 5–6)	Homophonic

asking the children to identify which they hear. On the third repetition, the teacher would clap a simple rhythmic *ostinato*, such as

to provide harmony for the song, and ask the children to reflect on how this rhythmic pattern differs from the previous sounds of either the steady beat or the rhythm of the song. After the children discuss and establish the parameters of **rhythmic *ostinato*** *(a short rhythmic pattern repeated as an accompaniment to a song)*, half of the children could then try clapping the *ostinato* or playing it on tone blocks while the other half sings, and vice versa. It will, of course, take several weeks of practice with a variety of simple rhythmic *ostinati* before the children will be able to successfully sing and play the *ostinato* accompaniment at the same time.

Johnny Works with One Hammer

Traditional children's song
Arranged by A. Montgomery

When introducing **partner songs** (*two songs that produce acceptable harmony when sung together*) or **rounds** (*part songs consisting of a single melody, where the voices begin one after another at equally-spaced time intervals*), it is helpful to follow a similar strategy. For example, with Grade 2–3 students, the teacher could ask the children to review the song *Make New Friends* by singing it while clapping the beat. After several repetitions, the teacher would then ask the children to sing the song while she or he sings something different—in this case, starting the song one measure after the children, as in a round. Discussion with the children should follow, in order to establish the parameters of how the harmonic concept of *round* is organized, and comparisons should be drawn with previously-learned harmonic concepts such as rhythmic *ostinati*, or pedal tones.

Make New Friends

Traditional English round

Next, the children should attempt the round with the class as one voice and the teacher as the other, giving the children an opportunity to gain practice at both beginning the round and coming in as the second voice. When secure, the children can try the round by themselves, with one half the class starting at "*1" and the other half starting at "*2." Again, considerable practice will be needed with a variety of rounds before the children will feel comfortable enough to sing the round in two parts without help from the teacher. Children in the later grades should gain experience with three-voice rounds and **canons** (*polyphonic music in which all parts perform the same melody, each voice entering after a specific time interval*), such as the *Alleluia Canon*. A variety of rounds and canons with recommendations regarding grade level can be found in Chapter 4.

Alleluia Canon

Attributed to Wolfgang Amadeus Mozart (1756–1791)

The detailed discussion of playing *bordun* patterns on barred instruments such as xylophones in Chapter 5 outlines which types of patterns should be presented at which grade level. It is recommended that students in Grades 2–3 begin with *simple* and *broken bordun* patterns, and that students in Grades 3–6 move on to *level* and *arpeggiated borduns*. As with the other types of harmony, introduction of harmonic concepts involving *borduns* often begins with the students engaged in hands-on experience with a *bordun*, both through listening and through playing, with these activities leading to reflection on how this kind of harmonic accompaniment compares with those previously learned.

The use of *borduns*, rhythmic *ostinati*, and melodic *ostinati* to accompany children's singing, in combination with partner songs and rounds either sung or played on the recorder, provides for a continued experience with polyphonic texture. The following arrangement of *Jesous Ahatonhia* (*The Huron Carol*) for Grade 3–4 students includes harmonic concepts such as rhythmic and melodic *ostinati* and a *bordun* accompaniment. Other examples of such harmonic arrangements appropriate for a variety of grade levels can be found throughout Chapters 5–14.

Jesous Ahatonhia
(The Huron Carol)

16th-century French melody
Huron text attributed to Jean de Brébeuf (1593–1649)
Arranged by A. Montgomery

continued

The introduction of the harmonic concepts of *I–IV–V chords* in Grades 4–6 should parallel the introduction of *fa* and *ti* and major and minor scales in the music class, thereby providing students with the theoretical knowledge needed to both select and play the appropriate notes of the chord.

Students in Grades 4–6 learn about I–IV–V chords in music.

I, IV, and V chords in G major

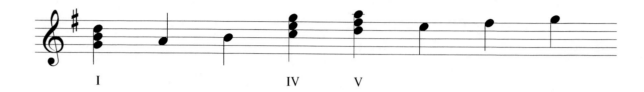

I   IV   V

Chordal accompaniments involving selected notes from I, IV, and V chords may be experienced using barred instruments, as in the arrangement of *I'se The B'y* (pp. 90–91). Accompaniments using homophonic accompaniments of complete I–IV–V chords may be experienced using the recorder, barred instruments (as in the bass xylophone), the voice, or other harmonic instruments available in the classroom (such as guitars or ukeleles). *Lukey's Boat* is an example of a song that may be accompanied using any of these instruments to play the appropriate I and V chords. *Acadian Lullaby* is an example of a song that sounds lovely with an accompaniment of I–IV–V chords:

Lukey's Boat

Maritime folk song

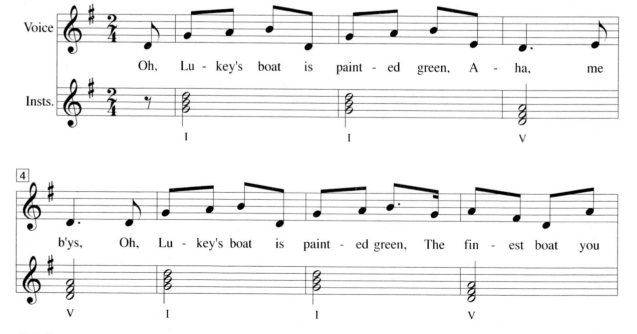

Acadian Lullaby

Traditional Acadian lullaby

continued

This version of Acadian Lullaby was collected by Helen Creighton. It is used here with permission of Nova Scotia Archives and Records Management, Halifax, Nova Scotia.

Recorded music is used to help students gain a deeper understanding of concepts from harmony.

Recorded music should also be provided for the children to experience harmony. *Ostinato* accompaniments can be heard in works such as the *Allegretto* movement from the *Sinfonetta* by Leoš Janáček (1854–1928) or *La morisque* by Tylman Susato (ca 1510–1570 or later); I–IV–V chord progressions can be heard in *Watermelon Man* by Herbie Hancock (b. 1940). Additional examples of recorded music for harmonic listening can be found in Chapter 7.

Questions for Discussion and Practice

1. What is the difference between harmony and texture? Why are the two taught in conjunction with one another?

2. Find two examples each of monophonic and polyphonic music in this textbook. Now do the same with homophonic music. Why is the latter a more difficult task?

3. Write a rhythmic *ostinato* to accompany an unaccompanied children's song in this textbook. Make sure your *ostinato* is complementary to the song (that is, it differs from the rhythm of the text). Is your completed piece polyphonic or homophonic? Why?

4. Find three rounds appropriate for Grade 4 (other than those found in this chapter or Chapter 4).

5. Find three songs in this textbook that could be accompanied with I–V or I–IV–V chords. Select one and write an appropriate accompaniment.

PART FOUR

Curricular Planning

Part IV provides vital information for the elementary music educator on curricular planning. Chapter 16 discusses the process of long range planning leading to the daily task of lesson planning. Two examples of lesson plans are presented, utilizing activities and strategies discussed in Chapters 4–5. Chapter 17 provides guidance as to the role of student assessment and evaluation. Prospective elementary music teachers will find a variety of helpful examples regarding assessment strategies.

CHAPTER 16

Daily and Long-Range Planning

SYNOPSIS

Chapter 16 examines the process of curricular planning in the elementary music class. The influences on teacher planning are discussed, as well as the importance of the teacher's role within the process of development. Specifics regarding selection and sequencing of yearly content, selection of learner-centered experiences, activities, and strategies, selection of authentic assessment measures, and the writing of the daily lesson plan are explored with the inclusion of a model example for planning.

Introduction

Curricular planning is the ability to translate educational goals into daily action.

Curricular planning—*the ability to bring educational goals into daily action*—is one of the most exciting and significant aspects of being an elementary music teacher. It is important to first lay the groundwork for teaching by learning about:

1. the structure of music and all its parameters, including appropriate sequencing;
2. the principle of the sound-before-symbol teaching process;
3. the types of authentic musical experiences and activities that are developmentally appropriate for children; and
4. the musical content, concrete materials, equipment, and teaching strategies that will result in a learner-centred environment in the music classroom.

Curricular
planning is
influenced by a
variety of factors
inside and
outside the
classroom.

However, the most important step towards effective teaching is the ability to bring this knowledge into action through the lesson plan and assessment procedures used on a daily basis.

Curricular planning is influenced by a variety of variables outside an elementary music teacher's classroom. These variables include:

- provincial educational goals and specific directives regarding music teaching;
- local school board educational goals and specific directives regarding music teaching;
- individual school educational goals and administrator's expectations regarding the role of the music in the elementary curriculum.

Factors inside the classroom include:

- the teacher's attitude to the role of music in the elementary curricula;
- the teacher's comfort level with providing music instruction;
- the teacher's knowledge of the basics of providing music instruction in the elementary classroom;
- the amount of time available for instruction each week;
- the class size and the grade level;
- the classroom space and the equipment, materials, and instruments available for instruction;
- and, most importantly, the nature of the individual population of children in the music class.

According to Eisner (1985)

> the role of the teacher in curricula decision making is important because the teacher serves as the interpreter of educational policy and because the teacher is the major mediator of what shall be taught—if not learned—in the classroom. (p. 129)

There are a variety of resources available to the elementary music teacher—including *Achieving Musical Understanding* (CMEA and CMEC, 2001), provincial and board music curriculum documents, and this textbook. Resources such as these can provide guidance for both **overall goals** (for example: *elementary music education should lead children towards the development of musical understanding*) and **general learner objectives** (for example, *the student will identify and respond to repetition and contrast in musical form*) of the music curriculum. However, such resources should be viewed only as *starting points* for curricular decisions. The elementary music teacher will still need to make judgments regarding the following issues.

1. *the selection and sequencing of yearly content* (for example, music and musical concepts) that will relate to the overall goals and general learner objectives prescribed in the curriculum
2. *the selection of learner-centred experiences, activities, and strategies* through which children will experience this content
3. *the selection of authentic assessment measures* with which to evaluate the children's progress and success at meeting the learner objectives
4. *the preparation of daily lesson plans* that will guide the daily instructional procedures of the teacher

Indeed, successful learning in the elementary music class is clearly dependent on teachers playing an *active* role in the curricular decision making of their individual classrooms (Montgomery, 2000).

Step 1: Selection and Sequencing of Yearly Content

Content in elementary music education refers to both the musical concepts taught and the music through which students experience them.

Yearly content in elementary music education refers to both the list of *musical concepts* that will be experienced by the students at a particular grade level, and the *music* through which these concepts will be brought to consciousness. As discussed in Chapter 2, such concepts are generally sequenced in an easy-to-complex **spiral progression**, providing for experience with musical concepts from each of the ten elements of music during each grade level.

Since most teachers in Canada utilize sequences established by their provincial or school board curriculum guides, or perhaps turn to *Achieving Musical Understanding* (CMEA and CMEC, 2001) for guidance, the first step is to *take the appropriate yearly list of concepts provided by such documents and place them into a logical **sound-before-symbol** teaching time frame in relation to the school year calendar*. This means you should count the number of lessons *projected* to take place over the year and make a timetable to determine approximately when to introduce each music concept to the students throughout the year.

For example, this textbook recommends that Grade 1 and Grade 5 students be introduced to the musical concepts listed in Table 16.1 (see pp. 12–13 for a complete list for all grades).

Table 16.1

Recommended Concepts for Labelling at Grade 1 and Grade 5
(summarized from Chapter 2, pp. 12–13)

Music Element	Grade 1 concepts	Grade 5 concepts
Beat, Tempo, and Metre	beat beat vs rhythm tempo: fast vs slow	6/8 metre
Dynamics	loud vs soft	as appropriate
Rhythm	rhythm rhythm vs beat *tah* and *ti-ti*, quarter note rest	*tim-ka, tam-ti*; 6/8: *ti-ti-ti; ta-ti; tam*
Pitch	high vs low melodic contour *soh-mi, lah*	*fa, ti*
Harmony and Texture	monophonic singing rhythmic ostinato pedal tones	I–IV–V chords
Form	phrase phrase form	theme & variations
Timbre	four voices non-pitched percussion pitched percussion	orchestral instruments
Expressive Elements	as appropriate	as appropriate

When the teacher places these concepts in a logical sound-before-symbol teaching time frame based on an average of two 30- to 40-minute lessons per week throughout the year, she or he can create timetables such as those shown in Tables 16.2 and 16.3.

These timetables, generally prepared in late August or early September, are of course merely projections based on the teacher's knowledge of the pacing of children's musical learning. Adjustments in scheduling throughout the year will be inevitable because of both individual student progress and a variety of external constraints (including interruptions such as school closures due to weather or special programming). Nonetheless, making such a musical concept timetable is an important step in the process of curricular decision making, as these timelines provide teachers with a clear sense of direction for daily planning.

Once the music concept timetable has been completed, the next task is to select the *music* for the year, based on the parameters discussed in Chapter 4 (developmental appropriateness, diversity of styles, a variety of music for singing, playing and listening, etc.). Teachers might match certain pieces of music with particular musical concepts, making sure that there will be an adequate repertoire upon which to draw from. It is recommended that students revisit music many times throughout the year as they move towards an understanding of different musical concepts, rather than learning a new piece of music for the introduction of each new concept. As a result, the children's familiarity with their classroom repertoire should provide them with an open window through which to view the inner workings of musical structure.

Continuing with the planning example for Grades 1 and 5 music curricula, a list of music appropriate for these grades (using only music found in this textbook) might look like Table 16.4.

Naturally, Table 16.4 is merely an exercise to illustrate how one might go about selecting musical content for a particular grade level. Teachers in their own classrooms would of course use a wide variety of resources from which to select their music including Canadian elementary music textbooks (for example, Harrison and Harrison, 2000), Canadian folk song collections (for example, Lehr, 1985; Pottie and Ellis, 1992; Wilkie, 1998), rhyme and finger play collections (for example, Opie and Opie, 1979), collections of rounds and canons (for example, Bolkovac and Johnson, 1996), collections of children's songs and recorder music (for example, Hackett, 1998), Orff instrumental arrangements (for example, Birkenshaw-Fleming, 1996), poetry collections (for example, Lee, 1974), world music collections (for example, Campbell et al. 1994), choral music (for example, Telfer, 1993), recorded music collections (Bowmar, 1981), and this textbook.

Upon completion of both this selection process (i.e., musical concepts and music) for the year, and the graphing of the musical concept list into a logical sound-before-symbol instructional timetable, the elementary music teacher is then ready to move forward to the second stage of the planning process.

Teachers need a plan to introduce musical concepts throughout the school year.

Music should be revisited by students several times during any one school year.

Select musical content from a variety of resources.

Step 2: Selection of Learner-Centred Activities and Strategies

As discussed in Chapters 1–2, it is recommended that elementary music education be rooted in the authentic musical practices of **performing**, **composing**, and

Table 16.2
Example of a Music Concept Timetable for Grade 1

	Beat, Tempo and Metre	Dynamics	Rhythm	Pitch	Harmony and Texture	Timbre	Form
Sep.	Aural intro and label: beat Reinforce: beat	Aural intro and label: loud vs. soft	Aural intro and label: rhythm Reinforce: rhythm	Aural intro: high vs. low	Aural intro: monophonic texture	Aural intro, label, reinforce: four voices and body percussion	Aural intro: phrase
Oct.	Reinforce: beat vs. rhythm Aural intro, label: fast vs. slow	Reinforce: loud vs. soft	Reinforce: beat vs. rhythm Aural intro: *tah/ti-ti*	Label, reinforce: high vs. low Aural intro: *soh-mi*		Aural intro, label, reinforce: non-pitched percussion	
Nov.	Reinforce: fast vs. slow	Create: loud vs. soft	Label, reinforce: *tah/ti-ti*	Create: high vs. low Aural intro label, reinforce: melodic contour			
Dec.							
Jan.	Create: beat, fast vs. slow		Aural intro: quarter rest	Label, reinforce: *soh-mi*			
Feb.			Create: *tah/ti-ti* Label, reinforce: quarter rest	Aural intro and label: *lah*			
Mar.			Create: *tah/ti-ti*, rest	Create: *soh-mi*	Aural intro and label: rhythmic *ostinato*		Label: phrase
Apr.				Create: *soh-mi-lah*	Reinforce, create: rhythmic *ostinato* Aural intro, label: pedal tone	Aural intro and label: pitched percussion	Reinforce: phrase Aural intro and label: phrase form
May							Reinforce: phrase form
Jun.							

Table 16.3
Example of a Music Concept Timetable for Grade 5

	Beat, Tempo and Metre	Dynamics	Rhythm	Pitch	Harmony and Texture	Timbre	Form
Sep.	Reinforce, create: beat and tempo, 2/4, 3/4, 4/4 metres	Reinforce, create: as appropriate.	Reinforce, create: all previous rhythms Aural intro: *tim-ka*	Reinforce, create: all previous tonic sol-fa and musical alphabet	Reinforce, create: rhythmic and melodic *ostinati, bordun,* canons, two- and three-part singing	Reinforce, create: non-pitched and pitched percussion, recorder, strings, brass, woodwinds	Reinforce, create: AB, ABA, rondo sectional forms
Oct.			Label, reinforce: *tim-ka* Aural intro: *tam-ti*	Aural intro: *fa* and *ti*			
Nov.			Label, reinforce: tam-ti	Label: *fa* and *ti*			
Dec.				Reinforce *fa* and *ti*			
Jan.	Aural intro: 6/8 metre						
Feb.	Label and reinforce: 6/8 metre		Label and reinforce: 6/8 versions of *ti-ti-ti-, tah-ti; tam*		Aural intro, label, reinforce: major and natural minor scales		
Mar.			Create *tim-ka* and *tam-ti*		Aural intro, label, reinforce: I-V chords		Aural intro, label, reinforce, create: theme and variations
Apr.	Create: 6/8 metre			Create: *fa* and *ti*	Aural intro and label, reinforce: I-IV-V chords		
May							
June							

Table 16.4

Example of a Musical Content List for Grades 1 and 5

(using music found in *Teaching Towards Musical Understanding*)

Grade 1	Grade 5
Are You My Children (p. 47)	*Alleluia Canon* (p. 302)
Body Fun (p. 68)	*Bonavist' Harbour* (pp. 128–29)
Bingo (p. 160)	*Circle 'round the Zero* (p. 164)
Bounce High, Bounce Low (p. 211)	*Coffee Canon* (p. 60)
Bow Wow Wow (p. 157)	*Dona Nobis Pacem* (pp. 175–76)
Brown Bear, Brown Bear (p. 246)	*En roulant ma boule* (pp. 246–47)
Bye Baby Bunting (p. 210)	*The Huron Carol* (p. 256)
Criss Cross (p. 218)	*I'll Give My Love an Apple* (p. 33)
Diddle Diddle Dumpling (p. 285)	*In the Bleak Midwinter* (p. 225)
Doggie, Doggie (p. 45)	*I'se the B'y* (pp. 90–91)
Hicketty Picketty (p. 72)	*Jack Was Every Inch a Sailor* (pp. 171–72)
Hey Hey (p. 47)	*Kelligrew's Soirée* (pp. 268–69)
Hop Old Squirrel (p. 217)	*The Lumber Camp Song* (p. 267)
Ickle Ockle (p. 86)	*My Bark Canoe* (p. 75)
Jelly in a Bowl (p. 131)	*The Nova Scotia Song* (pp. 264–65)
Jingle Bells (p. 162)	*The Ryans and The Pittmans* (pp. 280–81)
Lucy Locket (p. 154)	*Un canadien errant* (pp. 92–94)
Mary Had a Little Lamb (p. 209)	*Vive la canadienne* (p. 226)
One, Two, Tie My Shoe (p. 41)	
Percussion Fun (p. 78)	Plus: recorder music
See-Saw (p. 191)	*À Saint-Malo, beau port de mer* (p. 102)
Star Light, Star Bright (p. 238)	*Entendez-vous sur l'ormeau* (p. 110)
There Was an Old Woman (p. 43)	*Gavotte* (p. 108)
We Are Dancing in the Forest (p. 46)	*Le coq est mort* (p. 111)
Who's That? (p. 48)	
Plus: recorded music from chapter 7	Plus: recorded music from chapter 7
Plus: music composed by the children	Plus: music composed by the children

Classroom activities should be as multi-sensory as possible.

listening. Classroom experiences through which children engage in such behaviours include singing, playing classroom instruments, listening, moving, composing, improvising, and reading and writing music. Therefore, as teachers begin to organize monthly instruction to include appropriate learner-centred activities with which to explore musical concepts, they should make sure classroom experiences are as *multi-sensory* as possible.

Again using the planning example of Grade 1 and Grade 5 music, according to Table 16.2, during the month of November, the Grade 1 students are projected to be at various stages in the **sound-before-symbol** teaching process with the following concepts.

- aural, kinesthetic, and oral introduction: monophonic texture, melodic contour, *soh–mi,* and phrases
- labelling and reinforcing: *tah/ti-ti,* melodic contour
- reinforcing: beat, fast vs. slow, four voices, body percussion, and non-pitched percussion
- creating: loud vs. soft, melodic contour, and high vs. low

The Grade 5 students are projected to be experiencing the following concepts.

- labelling and reinforcing: *tam-ti,* and *fa* and *ti*
- reinforcing: *tim-ka*
- reinforcing and creating: beat (2/4, 3/4, and 4/4 metres), dynamics, all rhythms from Grades 1–4, all tonic sol-fa and staff names from Grades 1–4, polyphonic texture (*ostinati, borduns,* and rounds in two or three parts), and sectional forms (AB, ABA, and rondo)

Keeping in mind the overall goal of the curriculum—*to guide children towards the development of a comprehensive musical understanding,* that is, the ability to think and act musically with personal meaning—the reader can turn to Chapters 4–9 and 10–15 to locate a variety of classroom activities to support this goal that would be **developmentally appropriate** for use with the musical concepts listed for the month of November. Such activities are examples of the variety of choices that would be available to teachers as they begin to move towards the planning of the daily lessons for these two grade levels during this month.

Step 3: Selection of Authentic Assessment Tools

Assessment is a key component of the curricular planning process.

Planning for **formal assessment**—*the gathering and recording of evidence of student growth in musical understanding*—is an important part of the curricular planning process. Such assessment should be utilized on a regular basis as a part of the daily instructional process in order for it to be as natural and unobtrusive as possible. Thus, in preparation for writing daily lesson plans, the teacher should examine the learner objectives of the curriculum in conjunction with the list of activities and strategies to be used and determine a list of possible assessment tools with which to chart student progress. Chapter 17 provides specific guidance for this selection process.

Step 4: Preparation of Daily Lesson Plans

The long-range and monthly planning undertaken by the teacher prior to this point will prove to be very helpful as the teacher begins the excitement of daily lesson planning. Curricular instruction is most effective when built within a framework of long-term planning for musical growth and development. It is much easier to write a lesson plan for the first day of the month if the teacher has a general plan as to where he or she hopes to lead the students by the end of the month. Thus, teachers should think of the three steps of planning discussed earlier in this chapter as integral to the process of writing successful daily lesson plans.

Lesson plans may be written in many different formats. One of the most useful formats divides the plan into five sections:

Section 1: A list of *the main concept and the supplementary concepts* to be aurally, orally, and kinesthetically experienced, introduced with label and symbols, reinforced, or created during the lesson; these concepts come from the yearly and monthly sequencing chart made previously by the teacher.

Section 2: A list of *learner objectives* specifying what the student will do in the lesson in order to show appropriate (i.e., cognitive, psychomotor, or affective) "knowledge" of the concept; these objectives either come directly from the curriculum guide or are written by the teacher.

Section 3: A list of the *music, materials, and equipment* needed for the lesson—that is, everything!

Section 4: A *step-by-step teaching procedure* that is broken down into five parts: **opening**, **motivation**, **main activity**, **active change**, and **closure**.

- *opening*—a short section at the beginning of the lesson that warms up the children's musical ears, voices, bodies (for example singing a favourite song, echo-singing or echo-clapping, or identifying a mystery tune)

- *motivation*—a short experiential section that "sets-up" the main activity by preparing and focusing the children's attention towards the main concept being studied

- *main activity*—the central section of the lesson, where the children engage in musical activities that focus their learning towards the main concept

- *active change*—sometimes thought of as the "second part of the main activity," where the children apply their knowledge of the music concept to a different piece of music; it is often used as an assessment section

- *closure*—a short review of what has been learned during the lesson, often using recorded music that incorporates the concept

Section 5: a list of any *formal assessment* to be used during the lesson to determine students' success at meeting the learner objective(s) of the lesson (see Chapter 17 for specifics); this section is an integral part of the lesson plan .

Planning a music lesson requires a variety of thoughtful considerations by the teacher. These considerations might include answering questions such as the following:

- What stage are the children presently at with the main concept in relation to the sound-before-symbol teaching process? The answer to this question will determine whether the activities selected should be purely experiential, involve an "introductory lesson," utilize musical symbols, or invite the children to create something new with the concept.

- What ages are the children? Are they six-year-olds (Grade 1s), who generally require several changes in activities during any one lesson in order to keep them focused? Are they ten-year-olds (Grade 4s), who are capable of working cooperatively in small groups for a longer period of time?

- What kinds of concrete manipulatables are appropriate for use with the age group in question? What kinds of classroom management strategies could be built into the lesson to avoid discipline problems arising out of the use of manipulatables, classroom instruments, or movement activities in the classroom?

- How might the concept be approached in such a way as to facilitate learning by a diversified group of individual learners: some with strengths in kinesthetic learning, some with strengths as visual learners, and some preferring aural learning? Does the lesson include a variety of musical experiences, such as singing, moving, and listening? How might the lesson support children with special needs?

- Do the strategies you plan to use place the students in the middle of making, creating, or listening to music? Do they require the child to problem-solve or use critical thinking? How might the lesson be organized such that the children are able to derive the new knowledge from the experience itself, thus taking greater ownership in the learning process?

- Does the procedure you plan involve time for student reflection, whether verbal or written? Will the students be given time to talk about, explain, or interpret the decisions they make regarding the music they experience?

- If assessment beyond simply recorded observation is planned, is it authentic in reference to the musical task at hand?

A music lesson plan comes to life in the hands of a skilled teacher.

These questions, when answered by the teacher, should provide considerable guidance as to the writing of a stimulating and enjoyable music lesson for the children. Teachers might want to use such questions as a kind of checklist whenever they engage in writing a new lesson, in order to ascertain both the strengths and weaknesses of their projected plan. Teachers should be reminded however, that a lesson plan is only that—a plan. *The strength of the lesson comes not from what is written on the page, but from the ability of a skilled teacher to bring the lesson to life for the children.*

Sample Lesson Plans

The two sample lesson plans included below are based on the planning examples done previously in this chapter for lessons for Grades 1 and 5 in November.

Grade 1 Lesson (40 minutes)

Main concept: reinforce *tah* and *ti-ti*

Supplementary concepts
- reinforce: *singing voice* from the four voices, *beat vs. rhythm*, and the *non-pitched percussion timbres* of wood block and hand drum
- introduce: *sforzando*

Learner Objectives

1. The students will chant a rhyme containing *tah ti-ti* rhythms—*Criss Cross*

2. The students will write the *tah* and *ti-ti* rhythms of *See-Saw* using felt hearts and popsicle sticks

3. The students will read a mystery rhythm of a familiar song that has *tah/ti-ti* rhythms and identify its name—*Lucy Locket*

4. The students will sight-read a new rhythm pattern containing *tah ti-ti* rhythms

5. The students will recognize and clap along with a *tah ti-ti* rhythm heard in recorded music: the opening (1 minute 45 seconds) of the second movement of the Symphony no. 94 ("Surprise") by Haydn

Music, Materials, and Equipment

- Music: *Hey Hey* (p. 47), *Criss Cross* (p. 218), *See-Saw* (p. 191), *Lucy Locket* (p. 154), second movement of the Symphony no. 94 ("Surprise") by Haydn

- Equipment: a pair of claves, 25 baggies containing popsicle sticks and felt hearts, beat vs. rhythm stick, white board, 6 hand drums, 7 tone blocks and mallets, CD player, space for movement

Procedure

- Opening (6–7 minutes)

  Ask the children to review the song *Hey Hey* by singing it as a group. Next, invite a child to sing by herself or himself as the leader of the song, with the rest of the class singing the echo. Repeat this seven times, giving eight children a chance at individual singing. (Plan to repeat with eight more children at the next lesson.)

  Concept: reinforcing the four voices (singing, from Timbre) using individual singing.

- Motivation (7–8 minutes)

  (a) Play the rhythm of *Criss Cross* on the claves for the children as a mystery rhythm. Invite the children to identify the name of the rhyme.

  (b) Ask the children to keep the beat on their knees while chanting the rhyme. Have them chant the rhyme a second time while clapping the rhythm.

  (c) Pass out the hand drums to six children and the wood blocks to another seven. Invite the children with hand drums to play the beat, the children with wood blocks to play the rhythm, and the rest of the class to chant the rhyme. Do this twice so all the children get a chance to play one of the instruments. Collect instruments.

  Concept: reinforcing beat vs. rhythm (*tah* and *ti-ti*, from Rhythm) using playing classroom instruments

- Main Activity (10 minutes)

  (a) Play the melody of *See-Saw* on the recorder for the children as a mystery tune. Invite the children to identify the song.

  (b) Ask the children to sing the song while keeping the beat on their knees. Repeat, this time clapping the rhythm. Guide the children between keeping the beat and clapping the rhythm as you turn the beat-rhythm stick periodically from the side showing rhythm to the side showing beat, and back again.

  (c) Pass out baggies of manipulatables to children. Have them write the rhythm of *See-Saw* using popsicle sticks to represent the *tahs* and *ti-tis* and the felt hearts for the beats. Circulate around the room, putting appropriate marks (+, √, or **X**) in the grade book to record the success of each child at writing the rhythm.

  Concept: Reinforce *tah* and *ti-ti* (from Rhythm) using writing

- Active Change (10 minutes)

  Have the children read the rhythm of the familiar song *Lucy Locket* written on the board. Invite the children to read the rhythm by chanting *tahs* and *ti-tis* while keeping the beat on their knees. End by playing the game *Lucy Locket* with enough repetitions to give 12 children a chance to be the one to skip around the circle.

  Concept: Reinforce *tah* and *ti-ti* (from Rhythm) using reading, singing, and moving.

- Closing (5 minutes)

  Invite the children to sight-read the following *tah/ti-ti* rhythm off the board using rhythmic syllables while clapping. Repeat a couple of times.

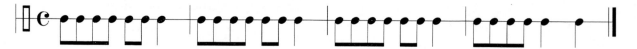

  Ask the children to listen for this rhythm in the recording of the second movement of Haydn's Symphony no. 94 ("Surprise"), which you will play for them, and invite them to quietly tap along on their tables when they think they hear the rhythm in the music (it repeats several times). Ask them to also listen for the "surprise" (the unexpected *fortissimo* chord that comes at the end of one of the repetitions of the rhythm), and to be prepared to reflect on its parameters at the end of the listening. Repeat.

  Concept: Reinforce *tah* and *ti-ti* (from Rhythm); introduce *sforzando* (from Dynamics) using listening.

Assessment

Based on Learner Objective 2: The teacher marks the children as successful (+), partly successful (√), or not successful (X) on a checklist while circulating around the room to look at the results of the individual work with the popsicle sticks.

Grade 5 lesson (50 minutes)

Main Concept: *tam-ti*

Supplementary concepts

- reinforce: rhythmic *ostinato*, polyphonic singing involving canons, timbres of tone blocks, hand drums, triangles, and recorders
- aural introduction: *fa* and *ti*
- label: *ti-tam* (variation of *tam-ti*)

Learner Objectives

1. The students will read the rhythm of a familiar song containing *tam-ti*: *In the Bleak Midwinter*

2. The students will play the rhythm of a familiar recorder piece containing *tam-ti*: *In the Bleak Midwinter*

3. The students will sing and play a canon containing *tam-ti* rhythms: *Dona Nobis Pacem*

4. The students will play a rhythmic *ostinato* containing *tam-ti* to accompany their singing of a familiar song: *Dona Nobis Pacem*

5. The students will sing a new singing game containing *ti-tam* rhythms: *Circle 'round the Zero*

6. The students will identify with movement when they hear the rhythm *tam-ti* in recorded music: *In the Bleak Midwinter*

Music, Materials, and Equipment

- Music—*In the Bleak Midwinter* (p. 225), *Dona Nobis Pacem* (p. 175), *Circle 'round the Zero* (p. 164), recording of brass quintet arrangement of *In the Bleak Midwinter*
- Equipment—30 soprano recorders, 4 tone blocks, 4 hand drums, printed music of *In the Bleak Midwinter* and *Dona Nobis Pacem*, CD player, digital video recorder, white board

Procedure

- Opening (5–6 minutes)

Have the rhythm of *In the Bleak Midwinter* written on the board. Invite children to read the rhythm using rhythmic syllables. Use this rhythm to play the Rhythm Erase game (p. 231). At the end, ask children to identify the name of the song that belongs to this rhythm.

Concept: reinforce *tam-ti* from Rhythm using reading

- Motivation (8 minutes)

Ask children to get out their recorders and the familiar music of *In the Bleak Midwinter*. Rehearse the piece making corrections as needed. Remind the children that personal tape recordings of their solo playing of the piece are due next week.

Concepts: reinforce *tam-ti*; and aural experience of *fa* and *ti* using playing the recorder

- Main Activity (20 minutes)

    (a) Review the familiar canon *Dona Nobis Pacem* by asking the children to sing it first as a regular melody (i.e., no canon). Invite four children to play the rhythmic *ostinato*

on tone blocks to accompany the singing.

    (b Divide the children into two groups. Ask Group 1 to begin the singing of the canon with Group 2 coming in at the correct spot as the second voice to make a two-part canon. Add the rhythmic *ostinato* accompaniment with four students from Group 1 playing the *ostinato* on tone blocks while four students from Group 2 play the *ostinato* on hand drum. Repeat a couple of times with different students having an opportunity to play the instrumental accompaniment.

    (c) Divide the children into three groups. Ask Group 3 to play the piece on their recorders. Perform *Dona Nobis Pacem* as a three-part canon with Group 1 singing and playing the rhythmic *ostinato* on tone blocks, Group 2 singing and playing the rhythmic *ostinato* on hand drums, and Group 3 playing the melody on recorders (with no *ostinato*). Record the performance on video and place in the students' portfolios for sharing with parents during parent-student-teacher conference night coming up in three weeks.

    (d) Homework: Ask the students to write a one-page reflection on the learning process required to bring the piece to this level of performance; add this to the students' portfolios day after tomorrow.

Concepts: reinforce *tam-ti* (from Rhythm), tone color of hand drum, tone block, and recorder (from Timbre), polyphonic canon in three parts (from Harmony and Texture) using singing and playing; aural introduction of *fa* and *ti* using singing and playing.

- Active Change (10–11 minutes)

  Teach the students the new song, *Circle 'round the Zero*. Ask the children to sing while keeping the beat on their knees. Sing again this time while clapping the rhythm. Hold a classroom discussion to figure out the rhythm of the first two measures, which contains a variant of tam-ti. Teach the children the game and play with a few repetitions.

  Concept: labelling *ti-tam* as a variant of *tam-ti* (from Rhythm) using singing and moving.

- Closure (5 minutes)

  Ask the children to listen to a recorded version of *In the Bleak Midwinter* played by a brass quintet, and invite them to use a movement of their choice in their own space to indicate every time they hear the *tam-ti* in the melody. Reflect on the different instruments in the brass family. Remind the children they will begin studying the individual instruments next week.

  Concepts: reinforce *tam-ti* (from Rhythm) and instruments of the brass family (from Timbre) using listening and movement.

Assessment

Based on Learner Objective 3: a videotape of performing music containing *tam-ti* in ensemble is placed in each student's portfolio along with her or his reflection on the learning process. In addition, advance notice is given regarding an upcoming assessment (the taped performance of *In the Bleak Midwinter*) that is due in the near future.

Questions for Discussion and Practice

1. What is meant by curricular planning? What variables in and out of a teacher's classroom may influence such planning? Why?

2. Why should the provincial or local board curriculum guide be viewed as only a starting point for curricular decision making? What role should the elementary music teacher play in this process?

3. Using the music concept sequence list from Chapter 2, make a year graph that places the concepts from Grade 2 into a logical sound-before-symbol teaching timetable in relation to a 38-week school year, averaging 90 minutes of music per week. Now repeat this exercise with Grade 4 concepts using the musical concept list from your provincial or local school board music curricula guide.

4. Using a variety of resources, select music to coordinate with the music concept list chosen for Grade 2 or 4 in question 3.

5. Write a Grade 2 or Grade 4 lesson plan based on the planning done in question 3. Use the seven-question checklist presented in this chapter to check for strengths and weaknesses in your lesson plan. Make revisions if necessary.

References

Birkenshaw-Fleming, L. (Ed.) (1996). *An Orff Mosaic*. New York: Schott Music.

Bolkovac, E., and Johnson, J. (1996). *150 Rounds for Singing and Teaching*. London: Boosey and Hawkes.

Bowmar Records (1981). *The Bowmar Orchestral Library*. Florida: C.P. Belwin.

Campbell, P., McCullough-Brabsob, E., and Tucker, J. (1994). *Roots and Branches*. Danbury, CT: World Music Press.

CMEA and CMEC. (2001). *Achieving Musical Understanding: Concepts and Skills for Pre-Kindergarten to Grade 8*. Toronto: Coalition for Music Education in Canada.

Eisner, E. (1985). *The Educational Imagination: On the Design and Evaluation of School Programs*. New York: MacMillan.

Hackett, P. (1998). *The Melody Book*. Upper Saddle River, NJ: Prentice Hall.

Harrison, J., and Harrison, M. (Eds.). (2000). *Canada Is Music*. Toronto: Gordon V. Thompson Music.

Lee, D. (1982). *Alligator Pie*. Toronto: MacMillan.

Lehr, G. (1985). *Come And I Will Sing You*. St. John's: Breakwater Books.

Montgomery, A. (2000). Elementary school music: reflections for the future. In B. Hanley and B. Roberts (Eds.), *Looking Forward: Challenges to Canadian Music Education*. Victoria, BC: Canadian Music Educators Association.

Opie, I., and Opie, P. (1979). *The Oxford Nursery Rhyme Book*. London: Oxford University Press.

Pottie, K., and Ellis, V. (1992). *Folksongs of the Maritimes*. Halifax: Formac Publishing.

Telfer, N. (1993). *When the Outports Sing*. San Diego: Kjos Music.

Wilkie, R. (1998). *Discovering Folksongs*. Waterloo, Ontario: Waterloo Music.

CHAPTER 17

Assessment and Evaluation

SYNOPSIS

Chapter 17 provides guidance for the role of assessment and evaluation in the elementary music classroom. Authentic music assessment is defined and a variety of classroom examples are provided. The potential for using portfolios in the elementary music class is also discussed.

Introduction

Student assessment is the fair and ethical tracking and recording of evidence of the students' growth and development.

Assessment may be informal or formal.

Student assessment and evaluation plays an important role in the classroom life of the elementary music teacher. Indeed, documenting student growth in musical understanding and placing a grade based on the value of that growth is an integral part of the teacher's responsibility. Educators are expected to *track and record evidence of this growth on a regular basis in a fair, and ethical manner* (**assessment**), and to make an official *judgment of the merit of this collected data* (**evaluation**) three or four times a year at report card time.

Student assessment may be **informal** (*unrecorded observations*) or **formal** (*recorded observations or other tools used for later evaluation*). Informal assessment usually consists of unobtrusive observations made by the teacher during instruction for the purpose of determining student progress. Such mental field notes guide the teacher in the design and implementation of curricula. Formal assessment is used when teachers want to record student responses as part of an ongoing collection of data on students' growth and development in musical understanding. Although such assessment is perhaps still unobtrusive, students should be informed when the teacher is recording their music behaviour.

Musically Authentic Assessment

Musically
authentic
assessment
gathers
information in
real music
making and
listening
situations.

The term **musically authentic assessment** refers to *assessment techniques that gather information naturally in real music making, creating, and listening situations*. As stated in Chapter 16, assessment should ideally be an integral part of the instructional process in the elementary music class. When student assessment can be integrated as a regular part of the lesson plan, it not only makes the assessment process more musically authentic but also informs teachers as to when they should move on in a lesson and when there is a need to review a topic area more thoroughly. For example, rather than giving a written multiple-choice test, a teacher might use students' musical compositions written in class as evidence of understanding of musical symbols. Objectives stated in the lesson plan provide guidance as to what will be assessed during instruction. The general goals of the curriculum provide direction for the creation of these objectives (see Chapter 16).

Student
assessment
should be
multi-faceted.

Often assessment is purely observational, with the teacher using a checklist to record evidence of a student's performance of a specific musical skill (such as keeping a steady beat while singing). At other times, the lesson might include a few minutes for students to write reflections on a group activity (such as creating movement to illustrate the form of a song) that was completed during the lesson. Further, a lesson might involve students writing eight-measure rhythms, performing them as introductions to a song during class time, recording their performance on videotape, and handing their brief compositions in to the teacher at the end of the lesson.

Clearly, quality assessment in elementary music education means that a *variety* of methods should be used to gather data about process and product. Since children are reaching towards musical understanding through activities in performing, composing, and listening, no one method of collecting data will give a complete picture of the child's developing ability to think and act musically.

Examples of Assessment Tools

The following list includes a number of assessment devices that are available to the elementary music teacher for use during or in combination with instruction.

1. *Teacher or student checklists*: Checklists (marked by the teacher with "+" to indicate *mastery*, "√" to indicate *emerging*, or "X" to indicate *still under development*) that describe musical behaviour in reference to specific abilities, such as:

   - the ability to use the correct voice (singing or talking) during singing-game activities in class, such as playing the solo part in *Are You My Children?* (p. 47, Grade 1)

   - the ability to play a *bordun* pattern with a steady beat to accompany classroom singing (p. 87, Grade 3)

   - the ability to play a recorder descant to accompany singing during small group work in class (pp. 92–94, Grade 5)

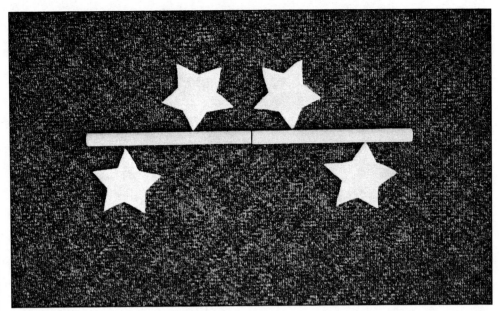

Example of a Grade 1 student's composition using iconic stars to represent the high and low pitches

2. *Recordings (audio tape, videotape or CD-ROM)*: Recordings of students' solo improvisations, solo performances, and solo or ensemble performances of class work (for example: a videotape of a student playing an *ostinato* accompaniment on non-pitched percussion during class singing, p. 74; an audiotape of an assigned recorder piece made by the student during lunch hour, pp. 100–111)

3. *Photographs*: A photographic record of students' musical compositions (for example, showing completed class work that required Grade 1 children to write a short melody using iconic stars to represent the high and low pitches, p. 237)

4. *Student journals that highlight aesthetic response*: Journals in which students describe their aesthetic response to hearing a selection of recorded music; for example, students might complete written reflections on how listening to a particular piece of music makes them feel—thus highlighting their discussion of particular structural elements within the music that caught their attention (pp. 145–150).

5. *Worksheets*: Students' worksheets that focus on reading and writing musical symbols or on discrimination responses made while listening to music (for example, circling iconic responses regarding the form of a song while listening, figure 17.1).

6. *Students' drafts and final musical scores*: Drafts and final musical scores of student compositions—ranging from four-measure rhythms written in Grade 1 (p. 127) to complete 20-measure songs with instrumental accompaniments written in Grade 6 (p. 134)

7. *Written tests*: Written tests that focus on cognitive understanding (for example, asking children to answer a question about brass instruments with a short essay describing the different instruments of the brass family, explaining details such as how the sound is made and how the pitch is changed, p. 277)

8. *Student journals that reflect on class projects*: Journals in which students describe class projects that involve singing, playing instruments, moving, composing or

Figure 17.1 • Instruction: Circle the picture that you think best illustrates the form of the song.

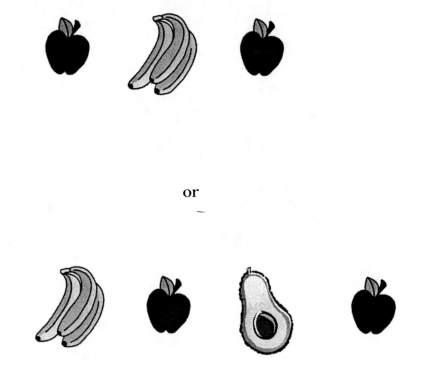

or

improving (for example, a student's reflections on the process of small group work in selecting appropriate rhythmic *ostinati* to accompany a familiar song, p. 272)

9. *Programs of performances*: Copies of programs for performances in which a student has participated, along with the student's self-assessment comments (for example, a student's written assessments of his or her performances both during school concerts and in context with music lessons outside of school)

10. *Students' research reports*: research reports written by students on subjects such as composers, musical styles, or performers, (for example, a written report on Canadian composer and jazz musician Oscar Peterson, using information found on the Internet, p. 278)

11. *Videotapes and peer evaluation of students' oral presentations*: A video recording of an oral presentation by one student on a composer, a musical style, or a performer, along with comments from other students in the class (for example, written reports on composers or performers that might include audio selections made by students to illustrate their findings—peers provide feedback as to the effectiveness of the "public" presentation)

12. *Videotapes of music-movement responses*: Video recordings showing students' music-movement responses to music. (for example, a videotape of small group work during class where students are asked to devise a movement sequence to illustrate the ABA form of a piece of music, p. 171)

Music Portfolios

Hard copies of these assessment tools can be placed in a student's **music portfolio**—*a file folder, box, or multi-media computer file containing evidence of a student's progress in elementary music education, collected over a particular period of time.* According to Beatty (2000), such portfolios provide an opportunity to "depict the artistic thinking process of the students and give meaning to their long-term development" (p. 201).

Students take ownership in the assessment process by helping the teacher to select the particular items to be included in the portfolio. Indeed, these portfolios can include a rich tapestry of a student's work, thereby giving the teacher, student, parent, and administrator a clearer picture of the student's musical growth and development.

Student work within the portfolios may be shared with parents at student-teacher-parent conferences held periodically throughout the year, usually near report card time. Students might lead their parents around the classroom to different centres (language arts, math, music, etc.), sharing work from their portfolios in each subject area with their parents. Since some of the work in the music portfolios will be on audio or videotape or on CD-ROM, the appropriate equipment should be available in the classroom for these events.

In addition, live performances during the conference evening, involving all of the children in the class, can be a wonderful way to give parents a glimpse into the musical education of their children. Be sure to invite the principal to attend as well; she or he may become a stronger advocate for the arts in education if she or he is made aware of all the wonderful activities that take place during elementary music class!

In summary, a wide variety of assessment tools are available to the elementary music teacher interested in "using assessment to support the needs of learners" (Wiggins, 1990, p. 2). Selecting authentic tasks embedded within the natural practice of performing, composing, and listening should provide valuable feedback to students regarding their progress in the development of musical understanding. In addition, the teacher will find a useful blend of information from which to continue to modify and design future curricula for the classroom.

Questions for Discussion and Practice

1. What is the difference between assessment and evaluation? Are music teachers responsible for both?

2. Briefly define authentic music assessment. Give three classroom examples.

3. Develop a worksheet you could use in a Grade 2 class to assess children's knowledge of rhythmic values appropriate for introduction in this grade.

4. Develop a checklist to record performance skills in singing appropriate for Grade 1. Now do the same for Grade 5.

5. Visit a local school and make a list of the kinds of assessment tools included in the elementary music class.

References

Beatty, R. (2000). Assessing for success in music education. In B. Hanley and B. Roberts (Eds.), *Challenges to Canadian Music Education*. Victoria, BC: Canadian Music Educators Association.

Wiggins, G. (1990). The case for authentic assessment. *Practical Assessment, Research and Evaluation*, 2(2). Available online at http://ericae.net/.

PART FIVE

Finale

Part V provides closing thoughts about the role of the elementary music teacher in the classroom. Advice is given regarding the need to become an advocator for the arts, the importance of continuing to grow as a musician, the significance of keeping abreast of new research and technology, and the value of lifelong professional development.

CHAPTER 18

Thoughts for the Future

Well . . . it is just about time to embark on your new life as an elementary music teacher. Are you ready? Are you excited? Are you up for the challenges?

There can be no doubt that one of the most satisfying and stimulating parts of your day as a teacher will be when you are busily sharing the gift of music with children. This gift is precious, as rich experiences with music are often what make us feel truly alive.

Music relaxes us, it comforts us, it inspires us, it draws us in and leads us to discover a wealth of emotions deep down inside ourselves. Indeed, elementary music education is the moment in the day when we have the opportunity to guide students towards this rich array of musical sounds through the development of a strong musical understanding – that ability to think and act musically with personal meaning. Whether as performers, composers, or listeners, we want children to experience music to its fullest, to reach inside the music through active interplay with its structure.

While reading through this textbook, you have had an opportunity to begin to think about many of the responsibilities you will have in the process of teaching elementary school music. Reflection on issues such as the selection of age-appropriate materials, the creation of a learner-centred environment, the choice of authentic experiences that place the child in the centre of music making, composing, and listening, the need to value individual's response to musical nuance has all been part of your journey towards the delight of sharing music with children.

As you begin to reach towards the moment when you will need to turn your reflection into classroom action, it may be useful to jot down a few notes to which you might refer to from time to time in the future. These musings from an experienced voice might be food for thought as you travel down the exciting road of teaching. Here are a few ideas in this direction.

Learn how to be an advocate for the arts! You may find that your colleagues, and/or administrators and/or parents sometimes need reminding about the significance of including music education in the elementary curriculum. Remind them, and yourself, of the importance of educating the whole child, of enhancing children's natural musical intelligence through the joys of making, composing, and listening to music. Advise them of the consequence of placing children in the middle of the music experience from which they develop the ability to think and act musically with personal meaning. Share the excitement of musical learning that happens in your classroom by inviting parents and administrators to see what actually happens in a typical music lesson in your class. Do this as part of your quarterly parent-teacher conferences to help illuminate the importance of what you do as a teacher. Indeed, if all the parents ever see is the Christmas or spring concert, why would they think the music curriculum is anything more than performing for the public on risers?

Continue to grow as a musician! Build your confidence by taking lessons on a new instrument, perform in a local community music ensemble, keep abreast of musical traditions past and present by visiting your local music store to buy a few CDs for your collection, volunteer to conduct the children's choir at your church or community hall. In order to help children make music, *you* need to make music. In order to help children turn on their ears to new sounds, *you* need to listen to a varied repertoire of music. In order to help children compose, *you* need to grab a little courage and dabble in the process yourself. Indeed, could you imagine teaching children to read books if you had never enjoyed a good book yourself?

Keep tuned in to research in elementary music education. Pay an online visit to the Canadian Music Education Resource Base at **www.culturenet.ca/merb** to search out information on various aspects of music teaching. Attend a research session in music education at a professional conference (for example, a conference of the Canadian Music Educators Association) and find out how these ideas might be used to enhance your instruction. Take a few minutes to read some of the research articles referenced in this textbook. They can lead you to a whole array of exciting professional reading that may find you eager to take a year's leave from teaching and go back to university to do an advanced degree.

Develop positive relationships with other elementary music teachers in your school board, in your province, and across Canada. Enjoy the support and professional development that can result from such relationships. Become an active member of one or more of the professional associations available to elementary music teachers, such as the Canadian Music Educators Association (**www. musiceducationonline.org/~cmea**), Carl Orff Canada (**www.orffcanada.ca**), the Kodály Society of Canada (**cnet.unb.ca/achn/kodaly**), and the Association of Canadian Choral Directors (**www.choralcanada.org**). Membership in such organizations opens up a whole world of excellent reading and discussion about the particulars of elementary music teaching through the associations' journals, newsletters, and other publications. Local, provincial and national conferences sponsored by a variety of these dynamic organizations can be just the boost of inspiration needed during a cold spell in January!

Keep abreast of technology and what it might do to enhance instruction in your elementary music classroom. Become familiar with the various software packages that can be used to teach children about musical symbols, instruments, and composing. Use the Internet to help children experience a wealth of musical styles from around the world. Hook up online with an elementary class in a different part of the world and record some of your children's music making to share between cultures. Music, although unique within cultures, may be used as a doorway through which children begin communicating and learning about each other. This will become especially important during the next decade as the global economy becomes even more connected.

Most of all, know that what you do with children is important! You provide the key that will unlock the door to a magical world of music making, composing, and listening. With your guidance and support, these children will benefit from the enjoyment of a richer and more aesthetic musical future.

Appendix
Musical Signs, Symbols, and Notation

The Musical Staff

Musical notation is written on a **staff** made up of five lines and four spaces. The bottom line is line 1 and the top line is line 5. Numbering of the four spaces works in the same way. Extra lines added above and below the staff as needed to notate pitches outside the staff are called **ledger lines**. There is an automatic space added with each ledger line.

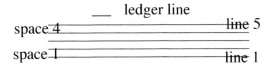

Bar Lines and Measures

Notes on the staff are organized into groups by vertical lines called **bar lines**. The space between two bar lines is called a **measure**. When the measures in a piece of music are numbered, the numbering starts with the first *complete* measure of the music. A double bar line is usually placed at the end of the music.

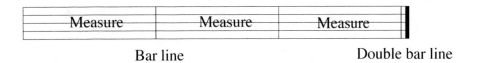

Bar line   Double bar line

Clefs and the Musical Alphabet

A **clef** is placed at the beginning of the staff to identify the lines and spaces by letter name using the **musical alphabet** : A–B–C–D–E–F–G. For example, the **treble clef** (the most common clef used in the elementary grades) identifies the second line of the staff (where the middle of the clef circles around) as the G above **middle C**. Thus, the bottom line is E, the space above is F, and so on. As notes move up the staff, the letter names proceed forward in alphabetical order. As notes move down the staff, their names move backwards in the alphabet.

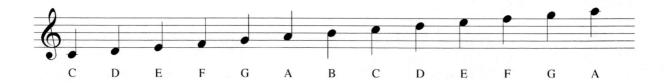

The **bass clef** identifies the fourth line of the staff (the line between the two dots) as the F below middle C. Thus, the bottom line is G, the space above is A, and so on.

The treble staff and the bass staff are combined to form the **grand staff**, which is used for piano music. The single ledger line between these two staves is called "middle C."

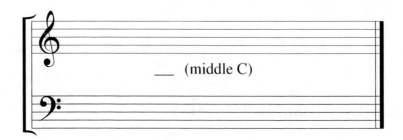

The One-Line Staff

A **one-line staff** is used to write the rhythm parts for non-pitched percussion instruments. The **rectangular clef** placed at the beginning of this staff indicates that there is no particular pitch attached to the line.

Distances between Notes on the Staff—Intervals

The distance between two notes is called an **interval**. Intervals can be grouped into four categories, according to size: **repeats**, **steps**, **skips**, and **leaps**. There are several ways to label intervals. Small intervals are often labelled by the number of half steps or steps they contain. Intervals are also given number labels (3rd, 4th, etc.) according to the number of lines and spaces on the staff from the bottom note to the top note.

- The interval between two consecutive notes that have the same pitch and letter name (that is, two notes that are written on the same line or space of the staff) is called a **unison** or a repeat.

- The interval between a note on a line and a note on the space directly above or below (or between a note on a space to a note on the line directly above or below) is called a **step**. Steps can be either **half steps (semitones)** or **whole steps (whole tones)**. Steps always have consecutive letter names (for example, A to B). Most of the notes on the staff are a whole step apart. The two exceptions are E to F, and B to C, which are only a half step apart; on the piano keyboard, these are the two pairs of white notes that do not have a black key in between. Another label for a step is a **2nd** (because, on the staff, there are only two lines or spaces involved: the line or space of the bottom note and that of the top note). A half step is a **minor 2nd** and a whole step is a **major 2nd**.

- The interval between two consecutive notes with a space or line skipped between them is called, appropriately enough, a **skip**. Skips are also called **3rds** (because there are three lines or spaces involved: the line or space of the bottom and top notes, and the line or space in the middle). A **major 3rd** is the equivalent of two whole steps, and a **minor 3rd** is the equivalent of a whole step plus a half step.

- The interval between two consecutive tones that are farther apart than a skip is called a **leap**. Intervals such as 4ths, 5ths, 6ths, and 7ths are all leaps. The interval of an 8th is called an **octave**.

Distances between notes on the staff

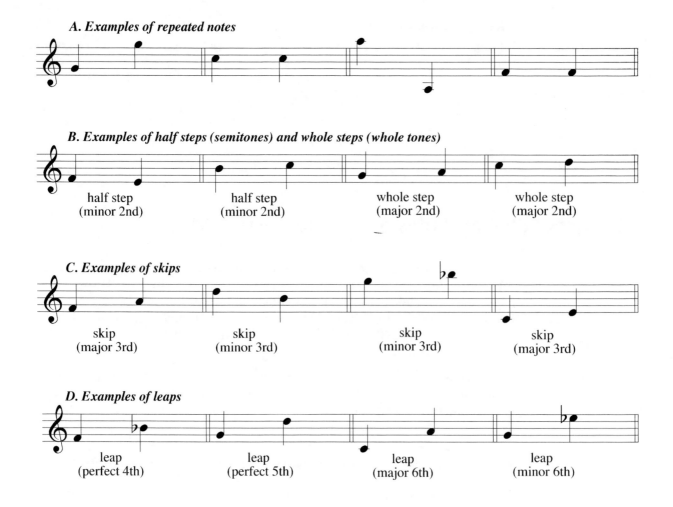

A. Examples of repeated notes

B. Examples of half steps (semitones) and whole steps (whole tones)

half step
(minor 2nd)

half step
(minor 2nd)

whole step
(major 2nd)

whole step
(major 2nd)

C. Examples of skips

skip
(major 3rd)

skip
(minor 3rd)

skip
(minor 3rd)

skip
(major 3rd)

D. Examples of leaps

leap
(perfect 4th)

leap
(perfect 5th)

leap
(major 6th)

leap
(minor 6th)

Accidentals

Accidentals are signs that are placed in front of a note on the staff to direct a musician to alter the pitch of the note by one **half step** (a **semitone**) A **sharp** sign placed before a note raises the note one half step; a **flat** sign lowers the note by one half step; a **natural** sign cancels a previous sharp or flat sign (or a sharp or flat in the key signature), thus making the note "regular" (i.e., natural). Accidentals apply only to notes at the pitch and within the measure in which they appear. In the example below, G♯ sounds a half step higher than G, and G♭ sounds a half step lower than G. The natural sign (♮) in front of the G in the third measure "cancels" the previous sharp, making the note G natural (or simply, G).

Accidentals

| G | G sharp | G | G flat | G sharp | G natural |

Key Signatures

A **key signature** is a group of sharps or flats placed on the staff directly to the right of the clef. The key signature directs a musician to sing or play sharps or flats for particular notes throughout the entire piece of music. For example, a key signature with two sharps (F♯ and C♯) directs the musician to "sharpen" all the Fs and Cs in the music (that is, to play or sing them as F♯s and C♯s), unless temporarily redirected by an accidental.

D   F♯   A   B C♯   D C♯   C   B   C♯ B A D

Key signatures contain a collection of either sharps or flats, but never both, and the sharps or flats always appear in the same order. Each key signature represents two keys, as indicated in the example below.

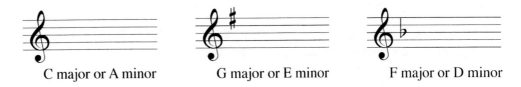

| C major or A minor | G major or E minor | F major or D minor |

Rhythmic Notation

Rhythmic notation shows the duration of individual notes on the staff. Different types of notes indicate different durations of sound. For example, a quarter note is longer than an eighth note but shorter than a half note. The relationship between whole notes, half notes, quarter notes, and so on, is exactly that which is implied by their fractional names. A whole note is equal to two half notes, or four quarter notes, and the same goes for rests, as is shown below.

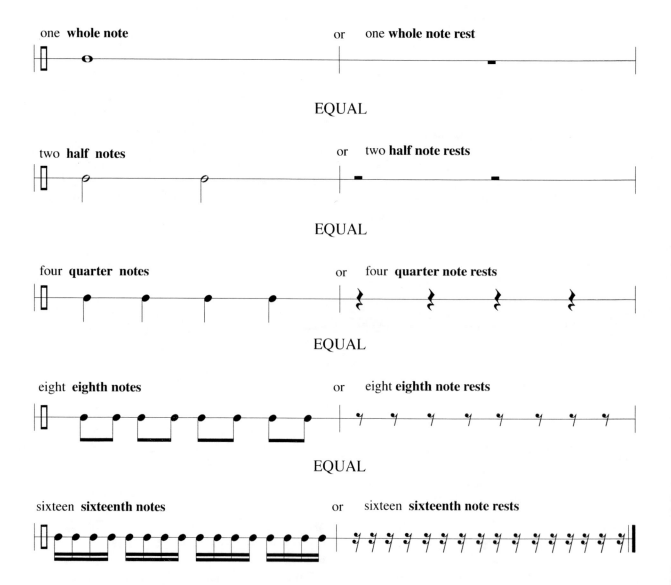

All rhythmic values except for the whole note have **stems**. The direction of the stem is determined by the location of the note on the staff. Notes on or below the second space are written with the stem on the right side of the note head, pointing upward. Notes on or above the third line are written with the stem on the left side of the note pointing downward.

Placement of stems

A **dot** added after a note increases the duration of the note by half the original value. For example, a dotted quarter note is equal in value to a quarter note plus an eighth note.

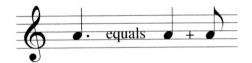

Rhythmic Syllable Names

Children use **rhythmic syllable names** (for example, *tah* and *ti-ti*), rather than traditional note names (for example, quarter note and eighth note) to label notes when they chant or clap rhythms in the classroom. With these syllables, the label of the rhythmic value coordinates with the actual sound of the rhythm when it is clapped.

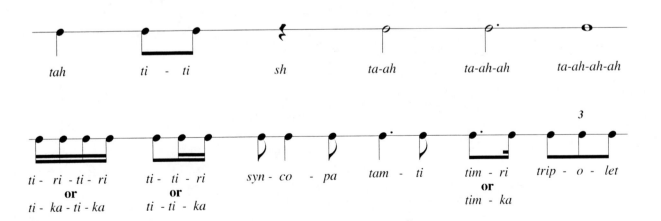

Metre

Time signatures (for example, 2/4, 3/4, or 4/4) are placed at the beginning of the staff just to the right of the key signature. In simple time, the time signature gives the musician two pieces of information. The top number indicates the number of beats in a measure; the bottom number specifies which rhythmic value is equal to one beat. This tells the musician how many beats to give each rhythmic value. For example, in 2/4 time, there are two beats to the measure and the quarter note receives one beat; in 3/4 time, there are three beats to the measure, and the quarter note gets the beat. The time signature also directs the musician as to which beats should receive a *slightly greater emphasis*. For example, in 2/4 metre, the first beat is felt more strongly than the second; in 4/4 time, the first beat is the strongest, and the third beat is stronger than the second and fourth beats.

2 - each measure contains two beats
4 - one beat is equal to the rhythmic value of a quarter note

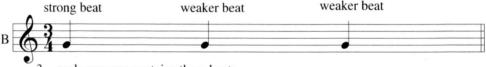

3 - each measure contains three beats
4 - one beat is equal to the rhythmic value of a quarter note

C = stands for *common time* or 4/4 meter

4 - each measure contains four beats
4 - one beat is equal to the rhythmic value of a quarter note

Compound time signatures (for example, 6/8, 9/8, 12/8) work almost the same way but the numbers do not identify the beat. For example in 6/8 time there are six eighth notes to the measure, but these eighth notes fall into two groups of three. There are two beats to the measure and the dotted quarter note gets the beat. The difference between 3/4 and 6/8 is that in 3/4 there are three groups of two eighth notes, but in 6/8 there are two groups of three eighth notes. In 9/8 time, there are nine eighth notes to the measure; there are three beats to the measure and the dotted quarter note gets the beat.

Tempo

A **tempo marking**,—for example, "**Moderato**"—is usually placed above the staff at the beginning of a piece of music (in the top left-hand corner) and may be accompanied by a specific **metronome marking**. Tempo and metronome markings may also appear throughout the score when needed to indicate tempo changes in the music.

There are many Italian terms used in music to direct the performer regarding tempo. Here are some of the more common ones:

Largo—a broad, very slow and dignified tempo

Lento—a very slow tempo

Adagio—a slow tempo

Andante—a walking tempo

Moderato—a moderate tempo

Allegretto—a cheerful and quick tempo

Allegro—a brisk and lively tempo

Vivace—a vivacious and fast tempo

Presto—a very quick tempo

Accelerando (*accel.*)—a gradual increase in tempo

Ritardando (*rit.*)—a gradual decrease in tempo

A tempo—return to the previous tempo

Dynamics

Dynamic markings are placed under the staff for instrumental music, and above the staff for vocal music. There is usually a dynamic marking at the beginning of the music, and additional markings are placed throughout the music, as needed. Unlike performance markings for tempo, most dynamic markings consist of letter abbreviations rather than the complete Italian word: for example, *f* stands for *forte* (loud) and *p* for *piano* (soft).

There are many Italian terms used in music to direct the performer regarding dynamics. Here are some of the more common ones:

pp (*pianissimo*)—very softly

p (*piano*)—softly

mp (*mezzo piano*)—moderately softly

mf (*mezzo forte*)—moderately loudly

f (*forte*)—loudly

ff (*fortissimo*)—very loudly

sfz (*sforzando*)—a sudden *forte* on the note or chord indicated

crescendo (or *cres.*)—a gradual increase in dynamics

decrescendo (or *decres.*)—a gradual decrease in dynamics

diminuendo (or *dim.*)—a gradual decrease in dynamics

Crescendo and *decrescendo*

Additional Symbols

Composers and arrangers use a variety of additional symbols in music to direct the performer regarding articulation, breathing, or sections to be repeated. Here are some of the most common of these symbols.

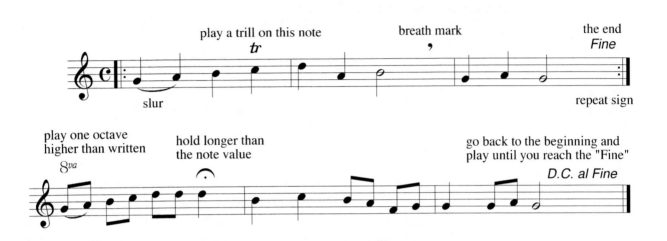

Scales

Notes may be grouped together into patterns called **scales**. The name or label of a scale depends on the order of whole steps (whole tones), half steps (semitones), or minor 3rds (a skip of three half steps) in the pattern. Composers usually choose notes from a particular scale when writing a piece of music.

A **major scale** consists of eight notes: there are half steps between notes 3 and 4 and notes 7 and 8; all the rest are a whole step apart. Major scales may start from any note on the staff. Notes in the major scale are sometimes labelled by using numbers 1 to 8. When using tonic sol-fa syllables, the notes of a major scale are labelled *doh, re, mi, fa, soh, lah, ti, doh*.

A major scale built on C

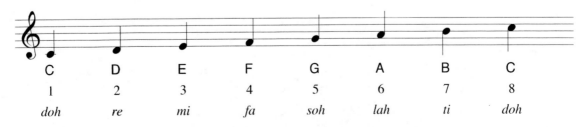

A **natural minor scale** is also made up of eight consecutive notes. Here the half steps occur between notes 2 and 3 and notes 5 and 6. Minor scales may also start from any note on the staff. Again, notes in a minor scale are sometimes numbered one to eight. When using tonic sol-fa syllables, the notes are labelled *lah, ti, doh, re, mi, fa, soh, lah*.

A natural minor scale built on C

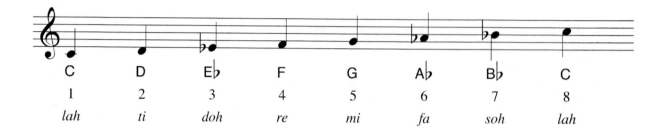

Two additional minor scales—the **harmonic minor scale** and the **melodic minor scale**—modify this pattern slightly. In the harmonic minor scale, the seventh note is raised by a half step. In the melodic minor scale, the sixth and seventh notes are raised by one half step going up, but these notes return to the original pitches of the natural minor scale going down.

A harmonic minor scale built on C

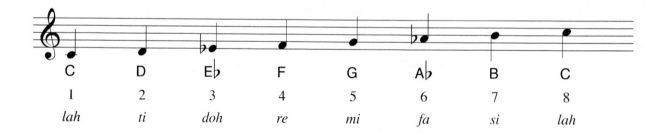

A melodic minor scale built on C

A **chromatic scale** consists of twelve consecutive notes one half step apart from each other. The chromatic scale may also begin from any note on the staff.

A chromatic scale built on C

Pentatonic scales consist of five notes. There are a wide variety of possible pentatonic scales, but the most common one by far consists of the notes *doh, re, mi, soh,* and *lah.* (This is also the scale that can be played on the black keys of a piano or other keyboard instrument.) The scale may begin on any of these tones, resulting in various patterns of whole-steps and minor-thirds.

A pentatonic scale built on C

Chords

Chords are used to accompany a song or an instrumental piece. They generally consist of three (or more) notes a skip apart on the staff that sound simultaneously. The size of the skips will be either a major 3rd (two whole steps) or a minor 3rd (three half steps). In the G chord shown below, for example, the bottom two notes are a major 3rd apart, and the top two notes are a minor 3rd apart.

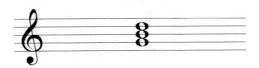

Often the actual notes of a chord are not written in the music, but instead are indicated by a single letter (for example, **C** or **c**) below the staff. This letter represents the bottom note in the chord. For example, the G chord above would be indicated by the letter "G" below the music in the place where the chord is to be played. Performers on harmonic instruments such as the piano or the guitar must learn how to interpret these letters in order to know which notes to play in the chord. Here are the labels and notes for some of the most common chords found in children's songs.

Common chords in children's songs

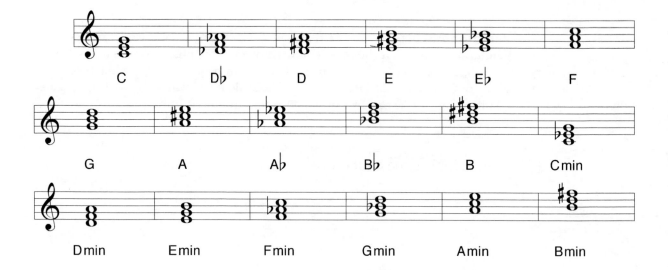

Glossary

a tempo—return to the previous tempo in the music

AB form—See **binary form**

ABA form—See **ternary form**

ABACA form—See **rondo form**

AA¹A² A³A⁴ form—See **theme and variations form**

absolute pitch names—the musical alphabet—A, B, C, D, E. F, and G—used to label the lines and spaces on the staff

a cappella—singing with no instrumental accompaniment

accelerando—a marking that directs the musician to make a gradual increase in tempo

accent—a marking that directs a musician to give a note special emphasis

accidentals—signs that are placed before a note on the staff to direct a musician to play or sing the note one half step higher (sharp), one half step lower (flat) or cancel a previous sharp or flat (natural)

accompaniment—musical parts that enhance and provide support for the melody of the music

active change section of a lesson plan—a section where the children actively apply their knowledge of the main music concept to a different piece of music

active listening—focusing on and responding to structural properties embedded within music while listening

adagio—a slow tempo

agogo bells—a metal non-pitched percussion instrument consisting of two conical bells of different sizes connected by a curved metal rod

allegro—a brisk and lively tempo

andante—a walking tempo

art music—See **classical music**

articulation—the way a note is started (for example, with or without tonguing for wind instruments)

assessment—the tracking and recording of student progress on a regular basis in a fair and ethical manner

Association of Canadian Choral Directors—a Canadian organization made up of choral directors and conductors

augmentation—a compositional technique for altering a melody by lengthening all the note values of the rhythm by the same proportion (for example the eighth notes become quarter notes, the quarter notes become half notes, etc.)

aural, kinesthetic, and oral activities—music classroom activities done during the first step of the sound-before-symbol teaching process that provide experience with musical concepts without the presence of a label and/or symbol for that concept

authentic musical encounters—music making, music creating, and music listening

autoharp—a box-like string instrument belonging to the zither family, with a number of chord buttons that damp the appropriate strings to produce specific chords; the player strums the strings with one hand while pressing one of the chord buttons with the other

axial (non-locomotor) movement—movements performed while in a stationary position

bar lines—vertical lines that divide the musical staff into measures of equal length

Baroque era—a historical style period of music lasting approximately from 1600 to 1750; representative composers include Johann Sebastian Bach, George Friderick Handel, and Georg Philipp Telemann

Baroque fingering (English fingering)—the most commonly used fingering on the recorder, modelled on fingering systems used in the sixteenth century

barred instruments—pitched instruments of the percussion family consisting of wooden or metal bars of gradated lengths laid across a boxed frame (for example, the xylophone)

bass clef—a clef sign that identifies the fourth line of the staff as F

bass drum—a skin non-pitched percussion instrument; this large drum sits sideways on a stand

bassoon—a low double-reed member of the woodwind family

beam—a horizontal line connecting the stems of two or more consecutive notes

beat—the steady pulse underlying music

beat awareness—the ability to feel a steady beat in music

beat competency—the ability to keep a steady beat while singing or playing an instrument

beat-movement activities—music activities that use movement to help children feel a steady beat

beat-movement teaching sequence—a simple-to-complex teaching sequence for using movement with singing, playing instruments, and listening during the sound stage of beat development

beat-rhythm sign—a reversible sign with a large iconic beat symbol (❤) on one side, and a pair of rhythm sticks on the other; the sign is used to direct children to alternate between keeping the beat and keeping the rhythm while singing or chanting

bebop—an important modernist movement in jazz developed by black musicians in Harlem in the mid 1940s as a revolt against the swing era; characteristics include a theme-solo-theme format and fast-moving melodies and chordal progressions, as exemplified in the music of Charlie Parker, Dizzy Gillespie, and Thelonious Monk

bell tree—a metal non-pitched percussion instrument consisting of a handle with a series of gradated bells stacked on top of each other, which ring when a metal-tipped mallet is pulled gently down across them

binary (AB) form—music that is organized into two contrasting sections (A and B)

blues scales—scales that are based on blues tunes: these scales resemble a major scale but some degrees of the scale—often the third and the seventh—are lowered

body awareness activities—movement activities that explore different ways to move various body parts

body percussion—use of the body as an instrument to make sounds such as snapping, clapping, stamping

bongo drums—a skin non-pitched percussion instrument consisting of two small drums, one slightly larger than the other, connected by a wooden bar

bordun—two notes—usually the tonic (I) and the dominant (V) of the key of the song—that are played as an *ostinato* accompaniment

brass instruments—a family of instruments consisting of differing lengths of brass tubing with a bell and a cupped mouthpiece (for example, trumpet, French horn, euphonium, trombone, and tuba)

breath mark—a small apostrophe-like sign generally placed just above the staff to indicate a place where an instrumentalist or a singer should take a breath in the music

breath support—use of proper diaphragm breathing to support the tone in singing or playing wind instruments

cabaça—a metal non-pitched percussion instrument consisting of a circular container with small metal beads attached to the outside; the player rolls the beads back and forth to produce a scratchy sound

call-and-response songs—songs consisting of alternating sections of calls sung by the leader (solo) and responses sung by the rest of the singers (chorus)

call chart—a chart outlining various aspects of a piece of music, such as the themes

Canadian Music Educators Association—the national professional association of music teachers in Canada

canon—polyphonic music for voices or instruments, in which all parts perform the same melody; each voice enters after a specific time interval, and imitates exactly the melody sung or played by the first voice (See also **round**)

Carl Orff Canada—a Canadian organization made up of members interested in the teaching approach inspired by the German composer and music educator Carl Orff

cello—the third largest member of the string family; the instrument is supported by a peg that rests on the floor, and is held by the player between her or his knees

changing metre—changes of metre at least once within a piece of music (for example, from 2/4 to 3/4)

chords—three or more notes, usually a 3rd apart, that are sounded simultaneously

chromatic scale—a scale made up of twelve consecutive notes, each a half step apart

circle dances—folk-like dances done in a circle, and often accompanied by the dancer's own singing

classical music—a generic term used to refer to art music composed during the Middle Ages, (ca 500–1450), the Renaissance (ca 1450–1600), the Baroque period (ca 1600–1750), the Classical period (ca 1750–1820), the Romantic period (ca 1820-1900), and the twentieth century and beyond (from approximately 1900 on).

Classical period—a historical style period lasting approximately from 1750 to 1820; representative composers include Franz Joseph Haydn, Wolfgang Amadeus Mozart, and Ludwig van Beethoven.

classroom teachers—elementary teachers with university-level training in elementary education who are responsible for teaching a variety of subjects including music to the children in their individual classrooms

clarinet—a single-reed member of the woodwind family

classroom instruments—instruments commonly played by children in the elementary music classroom (non-pitched percussion instruments, barred-instruments, recorder, etc.)

claves—a wooden non-pitched percussion instrument consisting of two rosewood sticks that are clicked together

clavicular breathing—a shallow upper-chest type of breathing that causes the shoulders to rise during inhalation

clef—a symbol placed at the beginning of the staff to identify the letter names of the lines and spaces. For example, the treble clef identifies the second line of the staff as the G above middle C.

closure—the final part of a lesson plan that reviews what has been taught in the lesson and provides a transition to the end of music class

coda—a short section placed at the end of a piece of music, usually to serve as an epilogue; *coda* is an Italian word meaning "tail"

common time (C)—a term and symbol used to indicate 4/4 metre

complementary *ostinato*—a rhythmic or melodic *ostinato* that sounds like an independent accompaniment line rather than a simple imitation of the rhythms or melody of the music

composers—people who create music

composing—the thoughtful writing down of new musical material with the opportunity to re-work if desired

compound metre—a metre in which the beat is divided into three equal parts over an even bottom number, such as 3/2, 6/8, or 9/8

concrete manipulatables—a variety of tools (such as popsicle sticks or mini flash cards) that are used in a lesson to provide children with hands-on experience in manipulating musical structure

concrete motivator—a unique object (such as a puppet, an article of clothing, or a picture) that the teacher shows the children to motivate them towards a particular song or rhyme

conducting patterns—specific gestures made by a conductor to indicate various metres

cone puppet—a puppet that can pop its head in and out of a cone-shaped barrel

conga drum—a skin non-pitched percussion instrument; this tall, funnel-shaped drum is open at the narrow bottom end and is played with various parts of the hands

countermelody—an independent melody written below the melody of the music that enriches the main melody by providing not only harmony but also musical contrast

cow bell—a metal non-pitched percussion instrument that produces a loud metallic sound when struck with a metal-tipped mallet

creative or exploratory movement—movement that is used to interpret music

crescendo—a gradual increase in dynamics

curricular planning—the ability to bring educational goals into daily action

D.C. al Fine (*da capo al Fine*)—a marking that directs the musician to go back to the beginning and repeat to the "*Fine*" marking; the literal translation of this Italian phrase is "from head to end."

decrescendo—a gradual decrease in dynamics

deep breathing—lower chest breathing that involves the diaphragm

descant—an independent and sometimes ornamental melody written above the main melody of the music that provides both harmony and decoration for the main melody

developmentally appropriate activity—an activity that matches the children's cognitive, psychomotor, and socio-emotional levels of development

diaphragm—a large muscular membrane that separates the abdominal and chest cavities

diatonic patterns—melodic patterns that use notes from the major scale (including *fa* and *ti*)

diatonic songs—songs that use notes from the major scale (including *fa* and *ti*)

diminuendo—a gradual decrease in dynamics

diminution—a compositional technique for altering a melody by shortening all the note values in the rhythm by the same proportion (for example, quarter notes become eighth notes, half notes become quarters, etc.)

Dixieland jazz—a small ensemble style of jazz that developed in New Orleans in the early years of the twentieth century; representative musicians include Buddy Bolden, Joe "King" Oliver, Kid Ory, and Louis Armstrong

dominant—the fifth note in the scale of a key

dotted note—a note that is followed by a dot; the dot increases the value of the note by one half (for example, a dotted quarter note is equal to a quarter note plus an eighth note)

dotted rhythms—rhythmic figures that involve one or more dotted notes

double bar line—two bar lines placed at the end of a piece of music

double bass (string bass, bass fiddle)—the largest and lowest member of the string family

double-reed instruments—instruments that have two reeds joined together at one end to help generate the sound (for example, oboes and bassoons)

drone—See **pedal tone**

duple metre—music with a metre in which beat units are grouped into two, such as 2/4 or 4/4

duration—the length of a note or a rest

dynamics—the loudness or softness of music

dynamic discrimination—the ability to hear the difference between music performed loudly and music performed softly

dynamic production—the ability to use dynamics effectively during performing or improvising

echo-clapping—immediately clapping back a rhythmic pattern that has just been clapped

echo games—games in which the teacher plays a short rhythm or melody and the children echo it back

echo-playing—immediately playing back (on the recorder or a barred-instrument) a melodic pattern that has just been played

echo-singing—immediately singing back a melodic pattern that has just been sung

elements of music—the various components of the structure of music: beat, tempo, metre, rhythm, dynamics, timbre, pitch, form, harmony and texture, and expressive elements

embouchure—the specific formation of the lips and corners of the mouth that is required when playing a wind instrument

emergent language literacy—the period of time during which a child is exposed to both verbal and written language and moves towards making appropriate associations between the two

end point of the beat—a physical spot at which the beat is felt kinesthetically

energy awareness activities—movement activities that explore the amount of force, speed, and weight that various motions require

euphonium—a valved member of the brass instrument family with the same range as the trombone

eurhythmics—a series of movement-based activities that allow the expression of musical nuance by using the entire body as a musical instrument

evaluation—an official judgement of the merit of the data collected during assessment

expressive elements—the particular emphasis given to a note during performance

falsetto voice—a male singer's soprano-like voice achieved by singing lightly, one octave higher than the normal vocal range

fermata—a sign placed above or below a specific note to indicate that the note should be held longer than its written value; *fermatas* are usually written outside the staff

fill-in-the-blank songs—a song in which a leader sings most of the song while the rest of the singers sing only the missing text of the song (indicated by a blank line in the music)

Fine—a marking that indicates where the music ends; *fine* is an Italian word meaning "end"

finger cymbals—metal non-pitched percussion instruments consisting of two small metal disks that make a tinkling sound when struck lightly together

first and second endings—signs in the music that indicate different endings to be used for subsequent repetitions

flat (♭)—an sign placed in front of a note or incorporated into a key signature that directs the musician to sing or play the note one half step lower

flute—a member of the woodwind family that has an open hole mouthpiece to help generate a sound

folk song—a song arising as an outgrowth of the daily life of a culture or a community, usually transmitted orally over several generations

form—the way music is structured into an organized journey

formal assessment—the gathering and recording of evidence of a student's growth in musical understanding

forte (*f*)—a marking that directs the musician to play or sing loudly

fortissimo (*ff*)—a marking that directs the musician to play or sing very loudly

four voices—the child's four natural voices: talking voice, whispering voice, shouting or playground voice, and singing voice

French horn—an instrument in the brass family that consists of a length of tubing curled up into a circular shape, ending in a large bell

fugue—polyphonic music that consists of a theme—called a "subject"—that is presented by one part and taken up imitatively in turn by the other parts; sometimes the subject is accompanied by a contrasting theme, which is called a "counter subject."

German fingering—a fingering system for the recorder that was developed in the early twentieth century as an attempt to simplify the instrument for beginners

glockenspiel—a high barred instrument that consists of metal bars (2 cm wide) of gradated lengths laid across a frame and is played by striking individual bars with a mallet

goals—broad educational statements used to direct general outcomes in the curriculum

gong (or tam tam)—a metal non-pitched percussion instrument consisting of a large, disk-shaped plate that produces a rich, long resonating sound when struck with a soft headed mallet

grand staff—the two-staff system that consists of a treble staff on the top and a bass staff on the bottom, with middle C between the two staffs; the grand staff is used to notate piano music

guiro—a wood non-pitched percussion instrument consisting of a hollow oval gourd with raised grooves on the outside that are scraped with a small stick

half step (semitone)—the smallest distance between two notes on the staff

hand drum—a skin non-pitched percussion instrument; the player holds this round, flat drum by the rim and taps it with the hand or the fingers

handbells—sets of small bells of varying sizes that together cover the notes of a scale

hand signs—a series of specific hand shapes that are used by children to kinesthetically show individual pitches

handle castanets—a wood non-pitched percussion instrument consisting of a handle with small wooden disks attached that rattle when shaken

harmonic discrimination—the ability to hear and identify two or more musical parts that are sounding simultaneously

harmonic minor scale—a minor scale in which the seventh degree of the scale is raised by a half step (a semitone) both ascending and descending

harmony—the simultaneous sounding of two or more notes

head voice—the child's natural, light, treble singing voice

hold—See *fermata*

homophonic texture—music made up of two or more parts that move together rhythmically but in different pitches; music made up of a melody with a chordal accompaniment

improvisation—the immediate extemporization of new musical material using the voice or an instrument

individual rhythmic values—specific note or rest durations

individual singing—classroom activities that provide children with an opportunity to sing by themselves

informal assessment—unrecorded observations of a student's progress in musical understanding

inner hearing—the ability to silently hear music in the head without the benefit of aural presence

instruments of the orchestra—instruments from the four instrument families (brass, woodwind, percussion, and strings) that traditionally make up a symphony orchestra

interval—the distance between two notes; intervals can be measured by whole and half steps, or by their relation to the major scale

introduction—a brief section placed at the beginning of a piece of music, usually to serve as a prologue

jingle bell—a metal non-pitched percussion instrument consisting of a handle to which three or four small bells are attached; the player shakes the handle to ring the bells.

jingle tap or clog—a *metal* non-pitched percussion instrument consisting of a handle with several pairs of thin, round metal disks loosely attached; when the instrument is shaken, the discs clink together

key signature—a pattern of sharps and flats placed on the staff directly to the right of the clef to indicate which notes are to be played sharp or flat throughout an entire piece of music (except when temporarily cancelled by an accidental); the key signature also identifies the key and scale associated with the music

Kodály Society of Canada—a national music education organization made up of members interested in the teaching approach inspired by the Hungarian composer and music educator Zoltán Kodály

label activities—classroom activities that take place during the second step in the sound-before-symbol teaching process that teach the label and/or symbol for a musical concept

leap—two consecutive notes that are farther apart than a skip; an interval of a 4th or larger

learner objectives—statements that specify what a student must be able to do to show a particular aspect of musical understanding

learner-centred—learning in ways that allow individuals to reach their potential through the most developmentally appropriate and positive routes possible

ledger lines—extra lines added above or below the staff as needed to notate pitches outside the staff

legato—smooth, flowing, connected

line dance—folk-like dances done in a line, usually accompanied by the dancer's own singing

linguistic intelligence—the bio-psychological potential to think linguistically

listeners—consumers of music

locomotor movement—movement that involves travelling from one space to another

main activity—the main section of a lesson plan, where the children engage in musical activities that focus their learning towards the main concept under study

major key—a key that is based on notes of a major scale

major 3rd—the interval distance between two notes that have one letter name between them and that are two whole steps apart (for example, C to E, or G to B, but not B to E flat or G sharp to C)

major scale—a scale consisting of eight consecutive notes: half steps (semitones) occur between notes 3 and 4 and notes 7 and 8; all other notes are separated by whole steps (whole tones)

mallet—a wooden stick with a small round tip made of wood, plastic, metal, wound yarn, or cloth that is used to strike percussion instruments

maraca—a wood non-pitched percussion instrument consisting of a gourd containing dried seeds that rattle when the instrument is shaken

measure—a short segment of music on the staff that is enclosed by bar lines

melodic contour—the linear shape created by the rise and fall of a melody

melodic minor scale—a minor scale in which the sixth and seventh notes are raised a semitone going up but return to the original notes of the natural minor scale going down

melodic *ostinato*—a short melodic pattern repeated over and over as an accompaniment

melody—high and low pitches strung together into an organized sequence; thought of by children as "the way the tune goes"

metallophone - a barred-instrument that consists of thick metal bars (6 cm wide) of gradated lengths laid across a frame and is played by striking individual bars with a mallet

metre—the periodic accenting of specific beats of the measure over others

metronome—a mechanical or electronic device used to show and/or sound a steady beat at a given tempo

middle C—the pitch that is notated on the single ledger line between the treble and bass clefs in the grand staff

mini flash cards—small flash cards that contain musical notation; they can be used by elementary school children to write rhythmic or melodic phrases of music

minor key—a key that is based on notes of a minor scale

minor scale—See **natural minor scale**

minor 3rd—the interval distance between two notes that have one letter name between them and that are a step and a half apart (for example, A to C, or E to G, but not A to B sharp or F flat to G)

monophonic texture—music written in only one part with no accompaniment

motivation part of a lesson plan—a short experiential section of a lesson plan; its purpose is to set up the main activity by preparing and focusing the children's attention towards the main concept being studied

multiple intelligence—the bio-psychological potential to think in certain ways

music—an ever-changing experience that is dependent on the dynamics of human interaction

music classroom experiences—the eight music experiences that take place in an elementary classroom: singing, moving, playing classroom instruments, listening, improvising, composing, reading music, and writing music

music concept timetable—a graph on which the musical concepts appropriate for teaching in any one grade level are placed in a logical sound-before-symbol timeframe in relation to the school year calendar

music literacy—the reading and writing of music notation

music notation—the symbols used to represent music for purposes of reading and writing music

music phonemic awareness skills—the sensitivity to the musical phonological structure of music

music portfolio—a file (a folder, a box, or a multi-media file on computer) that contains evidence of the student's progress in musical understanding, collected over a specific period of time

music specialists—elementary teachers with university-level training in music and music education, whose main responsibility is to teach music classes

music reading and writing readiness—the readiness of children to begin learning to associate musical symbols with aural sounds

musical alphabet—the letters of the alphabet used to name the lines and spaces on the staff: A, B, C, D, E, and G

musical concept (musical construct)—the smallest unit of a musical element

musical intelligence—the bio-psychological potential to think musically

musical multiculturalism—music from many different cultures

musical phoneme—the smallest sound unit in music; a note distinguished by frequency (pitch) and duration (rhythmic value)

musical phrase—a musical sentence generally ending with a pause or breath

musical semantics—the meaning made of music based on a musical syntax that is socially and culturally shared to some degree by the individuals within a culture

musical structure—the building blocks of music: beat, tempo, rhythm, pitch, timbre, harmony and texture, form, expressive elements, and metre

musical styles—similarities in musical patterning that are shared by a group of musical works (for example, music from the Baroque period, or a particular kind of jazz)

musical syntax—culturally accepted rules within a musical style that govern the combination of musical phonemes into sound sequences

musical understanding—the ability to think and act musically with personal meaning

musically authentic assessment—assessment techniques that gather information naturally in real music making, creating, and listening situations

musician's way of keeping the beat—discreetly tapping the toes inside one's shoes

musique concrète—a composition technique that involves collecting sounds on audio tape and re-editing them into a cohesive piece of music; the term dates back to early experiments made by Pierre Schaffer at the French radio studios in Paris in the late 1940s.

natural minor scale—a scale made up of eight consecutive notes; there are half steps between the notes 2 and 3 and notes 5 and 6, and all the rest are whole steps

natural sign(♮)—an sign placed in front of a note that directs a musician to cancel a previous sharp or flat referring to that particular note

neighbour tone (auxiliary tone)—a non-chord tone positioned above or below a chord tone in a melody that is approached and left by step

non-chord tone—a note that is not part of the harmony (i.e. the chord) at the moment it occurs

non-locomotor movement—movement that is performed in a stationary position

non-pitched percussion instruments—percussion instruments that sound only one pitch

non-programmatic music—music that is written without reference to a non-musical idea such as a story or a description of a scene

note music—music that children are able to access through reading notation

note teaching of a song—teaching a song using some or all of the notation

note head—the round portion of a note

note placement—the placement of children's natural singing range in relation to the range of a song (i.e., the portion of the children's vocal range that is used in the song)

oboe—a high double-reed instrument belonging to the woodwind family

octave—an interval of eight notes; the top and bottom notes have the same letter name

one-line staff—a single line used to write non-pitched percussion parts

opening part of a lesson plan—a short section of a lesson plan that provides a warm-up for the children's musical ears, voices, and bodies

ostinato—an short melodic or rhythmic pattern that is repeated over and over as an accompaniment

part-singing—vocal music with more than one part

partner songs—two songs that produce acceptable harmony when sung together

passing tone—a non-chord tone that is positioned a step between two different chord tones in a melody, and is approached and left by step, as in a scale (See also **non-chord tones**)

patsching—patting the thighs to the beat (the word is derived from the German verb *patschen*, meaning "to slap")

pedal tone (drone)—a single note—usually the tonic note (I) of the key of the song—that is used as an *ostinato* accompaniment

pentatonic patterns—melodic patterns containing notes that are based on a pentatonic scale

pentatonic scale—a scale made up of five notes; the most common pentatonic scale contains five notes of the major scale: *doh, re, mi, soh*, and *lah*; songs or melodic patters built on this scale can start on any of these notes.

pentatonic songs—songs with tunes that are based on a pentatonic scale

percussion instruments—a family of instruments that are struck, shaken, or scraped, including both pitched and non-pitched percussion instruments

performers—people who make music

phoneme—the smallest sound unit in language

phonemic awareness skills—sensitivity to aspects of the phonological structure of language, such as rhyming, alliteration, or phonemes

phrase—a complete musical sentence, usually delineated by a pause or a breath

phrase form—the arrangement of individual musical phrases into a structure of same, different, and/or similar phrases; individual phrases are usually labelled with small letters (*a, b, c*, etc.)

phrase-by-phrase approach—an approach used when teaching a song by rote, in which the children hear and echo back the song one phrase at a time

piano (*p*)—a marking that directs the musician to play or sing softly

pianissimo (*pp*)—a marking that directs the musician to play or sing very softly

piggy-back songs—songs that combine a familiar melody with new or different words

pitch—the highness or lowness of a note

pitch discrimination—the ability to determine one pitch from another, and to hear a succession of pitches

pitch matching—the ability to sing back the same pitch immediately after hearing it sung or played

pitch monitoring—the ability to hear and focus on one's own vocal pitch

pitch production—the ability to manipulate one's singing through a range of pitches

pitched percussion instruments—percussion instruments that produce more than one pitch

polyphonic texture—music made up of two or more independent parts

program music—music that is written in reference to a specific non-musical idea or story

range—the distance between the highest and lowest note of a song, a voice, or an instrument

ratchet—a wood non-pitched percussion instrument that consists of crank-like device produces a clacking sound when turned

recorder—a small flute-like instrument belonging to the woodwind family

rectangular-shaped clef—a clef that is placed at the beginning of a one-line staff to indicate that the notes on the staff have no particular pitch

refrain (chorus)—a section of music that is repeated after each verse of a song

reinforcement activities—music classroom activities that take place during the third step of the sound-before-symbol teaching process and may include the use of music notation

repeat signs—signs used in music notation to indicate repetition; the music enclosed between the repeat signs is to be repeated

rests—musical symbols that represent silence in music

reversible sign with a face—a double-sided sign with a face on each side; on one side the mouth is open and on the other side it is closed. The sign is used to direct children to alternate between singing out loud and singing silently "in their heads."

review song—a song used in a lesson that has been previously taught to the children

rhythm—a sequence of durations of notes and/or silences over a steady beat; thought of by children as "the way the words sound"

rhythm vs. beat—the difference between the basic beat of the music and the rhythmic patterns of the notes

rhythmic *ostinato*—a short rhythmic pattern that is repeated over and over as an accompaniment

rhythm sticks—a wood non-pitched percussion instrument consisting of two sticks that make a tapping sound when hit together

rhythmic patterns—combinations of individual rhythmic values

rhythmic syllables—a mnemonic device for verbalizing rhythm, using syllables such as *tah* or *ti-ti*

ritardando (rit.)—a marking that directs the musician to decrease the tempo gradually

Romantic period—a historical style period of music lasting approximately from 1820 to 1900; representative composers include Franz Schubert, Robert Schumann, Frédéric Chopin, Johannes Brahms, and Felix Mendelssohn

rondo (ABACA) form—music that is organized into three contrasting sections, with the first (A) section repeated after each contrasting (B or C) section

rote/note observation method—a variation of the rote method for teaching a song, where children are given the notation of the music to look at while the teacher sings the song

rote music—music that children can learn by rote

rote teaching of a song—teaching a song orally without the use of notation

round—a part song consisting of a single melody that is sung in canon by several voices, where each voice sings the whole song several times; the voices begin one after another at equally-spaced time intervals (See also **canon**)

sand blocks—a wood non-pitched percussion instrument consisting of two small square blocks covered with sandpaper on one side that are rubbed together to produce a swishing sound

saxophone—a metal single-reed member of the woodwind family

scale—a group of pitches arranged in ascending and/or descending order

score—a form of notated music in which all the individual vocal and or instrumental parts of a composition are written together on separate staves, following a traditional order on the page

sectional form—the arrangement of larger sections of music made up of several phrases into a structure of same, different, or similar sections, usually labelled with capital letters (A, B, C, etc.)

semantics—the way in which meaning is assigned to or carried by sound sequences

semitone—a half step; in Western music—the smallest interval between two notes on the staff

sforzando (sfz.)—a marking that directs the musician to make a sudden strong *forte* on a note or chord

sharp sign(♯)—an sign placed in front of a note or incorporated into a key signature that directs the musician to sing or play the note one half step (semitone) higher

sight-reading—reading music from notation that has not been previously learned

sight-singing—the sight-reading of vocal music

simultaneous imitation—the simultaneous copying of body movement performed by a leader

single bass bars—large, single wooden bars laid over a resonating box that sound one low pitch when struck with a mallet

single-reed instruments—woodwind instruments that have a single reed attached to a mouthpiece to help generate the sound

skip—two consecutive notes with one note skipped between them; two consecutive notes that are the interval of a 3rd apart

sleigh bells—a metal non-pitched percussion instrument that consists of a handle with 10 to 20 large bells attached; the bells make a jingling sound when the player shakes the handle

slur—a curved line connecting two or more notes in a melody that directs the musician to connect the notes smoothly; for wind players, only the first note of the slur is tongued

sopranino recorder—the highest and smallest instrument of the recorder family

sound-before-symbol teaching process—a process in which students experience music aurally, kinesthetically, and orally before they label and read its symbolic representation

spatial awareness activities—movement activities that explore moving the body within personal space and through space at different levels and by different pathways

spiral progression—the progressive study of more sophisticated musical concepts from each of the ten elements of music during each grade level

spoons—a wood non-pitched percussion instrument consisting of two parallel spoons joined together at one end that make a clicking sound when slapped against the knee

staccato—short and detached; in musical notation, *staccato* is indicated by a dot below the note head (or above the note head, if the note stem is down)

staff—the lines and spaces on which musical notation is written

staff board—a staff laminated on poster board that is used by individual students to write music

starting note—the first note that is sung or played in the music

stem—a vertical line that is attached to the note head of all notes except whole notes

step—the distance between two consecutive notes on the staff (for example A to B or F to G). See also **half step** and **whole step**

stepping-beat motions—beat movement using the feet that does not involve travelling from space to space

stick notation—a short-cut for writing rhythmic notation using only stems with no note heads attached

story songbooks—picture books that contain the text of familiar children's songs as either part or all of the story

string instruments—a family of instruments that have several strings stretched over a resonating box, including the violin, viola, cello, and string bass

structured movement—movement that is directly related to music, such as action songs, singing games, and dances

student journal—a collection of short reflective essays written by a student about classroom music activities

subdominant—the fourth note of a scale or key

suspended cymbal—a metal non-pitched percussion instrument consisting of a large metal disk hung by a string that, when struck, produces a long resonating sound

swing—a style of jazz that became popular in the 1930s and is often associated with big bands; representative musicians include Duke Ellington, Tommy Dorsey, Benny Goodman, and Count Basie

symphony—a musical composition for orchestra that usually consists of several movements

syncopation—a shift of accent from a strong beat to a weak beat

syntax—the rules governing the combination of phonemes into sound sequences

tableau—a frozen picture created with body shapes

tam-tam—See **gong**

tambourine—a metal non-pitched percussion instrument consisting of a hollow wooden round frame with several small, flat metal disks attached, which make a jangling sound when the instrument is tapped or shaken

teacher checklists—an assessment tool used to record student success in specific music behaviour using a series of pre-determined check marks

temple blocks—a wood non-pitched percussion instrument consisting of a series of gradated wood blocks attached to a stand; the blocks produce a tick-tock sound when struck with a mallet

tempo—the speed (fast or slow) of the beat

tempo discrimination—the ability to hear the difference between faster and slower tempos in music

tempo production—the ability to use tempo effectively during performing or improvising

ternary (ABA) form—music that is organized into two contrasting sections (A and B) with a return of the first (A) section at the end

texture—the nature of the harmony of a piece of music in relation to the number and type of musical pats; for example, music might have a monophonic texture (one part) or a polyphonic texture (two or more independent parts).

tie—a curved line that joins two notes of the same pitch; a tie directs the musician to sustain the pitch for the total value of the notes connected by the tie

theme and variations form (AA^{1}A^2 A^{3}A^4)—music that is organized into several sections: a theme (melody) followed by several variations, in which the original theme is altered in one or

more ways through different compositional techniques

timbre—the tone colour of an instrument or a voice

timbre discrimination—the ability to determine one timbre from another

timbre exploration—classroom experiences that allow children to try out timbres of different instruments

time signature—a symbol placed at the beginning of the first staff in a piece of music, just to the right of the key signature, that indicates the metre of the music. In simple time, the top number specifies the number of beats in the measure, and the bottom number specifies the rhythmic value that is equal to one beat. (For example in 2/4, there are two beats to the measure and the beat is equal to one quarter note.)

tone block—a wood non-pitched percussion instrument consisting of a hollow wooden tube with a handle attached; the player holds the tone block by the handle and strikes it with a mallet

tonic—the first note in the scale or the name of the key signature

tonic sol-fa—a system of syllable names (*doh, re, mi, fa, soh, lah, ti*, etc.) that are used to identify particular pitches in a melody; tonic sol-fa is used to help children learn the intervallic relationships between pitches. This system is often referred to as "moveable doh" because *doh* always labels the tonic note of the major key of a song; *lah* identifies the tonic note of a song in a minor key.

traditional rhythmic names—the traditional labels used for individual rhythmic values such as quarter note, eighth note, etc.

treble clef—a clef that identifies the second line of the staff as the G above middle C

triangle—a metal non-pitched percussion instrument consisting of a solid metal rod formed into a triangular shape that is hung from a string and struck with a metal beater

triple metre—a metre in which the beat units are groups of three (for example, 3/2, 3/4, or 3/8, 9/8)

trombone—an instrument of the brass family that uses a double telescopic slide to change the length of tubing and thus alter the pitch

trumpet—the highest instrument in the brass family

tuba—the lowest instrument in the brass family

tuning fork—a solid piece of metal shaped into a two-pronged fork that when struck, produces a specific pitch (for example, A 440)

twelve-measure blues pattern: a chord progression that forms the basis of a traditional blues (for example, I–I–I–I^7–IV–IV–I–I–V^7–V^7–I–I)

ukulele—a small, four-string instrument belonging to the guitar family

unison—two notes that have the same pitch; on the staff the two notes will be written on the same line or space

upbeat—a weak beat that precedes the first strong beat of the following measure

verse—the main portion of a verse-refrain song; the melody of the verse is sung several times with different text

vibra slap—a wood non-pitched percussion instrument consisting of two thin wooden strips attached together at one end; the strips slap against each other when one strip is hit against the side of the body

vibrato—a slight fluctuation in pitch that enriches the timbre of a musical sound; on string instruments such as the violin, vibrato is produced by rocking the finger on the string; vocal vibrato is characterized by a fluctuation in both intensity and pitch

viola—an instrument in the string family that is slightly larger and slightly lower than the violin

violin (fiddle)—the highest instrument in the string family

whole-song approach (global approach)—an approach used when teaching a song by rote, in which the children hear and echo back the whole song on each repetition

whole step—a combination of two half steps; a whole tone

whole-tone scale—a scale made up of six notes, each a whole step (whole tone) apart

wind chimes—a metal non-pitched percussion instrument consisting of a series of metal cylinders suspended by strings from a wooden frame

wind instruments—instruments in which sound is produced by air blown through a tube

wood block—a wood non-pitched percussion instrument consisting of a hollow rectangular chunk of wood that is struck with a mallet

woodwind instruments—a family of wind instruments that consist of an enclosed pipe with tone holes, and have one of three types of sound-producing mechanisms: a single reed attached to a mouthpiece (clarinet, saxophone), a double reed (oboe, bassoon), an open mouthpiece (flute, recorder)

world music—music from many different cultures around the world

xylophone—a barred instrument consisting of wooden bars (6 cm wide) of gradated lengths laid across a frame, and played by striking individual bars with a mallet

Music Index

Note: For musical scores and rhymes that appear in the book, the first page number listed is always the score for the song or the text for the rhyme.

RECORDER MUSIC

RHYMES

SONGS

STORY

Subject Index

hold. *See* fermata
homophonic texture, 62, 298

improvising, 113–115
    activities for teaching, 115–123, 291
    creating a positive learning environment, 114
inner hearing, 51–52
instruments
    barred, 66, 82–94
    classroom, 65–66
    non-pitched percussion, 66, 68–81
    orchestral, 274–278
    other, 278
    pitched percussion, 66, 82–94
    recorder, 66, 95–111
intervals, 29, 234, 339–340
introduction, 127
Inuit and First Nations traditional songs, 10, 138

jazz style of music, 10, 138
jingle bells, 79
jingle tap, 79

key signatures, 234, 341
Kodály Society of Canada, 335
Kodály, Zoltán, 16, 186

label stage of the sound-before-symbol process, 15,
        204–205, 221–222, 241–245, 315–316
language
    emergent literacy, 180, 215
    parallels with music, 3
    phonemic awareness, 215
    phonology, 3
leap, 29, 339–340
learner objectives, 312
ledger lines, 337
legato, 279
lesson planning, 318–320
    examples, 320–325
    factors to consider, 319–320
    parts of a lesson plan, 319
    relationship to long-term planning, 319–320
listening, 136–137
    classroom space and equipment, 20
    musical preference research, 138–139
    planning for listening activities, 137–143
    program music and movement, 176–177
    recorded music examples, 144–150
locomotor motion, 153, 192

main activity part of a lesson plan, 319
major
    key, 14
    scale, 89, 347
    third, 339–340
male voice, 28–29
mallet, 67
maraca, 80

measure (bar), 213, 337
melodic
    contour, 29, 234, 238–241
    minor scale, 258, 348
    ostinato, 52–53, 308
melody, 234, 249–252
metallophone, 82–83
metre, 211
    activities for teaching, 211–214
    compound, 213, 344–345
    conducting patterns, 213
    duple, 173, 211–213, 344
    strong/weak beats, 211–213
    time signature, 213, 344
    triple, 173, 211–213, 344–345
metronome, 210, 345
middle C, 338
mini flashcards, 230, 251
minor
    key, 14
    scale, 253–258, 348
    third, 49, 235, 339–340
monophonic texture, 29, 299
motivation part of a lesson plan, 319
moveable-*doh*, 184–185
movement, 152, 156–157
    action songs, 159
    body awareness activities, 156
    chasing games, 165
    circle games, 162–164
    clapping games, 160–161
    creative, 19, 171–172, 176–177
    dances, 167–171
    energy and time awareness activities, 156
    establishing a movement vocabulary, 155–156
    eurhythmics, 172
    finger plays, 158–159
    locomotor, 153, 192
    non-locomotor, 153, 192
    passing games, 166, 198
    physical space and equipment, 19–20
    planning for positive experiences. 153–154
    program music, 176–177
    singing games, 154–166
    spatial awareness activities, 155
    structured, 19, 173–176
    tableau, 177
multiple intelligence, 2
multiple learning perspectives, 13–14, 317
musical intelligence, 3
musical meaning, 4, 334
musical multiculturalism, 6
musical structure, 4–5, 9–10, 140–142
musical thinking, 2
music literacy, 16–17, 179–188, 221–227, 244–245
music specialists, 21–22
musique concrète, 125
mystery beat games, 204–205

mystery rhythms, 228
mystery tunes, 51–52, 250–251

natural
   minor scale, 253, 348
   sign, 340–341
nature of
   music, 2, 4
   music education, 2–3
   music understanding, 4, 5–7
neighbour tones, 120
non-locomotor movement, 153, 192
non-pitched percussion instruments, 68–69, 270
   activities for teaching, 50, 69–78, 116–118, 125–129,
      271–274
   developmental appropriateness, 66–67
   metal, 78–79
   purchasing, 81
   skins, 81
   woods, 80
non-programmatic music, 177
note heads, 342–343
note teaching of a song, 36–37

oboe, 277
octave, 235, 339–340, 347
one-line staff, 339
opening part of a lesson plan, 319
orchestral instruments, 270, 274–276
   book and video resources, 277–278
   brass family, 274, 277
   percussion family, 276–277
   string family, 275–277
   woodwind family, 275, 277
orchestration of barred instruments, 94
Orff, Carl, 16, 82
ostinato
   activities for teaching, 74–78, 126–127, 300
   complimentary, 126–127
   melodic, 92, 308
   rhythmic, 74, 296–297, 300

parent-teacher conferences, 331
part-singing, 52–61
partner songs, 55–56, 301
passing tones, 120
patsching, 67, 85
pedal tone (drone), 85–86, 195
pentatonic
   accompaniments, 84–89
   patterns, 49
   scale, 85, 349
   songs, 85–89
percussion instruments
   non-pitched, 50, 68–81, 125
   orchestral, 274–278
   pitched, 50
phonemes
   language, 3

music, 3
phrase, 284
phrase-by-phrase approach for teaching a rote song,
   35–36
phrase form, 284
   activities for teaching, 284–288
piano, 261–263, 346
pianissimo, 261–263, 346
piggy-back songs, 49
pitch, 233–234
   absolute pitch names, 186–187, 252–253, 337–338
   accidentals, 258
   activities for teaching, 234–258
   discrimination, 37, 233
   hand signs, 50
   high vs low, 234–238
   introducing new tonic sol-fa notes, 185, 244–245
   key signatures, 258
   matching, 44–48
   melodic contour, 29, 238–241
   melody, 234, 249–252
   monitoring, 37
   production, 37, 234
   scales, 253, 347–349
   strategies for developing in-tune singing, 37–52
   tonic sol-fa syllables, 241–245
pitched percussion instruments, 50, 82–84, 270
   activities for teaching, 84–94, 129–131
pizzicato, 280
planning
   assessment, 318, 327–331
   curricular, 311–312
   lesson, 318–325
   long-range, 312–318
   music concept timetable, 314–316
   yearly content, 314, 317
polyphonic texture, 29, 62, 297, 301–302
pop music, 10
program music, 177–78
pulse. *See* beat
puppets, 44–48, 51, 236

quarter notes, 342–343
question-and-answer songs, 44–48, 115

range
   of barred instruments, 83
   of the child's voice, 26
   of the recorder, 95
   of a song, 29, 38
ratchet, 69
reading music
   absolute pitch, 186–187, 234, 252–253
   hand signs, 50, 186–187
   principles of instruction, 181–188
   readiness, 180–181
   rhythmic syllables, 183–184, 231, 343
   sequence of instruction, 183, 188, 221–227, 244–245

tonic sol-fa, 184–186
value, 16–17, 179–180
recorded music, 140
  activities for teaching, 140–143
  examples of, 145–150
  how to choose, 140
recorder, 67, 95–96, 111
  articulation, 98
  care of, 97
  echo games, 99
  embouchure, 98
  fingering chart, 99
  fingering types, 96–97
  hand position, 97–98
  music examples, 100–111
  note teaching sequence, 99
  types, 95–96
rectangular-shaped clef, 339
reinforce step of sound-before-symbol, 15, 204–205, 315–316
rests, 342
review song, 221, 244
rhythm, 215–216
  activities for teaching, 216–231
  criteria for selecting songs, 29, 222
  individual rhythmic values, 219, 221
  introducing new rhythms, 221–227
  patterns, 228–231
  rhythm vs beat, 219–220
  sequence for teaching rhythms, 183
  traditional names, 221
  the way the words sound, 215–219
rhythm sticks, 80
rhythmic
  ostinato, 74, 126–127, 300
  syllables, 36, 183–184, 231, 343
ritardando, 345
rock music, 10, 138
Romantic style of music, 10, 138
rondo (ABACA), 121–123, 290–291
rote teaching of a song
  phrase-by-phrase approach, 35–36
  whole song approach, 35
rounds, 52, 54
  how to teach, 301
  music examples, 54–61

sand blocks, 80
saxophone, 277
scales, 253, 347–349
  blues, 120, 258
  chromatic, 258, 349
  major, 253–254, 347
  minor, 253, 256–257, 348
  pentatonic, 85, 349
  whole tone, 258
sectional form, 288–292
  activities for teaching, 95, 121, 171–172, 284–294
  binary (AB), 121, 290–292

fugue, 290
rondo (ABACA), 121, 290–291
ternary (ABA), 95, 289–290
theme and variations, 121, 290, 292
semantics
  language, 3
  music, 3–4
semitone. *See* half step
sforzando, 266, 268–269, 346
sharp sign, 340–341
sight-reading, 181–188, 241–245
simultaneous imitation, 67
singing, 11, 25
  a cappella, 85
  breath support, 27
  changing voice, 33
  children's choirs, 62
  children's singing range, 26, 38
  classroom space and equipment, 20
  criteria for song selection, 29–34
  exercises, 27–28
  falsetto voice, using, 29
  good tone, 28
  hand signs, 50, 186–187
  head voice, 26
  individual, 44–48
  in harmony, 52–61
  posture, 27
  rounds, 52–61
  story song books, 50
  strategies for developing in tune singing, 37–52
  teaching a new song, 34–37
  tonic sol-fa, 184–185
  vibrato, using, 26
  vocal model, 26
  young children's, 25–26
singing games, 154
  action songs, 49, 159
  chasing, 165
  circle, 162–164
  clapping, 160–161
  how to teach, 157–158
  line, 167
  passing, 166
  value of, 154
single reed instruments, 277
sixteenth notes, 342
skip, 29, 339–340
sleigh bells, 79
slur, 347
sopranino recorder, 95
song teaching methods
  note, 36–37
  rote, 34–36
  rote-note combination, 36
sonic properties of music. *See* musical structure
sound-before-symbol teaching approach, 15–16, 180–181, 190, 192, 204–205, 215, 133, 260, 283, 296, 314–316

spiral progression of musical concepts, 11
spoons, 80
staccato, 279
staff, 234, 337
   grand, 338
   percussion, 339
   traditional, 242, 337
stems, 342–343
step. *See* whole step
string bass, 277
string instruments, 274–278
structure of music, 4–5, 9–10, 140–142
styles of music, 10, 138
suspended cymbal, 79
swing style of music, 10, 138
syntax
   language, 3
   music, 3, 9–10

tambourine, 79
tam-tam, 79
temple blocks, 80
tempo, 205
   activities for teaching, 206–210
   discrimination, 205–206
   markings, 206, 345
   production, 205, 207–210
ternary form (ABA), 95, 121, 290–292
texture, 297
   homophonic, 62, 298
   monophonic, 29, 299
   polyphonic, 29, 297
   sequence for teaching, 299,
theme and variations form, 121, 133–134, 290–292
thirds
   major, 339–340
   minor, 49, 339–340
timbre, 270
   activities for teaching, 69–81, 125, 270–278
   discrimination, 69–71, 271–272
   exploration, 67–68, 116
time signature, 213, 344–345
tone block, 66, 80
tonguing (recorder), 98
tonic note
   chord, 89, 305–308
   note, 85
tonic sol-fa, 36, 184–185
treble clef, 234, 252–253, 337–338
triangle, 79
trill, 347

triple metre, 173, 211–213, 344
triplet, 184, 222
trombone, 277
trumpet, 277
tuba, 277
tuning fork, 38

ukulele, 66
unison (repeat), 339–340

viola, 277
violin, 277
vocal model
   female, 26
   male, 28–29
   teacher, 26–29
voice
   breath support, 27
   changing, 34
   chest, 26
   children's, 25–26
   exercises, 27–28
   falsetto, 29
   four children's voices, 39–41
   head, 26–27
   male, 28–29
   teacher vocal model, 26
   vibrato, 26

Western art music, 10
Western popular music, 10
whole notes, 342
whole song approach for teaching a rote song, 35–36
whole step, 29, 339–402
whole tone scale, 258
wind chimes, 79
wood block, 67, 80
woodwind instruments, 274–278
writing music
   absolute pitch, 186–187
   composing, 125–134
   hand signs, 50, 186–187
   principles of instruction, 181–188
   readiness, 180–181
   rhythmic syllables, 183–184
   sequence of instruction, 183–188
   tonic sol-fa, 184–186, 343
   value, 16–17

xylophone, 67, 82–83